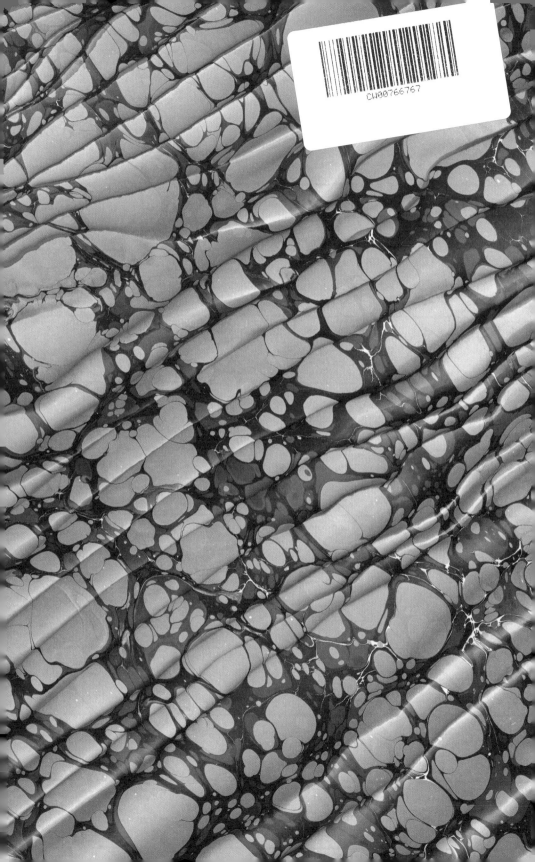

Suppliers to the Confederacy
British Imported Arms
and Accoutrements

Craig L. Barry and David C. Burt

Schiffer Military History
Atglen, PA

Acknowledgments

Special thanks for all the help in researching the accoutrements section of this book go to Mr David Jarnagin, of C&D Jarnagin & Co, without whose invaluable help and guidance this publication would not have been possible.

Also special thanks to Tim Prince of College Hill Arsenal for also sharing his knowledge and expertise. And Shannon Pritchard of Old South Military Antiques (http://www.oldsouthantiques.com) for sharing pictures and information of the Connell cap pocket and the "reconstructed cap pouch."

A big thank you is also due to the staff at the South Carolina Confederate Relic Room & Museum and to Gordon Jones at the Atlanta History Center. Other thanks go to: Neill Rose, Bob Williams, Will MacDonald, and C.L. Webster for providing other information and photographs for the book.

Book Design by Stephanie Daugherty.

Printed in China.
ISBN: 978-0-7643-4248-6

We are interested in hearing from authors with book ideas on related topics.

Published by Schiffer Publishing Ltd.
4880 Lower Valley Road
Atglen, PA 19310
Phone: (610) 593-1777
FAX: (610) 593-2002
E-mail: Info@schifferbooks.com.
Visit our web site at: www.schifferbooks.com
Please write for a free catalog.
This book may be purchased from the publisher.
Try your bookstore first.

In Europe, Schiffer books are distributed by:
Bushwood Books
6 Marksbury Avenue
Kew Gardens
Surrey TW9 4JF, England
Phone: 44 (0) 20 8392-8585
FAX: 44 (0) 20 8392-9876
E-mail: Info@bushwoodbooks.co.uk.
Visit our website at: www.bushwoodbooks.co.uk
Try your bookstore first.

Contents

Foreword

Unless you have put in the time it takes to do the research to really study military equipment that was made over a hundred and fifty years ago this topic is hard at best; now include the fact it is a foreign system and the task becomes even harder, and all the while stating it is the country that, at the time, the sun never set on its empire. The issues become even harder to understand since the Colonel system did not end until after the Crimean war. Change to this system was first attempted in the middle 1700s, and it took one hundred years to fully end it. This means establishing pattern types is very hard at best, since the Crown was trying to get control over its military supply system. Knowing this, and the large amount of ambiguity over what was brought and what made it through the blockade means any study will give us clues as to what the Confederate soldier might have used in the field. This, along with the fact that the original market in the United States has been inundated with English made gear that was never here during the Civil War, or are outright fakes brought in from England in the 1960s, makes you really question the original examples. This project was no easy task, and there are going to be chances for mistakes, but that the authors have been willing to take on the task to help us all to understand what could have been used by Confederate troops in the field is no mean feat.

I admire the authors for their hard work to unravel this very confusing subject.

David Jarnagin
January 2012

Introduction

The Industrial Revolution in England began in the mid-18th century. It marks a major turning point in human history; almost every aspect of daily life was eventually affected. The change from manual labor assisted by draught animals to machine based manufacturing spread through Europe and North America by the 19th century. For the first time in history, per capita income rose faster than the population. Whether the Industrial Revolution was a true "revolution" or more of an "evolution" is a question best left to history and the economists, which is not to be debated here. History tells us that beginning with textiles the factory system became the new model for efficient use of labor, and Manchester became the hub for the cotton mills, peaking in the mid-19th century with 108 factories. The plantations of the southern United States were the largest source of the cotton which fueled these mills. A visitor to Manchester from Germany during that era noted:

> It is a famous great factory town. Dark and smoky from the coal vapours, it resembles a huge forge or workshop. Work, profit and greed seem to be the only thoughts here. The clatter of the cotton mills and the looms can be heard everywhere. Everything in the factory happens with admirable precision and neatness and at the same time with great speed...it seemed as if all these wheels were really alive and the people occupied with them were machines. [1]

In terms of social structure, great wealth was created for the businessmen that owned the factories, putting them in the realm of wealthy gentlemen and landed gentry, but not quite up to nobility. The factory owners were a new category of social strata. For workers, the transition was not without conflict. Tradesmen in the crafts increasingly saw their livelihoods disappear, and their way of life along with it. In general, and for obvious reasons, "skilled labor" and the trade guilds resisted the American system of manufacture by machinery up until the time it was forced upon them.

The gun trade was one of the last industries to eliminate the crafts in favor of machinery, and a good case can be made that they waited too long to do so. For hundreds of years Ordnance (known as the War Department after 1854) had procured almost all necessary military items domestically through the private commercial sector. The gun makers of London and Birmingham had mostly been up to the task of supplying the British Army with enough firepower to keep their troops among the world's elite. That changed with the advent of the new Enfield rifle pattern of 1853 and the onset of the Crimean War. The first orders in October 1853 from Ordnance demonstrated the shortcomings of a system dependent on a large number of independent, specialized craftsmen. The initial Enfield rifle deliveries were late, incomplete, or failed to pass an inspection with gauges. The gun makers, for their part, offered up excuses rather than apologies. For example, it was suggested that the Birmingham made Enfield rifles were good enough, but the government inspectors at the Tower were just too strict. Faced with the evidence such as it was, the irony of the situation was a final slap in the face for Ordnance. The usually provincial British government was forced to place orders with foreign gun makers at Liege (Belgium), St. Etienne (France), and Robbins & Lawrence (U.S.) for military arms in order to meet their immediate needs.

The existing Ordnance contract system remained in place for the next few years while the Government modernized and prepared to open their own manufacturing facility at Enfield Lock to produce interchangeable parts for military arms. An intentional side effect was to reduce their dependence on the commercial gun makers. Rather than immediately modernizing operations and competing for the business, the Birmingham and London Gun Trade instead spread rumors that the new machine-made weapons would be horridly expensive, and how they would lack the "higher quality" of the hand finished arms. The opposite proved to be the case:

> Man's handiwork is at all times short of perfection, and, moreover, the work of one man differs materially in point of excellence from that of another. In spite of our claim to be a nation possessing the most skillful mechanics in the world, it may be questioned whether the bore of any two rifles is exactly similar. Of late years some curious facts have

come to light. For instance, it is stated that the best Birmingham manufacturers have never approached nearer to accuracy in the bore of the piece than the 350th of an inch,—a degree of accuracy sufficiently startling when we endeavour to "realize" that minute fraction of an inch; but we are assured that Mr. Whitworth, in the hexagonal bore of his rifle, has positively attained an accuracy up to the 5000th of an inch—one of those astounding facts of art as difficult to prove to the senses as anything that we deem mysterious or miraculous. [2]

In the mid-1850s the Worshipful Company of Gun-makers (London) and the Birmingham Small Arms Trade registered disbelief when they found that Enfield rifles produced by machine at Royal Small Arms Manufactory could be taken down, the parts placed in a heap, and the disassociated parts re-assembled back into rifles with no fitting required. The commercial handmade military arm had long been "set-up" or assembled from boxes full of parts which were "juggled until one was found that fit." [3] The government made Enfield rifles were not only better, but also significantly less expensive to produce. Ordnance claimed a savings of £131,085 during 1861-2 over the cost of the same number of rifles at prices previously paid to the Gun Trade. [4] And yet, the traditional methods of the gun makers, largely unchanged since the medieval period, lingered for another decade. It was boosted by the suddenly enormous demand for military arms created by the U.S. Civil War, as well as international demand from political upheaval worldwide. In economic terms, the gun trade became victim of the phenomenon of a spike in short run demand.

A certain lack of understanding exists about the inner workings of the gun trade during the final halcyon days of the handicraft era. Much has been written about the role of the Enfield rifle as the standard Confederate infantry arm of the U.S. Civil War, as well as its wide use by the Union early on, but comparatively little research has been published about the gun makers that produced these weapons. Confusion persists about their comparative level of quality and serviceability. Unsolved mysteries include how so many Enfield rifles were made for export so quickly and by whom? Did any certain gun makers only supply weapons to one particular side or the other? Did the British Government contribute small arms to the Confederacy? From which factories did the majority of Enfield rifles used in the U.S. Civil War originate? Which were the largest and which were the best gun making firms? How were these arms manufactured? Where did the raw materials come from? What was the meaning of the various markings found on these arms? What about the gun makers themselves?

Eventually, by the mid-1860s, even Birmingham Small Arms was ready to admit the handmade era was largely over and begin manufacture of military arms by machine. [5] However, the market was no longer there; with the end of the U.S. Civil War in 1865 both the Birmingham and London gun makers did not see large scale commercial military contracts again, at least not in the 19th century. The Gun Quarter in both cities all but collapsed, and the days of outworkers "making between £20 and £50 a week and lighting cigars in pubs with £5 notes" were over. [6] The English Gun Trade produced a million or more weapons from 1861 to 1865, the majority of which went to the Southern States. [7] The Gun Trade provided employment for thousands of craftsmen, and then it suddenly ended.

With an eye to preserving the history of this bygone era, researchers Craig L. Barry and David C. Burt have collaborated on the following monograph about the English Gun Trade and Accoutrement makers for their new book *Suppliers to the Confederacy*. This research includes the discovery of lost information on many of the commercial gun makers. We hope to provide a fresh look at the incredible impact the English had on supplying the Confederacy and its effect on the U.S. Civil War. The new research also looks at all the implements and accoutrements issued with the Enfield rifle musket, including the cap pocket, pouch, ball bags and knapsacks, right down to the muzzle stopper. Each piece of equipment is examined in great detail and is accompanied by detailed photographs, and discusses most of the patterns of British equipment carried by Confederate soldiers and how they were supposed to be used. The book also looks at how this equipment was purchased, from where and by whom, and how it was shipped over to the Confederate States.

Craig L. Barry, Murfreesboro, Tennessee
David C. Burt, Congleton, Cheshire, United Kingdom

CHAPTER ONE:
British Accoutrements in Confederate Service

D uring the industrial revolution—especially during the mid-1850s—the British army's weapons and equipment underwent significant changes. Following the Crimean War (1854-56) and the Indian (Sepoy) Rebellion in 1857, it was found that most equipment was not up to the rigours of life in the field. Many accoutrements would have to be upgraded, and from 1859 to 1865 there were over sixty changes to equipment to try and improve the soldier's kit. The items of equipment most altered were the knapsack, pouch (cartridge box), and ball bag, together with the introduction of a new cap pouch.

What follows are the details of the new official patterns of the British army accoutrement set that accompanied the P53 Enfield rifle musket imported by the likes of Huse, Anderson and Bulloch to equip the fledgling Confederate forces, as well as some volunteer equipment that also made its way over. And although not actually part of the official accoutrement set, the imported knapsack is examined, as well as a focus on Confederate copies of British equipment.

The Snake "Hook" Waist Belt

The snake buckle itself dates to antiquity, appearing in the 3-piece style we are familiar with by the 16th century. The snake was intended as a symbol of wisdom, the eternal, the universe, and the world of regeneration and rebirth. The snake buckle experienced a revival of popularity in British martial fashion in the late 18th century, after which it saw continuous use with British regulars, volunteers, and colonial forces, as well as constabulary organizations and school uniforms through to the 20th century. In Britain, these buckles appeared in endless variation in size and detail throughout their long period of service, owing in part to the fact that uniform design and procurement was largely left to the discretion - or whim - of the regiment's colonel (generally a peer of the realm), who for all intents and purposes "owned" the regiment.

The actual snake belt itself had been in use by the British army rifle regiments since around 1800. However, it was not introduced into the other regiments of the British army until 1850; until then the accoutrements had been suspended from the cross-belts. The pattern was altered in 1854, with the List of Changes noting: *Buff Infantry Pattern 1850 belt altered to Pattern 1854.* In 1859, the waist belt for the volunteer regiments was described as: *A brown leather waist belt with snake.* [1]

In the 1860s British regulations for Rifle regiments called for "a waist belt of black leather with a snakehook clasp" and "Belts, black leather, with snake hook." The belt was to be "2 inches" wide and the "weight to be 5 ½ oz"; and it was to have a teardrop style tongue. [2]

The teardrop tongue and brass snake hook of an original snake belt supplied by S. Isaac Campbell & Co. (Courtesy Shannon Pritchard Old South Military Antiques)

Pictured (on the previous page) is a copy of the Pattern 1854 snake *hook* waist belt as supplied to the Confederacy by the British commission house of S. Isaac Campbell & Co, London. The regulation teardrop tongue is 6 1/8 inches in length, and is attached to the belt using a unique *blind stitch* where the stitching does not appear on the face of the belt.

This *blind* or *tunnel* stitch joined the teardrop keeper to the belt; it is used to join the two adjacent pieces of leather together. From looking at the belt, it appears that the two edges are merely laid side by side and the stitching is only visible from the rear of the belt. This *tunnel* or *blind* stitch was used on the waist belts and to attach the tab to the flap on the P1860 pouch.

Full view of the SIC&Co waist belt. (Shannon Pritchard)

The belt width is 1 ¾ inches wide; made from 8oz black waxed flesh *(Leather finished on the rough side)* leather, which has been dyed on both sides. It is totally hand sewn, with the snake hook itself measuring 1 ½ inches in length and ½ inch in width. The main differential of the SIC&Co belt and the regulation belt is the snake hook is attached to the wrong side of the belt, on the side of the teardrop tongue, as opposed to the regulation belt which has the snake hook on the opposite end. It is also not as wide as the regulation belt being some 1 ¾ inches instead of two inches.

Another variation of the S. Isaac Campbell & Co P54 waist belt was this time made from black bridle *(smooth out finish)* leather.

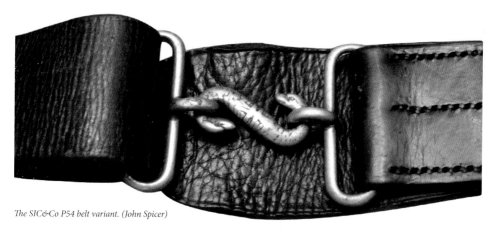

The SIC&Co P54 belt variant. (John Spicer)

This model exhibited differing features to the standard belt: the first was the lack of the tunnel stitch to attach the tongue to the belt. Instead, it was attached using three rows of visible stitching; and the snake hook this time is attached to the opposite end of the belt. It still uses the same size and style of snake buckle.

The belt pictured (on the following page) is a sword belt supplied by the company for the Confederacy. This is a commercial copy of the black leather sword belt as in British regulations for Staff Sergeants. It is constructed from black bridle leather and uses a smaller than normal snake buckle as compared to the company made P54 variety with a flower in the center. It features two brass "O" rings to which the separate pieces of the belt are fastened. The four rows of stitching between the tongue and the front ring is actually one long piece of leather folded over three times and hand sewn.

The most likely reason for S. Isaac Campbell & Co's suppliers manufacturing belts from both bridle (*smooth out*) and waxed (*rough side out*) is probably simply due to supply and demand. Since the leather supply on the market cannot be run up in a hurry (it can take 6 to 9 months) other stocks would be used, especially for the manufacture of belts where the finish would not matter too much. Since the supply of top quality bridle leather would quickly dry up, and would take time to replace, waxed leather of the correct weight and thickness could easily be substituted.

An original S. Isaac Campbell & Co stamped sword belt. (Gunbroker.com)

Surviving buckles on the SIC&Co waist belts were usually made of brass, with the two most common designs being a buckle with a double headed snake with an ornate leaf in the center of the snake with two horizontal bars in the middle of the leaf. The other most popular style has a circular flower pattern also in the center of the snake itself; these buckles could measure anywhere from 1 ⅜ to 1 ⅞ inches. S. Isaac Campbell & Co was also known to use a single headed snake buckle from time to time, but these are quite rare.

There are some snake buckles on existing Confederate used belts that are nickel plated. The British army regulations in the 1860s called for a *silver snake clasp and mountings* for officers, paymasters, quartermasters and medical officers of the rifles. It is most likely these officer styles of buckle were pressed into service by the commercial manufacturers for use on the exported belts. These buckles were described in period manuals as *silver plated*.

Tens of thousands of these belts were being exported by Major Caleb Huse, Chief purchasing Agent for the Confederate Ordnance Department, from the commission house of S. Isaac Campbell & Co, and – who would buy them from various individual contractors – to Alex Ross and Co, who provided their own to the regulation standard. The commercial copies of the Rifle regiment's snake hook waist belt would have been particularly popular with Huse, for they were of a simple and practical design and bore no regimental markings, unlike the belts for enlisted men and officers in Line and Guards regiments, where the regulations called for a belt with a *Brass Union Locket*. This locket would have had the regimental number in the middle of the plate and would have been totally unsuitable for Huse's requirements.

The smaller snake hook variety with the flower in the center.

The belt styles and leather used by the commercial makers differed greatly, indicating that volunteer belts and outdated surplus belts were widely purchased. Some belts exist today with rectangular tongues as opposed to the more common teardrop style, and some have no tongue at all, like the one belonging to Private Henry Marsh of the 2nd Georgia Cavalry (Below). Colors of leather

Snake hook waist belt of Private Henry Marsh of the 2nd GA Cavalry. Note no tongue on the belt. (Atlanta History Center care of David Burt)

also vary from black, brown, to buff leather, both rough out and smooth. It seems as long as it was serviceable it was accepted.

Initial shipments of the waist belt began almost immediately when the war began, with the first invoices dated December 23rd and 31st 1861. These were for 2,350 *waist belts* and all the other accoutrements that went with them.

Surviving specimens of the snake hook belt were found and taken as souvenirs from various battlefields; one such belt was taken from the body of a Confederate soldier at Gettysburg by a Captain W.H. Warner of the 40th New York Infantry. This particular one is described as *russet* (brown). There are at least three existing enlisted men's snake belts bearing the cartouche of SIC&Co in museums and private collections, and there are also surviving officers' sword belts, also with the snake hook.

This P1855 white enamelled leather British cavalry sword belt was used by an unknown Confederate during the Civil War. This style of whitened buff leather sword belt (below) was the regulation for all cavalry except the Household Cavalry. First authorized in 1855, it was first worn by the 1st King's Dragoon Guards in 1857 and subsequently by all Cavalry regiments. [3] This belt was just one of some *5,392 Cavalry saber-belts* that had been imported by Huse by February 1863. [4]

The P1855 white enamelled snake hook sword belt. (MOC David Burt)

Another whitened buff snake hook belt was recovered from the Antietam Battlefield; it was an enlisted man's belt with a snake buckle measuring 62 x 87. Written on the belt is the following inscription, "Taken from the body of a dead rebel soldier at Antietam by a member of the 1st Massachusetts Battery Light Artillery."

The snake hook belt was very popular amongst Confederate soldiers, and it can be seen in numerous photos of both enlisted men and officers alike, as is seen in this photo of an unidentified soldier.

The snake *hook* waist belt was still in use in the British military as late as the First Word War, and was still in use for British school children as late as the 1960s.

CS soldier with his snake hook belt.

White enamelled sword belt. (David Burt)

The 1856 - 57 Percussion Cap Pouch

The cap pouch was used for carrying the percussion caps used to fire the P53 Enfield rifle musket. These caps were placed on the nipple of the gun, and when the trigger was pulled the hammer struck the cap, which ignited, setting off the powder in the barrel. According to some historians, this angled sleeve cap pouch was first introduced in 1845. There is no actual evidence of this type of percussion cap pouch being issued at this time in any army manual or journal. In fact, the shoulder belt which carried the ammunition pouch did not come into service until 1850, when the cross-belt with breastplate at the intersection was replaced with the lighter and more convenient single shoulder belt to carry the pouch. [1] The first mention of any type of cap pouch was in 1841; it was written:

An original P56/57 Confederate cap pouch. (Courtesy of the Military & Historical Image Bank)

> The caps intended for immedi-ate use are carried in the small pouch made of patent leather on the outside for better resistance to the wet. This pouch is attached in infantry regiments to the coat on the right side by means of a ring, and so fixed as to be clear of the belt. [2]

In 1847, it was mentioned that *caps required for immediate use are to be carried in the pocket attached to the ball bag, no separate cap bag being required.* [3] During the Crimean War (between 1854-56), most regiments still wore the cap pouch on a ring attached to the tunic. However, some troops in the Coldstream Guards took to copying Russian troops they saw that were utilizing a cap pouch on the shoulder belt on the chest. Some men in the unit started sewing their tunic mounted cap pouches onto their shoulder belts in the Russian way. As most of the fighting was done whilst wearing greatcoats in the bitter cold of the Russian winter, it proved to be a very popular way of wearing it, as finding the cap pouch attached to the tunic under the greatcoat proved to be very problematic. [4]

The first mention of the shoulder belt carried cap pouch is in 1857 during the Sepoy rebellion in India. A military magazine of that year mentions *A shoulder belt; on the same belt also a cap pocket.* [5] There are also period drawings and watercolors of British soldiers from the Sepoy rebellion wearing the belt mounted cap pouch. By 1864, British army regulations for Guards, Line and Highlanders describe it as *a small pouch for percussion caps on a shoulder belt*. For Guards, Line and Highlanders it was to be made from *white buff leather*, and for Rifle regiments to be made from *all black leather*. [6] It seems from the evidence that the origins of this cap pouch came during the Crimean War, when some Guards units sewed their cap pouches to the shoulder belt. Wearing the cap pocket in this fashion meant that it could be carried on the outside of all clothing, mean-ing that in cold climates caps could easily be accessed. This new belt mounted cap pouch would become a regulation item of the kit sometime between the end of the Crimean War in February 1856 and the beginning of the Sepoy rebellion in May 1857.

Original Confederate used buff leather cap pouch from the Museum of the Confederacy. (David Burt)

It is this style of cap pouch that Huse started to export to the Confederacy in large numbers from early 1862. It was designed to fit onto the pouch (cartridge box) sling, hence the angled belt sleeve; and there are numerous photographs of Confederate soldiers wearing them, either on the waist belt or, as they should be worn, on the pouch belt.

The rear of the Davis cap pouch. (David Burt)

This particular one (pictured right) was owned by a soldier named Davis from the 37th North Carolina Infantry, and was reported to have been picked up by a Union soldier on a battlefield in 1864, who miss-identified it as a *coin purse*. It is made from *rough out* whitened buff leather, which was regulation for British guards, Line and Highlander regiments. [7]

The second one featured here is another surviving British import cap pouch in a private collection that was worn by Corporal Timothy Connell of the 1st Virginia Infantry.

Cap pouch and belt of Corporal Timothy Connell 1st Virginia Infantry C.S.A. Note it is worn on the waist belt. (Courtesy Shannon Pritchard Old South Military Antiques)

This cap pouch is hand sewn from black bridle leather with a small brass finial for fastening, and as can be seen, it was again worn on the waist belt instead of on the cartridge box belt. The belt itself is not of British manufacture, and was probably a belt that had been especially made for him. Timothy Connell enlisted in Company C, 1st Battalion Virginia Infantry, on June 20, 1861. He was promoted to 4th Corporal in November 1861 and 2nd Corporal in June 1862. Connell served the Confederacy for the entire war from June '61 until his capture at Farmville, Virginia, on April 7, 1865.

As can be seen in the case of the Connell cap pocket, it must have been quite alien to many Confederate

The cap pocket of Cpl T Connell. (Shannon Pritchard)

soldiers to be issued this type of pouch and to wear it on the pouch belt when other comrades were issued a Confederate manufactured one and wore them on the belt, as is witnessed in the photograph (below). This is an unidentified Confederate infantryman who is wearing the cap pouch on the pouch belt as it was intended, but in this case he is wearing it the wrong way around.

The first S. Isaac Campbell & Co invoices to the Confederacy for accoutrements starting in late 1861 do not mention any cap pouch at all. They first start to mention the cap *pocket* in January 1862, and from then on cap *pockets* were purchased in ever greater amounts, as can be seen by photo evidence and surviving examples in museums and private collections. It has to be remembered that the ball bag provided by SIC&Co provided for the British volunteers already had an internal cap pocket, and therefore there was no need for the belt mounted version to be provided by the company. By 1862, with the ball bag proving ever more unpopular amongst Confederate troops, the *cap pocket* began to be provided in much larger numbers by the firm, as the soldiers preferred to load their weapons with caps taken directly from a separate cap pouch. It is highly likely though that cap pockets and ball bags would have been sold together to the Confederacy by Alexander Ross & Co, as they provided the regulation ball bag, which did not have an internal cap pouch and therefore would have needed to have

Unidentified CS soldier wearing full British accoutrements, but he is wearing the cap pouch the wrong way around. He is again issued with the "short" Enfield, and has the snake hook waist belt. (Herb Peck)

been supplied with a separate cap pocket. One of the very first shipments of accoutrements to reach the Confederacy from England mentions "896 buff cap pockets," which were sent to Nashville from the Atlanta arsenal on November 25, 1861. These would have almost certainly been supplied by Ross & Co., and provide solid evidence of the cap pocket being used from the very outset of the war.

Both Huse and SIC&Co refer to them as *pockets* [8], which was quite correct at the time. The official British Army regulations called it a *pouch for percussion caps*, but in the manual *Equipment of Infantry* complied by Captain Martin Petrie in 1865, as well as that description, it does also refer to the belt mounted cap pouch as a *cap pocket*. [9]

The British regulation P'56-57 cap pocket measured some 2 ⅞ inches in length and 3 ⅝ inches in width, with the sleeve measuring 3 ⅛ by 3 inches, and they were fastened by a brass finial.

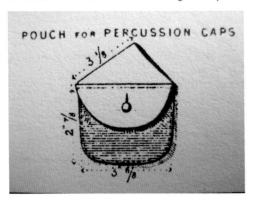

The inside of the pouch was constructed without any lamb's wool, unlike CS and Union manufactured cap boxes, although the ones attached to the sergeant's pouch did have a fur lining. Most surviving examples are made from black bridle or whitened buff leather, indicating that the cap pockets exported to the Confederacy were commercial copies of British rank and file infantry and rifle regiments.

The official steel engraved plate showing the cap pouch and dimensions. Equipment of Infantry by Captain M. Petrie, published in 1865.

The Pattern 1861 Ball Bag

S. Isaac Campbell & Co Ball Bag in the SCCRR & Museum, Columbia, SC. (Courtesy SCCRR & Museum)

Pictured here is an original Confederate used P1861 ball bag. This one (above) was supplied by S. Isaac Campbell & Co, and features their cartouche on the inside of the flap.

This particular one is a close copy of the official British army style one, but this one was an SIC&Co ball bag intended for the volunteer rifle regiments, and it differs in certain ways from the official pattern bag. The main differential in this SIC&Co model is the use of an internal cap pouch on the inside. This particular feature was not used on the regulation ball bag; only a leather tube for the oil bottle was used, as caps were meant to be carried in a cap pouch on the shoulder belt. This particular ball bag is also larger in size than the regulation bag and measures some

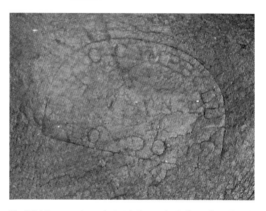

The SIC&Co cartouche on the inside flap on the Ball Bag. (David Burt)

seven inches in width and six inches in height, compared with the British army standard ball bag, which measured 4 ¼ inches in height and 7 ⅛ inches in width. This style of bag would have been made by the company for the newly formed volunteer companies, and as a result would not have to conform to any official regulations. This ball bag belonged to a Private Gunter of the 2nd S.C. Volunteers, and is made from black waxed leather dyed on both sides.

The regulation Pattern1861 *Ball Bag*, as it was termed (the British Army never referred to it as an Expense Pouch), was the British army's newest piece of equipment to be used with the P53 Enfield rifle musket. There were no less than three different ball bags issued through 1859 alone; one such patterned on May 5, 1859, was for a *brown leather ball bag, to hold ten rounds, for Cape Mounted Rifles.* Another pattern dated July 13, 1859, for the volunteer rifle regiments called for a *ball bag containing cap pocket*; this was to slide on the waist belt and contain ten rounds of ammunition. And finally, on October 21, 1859, another pattern called for *A brown leather ball bag to hold ten rounds, with zinc oil bottle, for Commissariat Staff Corps.* [1]

The final style of ball bag adopted by the Regular army was first put to trail in 1860, with the British Army List of Changes reporting *186 - Ball Bag with Loop 25th December 1860. Waterproofed by paint inside to govern supply of 1,000 for trial.*

The closure tab is stitched through the flap itself, and therefore does not utilize the "tunnel" stitch.

And it was finally accepted into service in 1861, with the LOC's recording:

> 371- Ball Bag, Buff Leather - 10th September 1861. With broad flap and painted inside. With leather tube for oil bottle. Buff Leather for Guards, Highland Battalion, Battalion of the Line.
> Black leather for Rifle Regiments. Leather to be rough side out. Weight of the bag to be, complete with oil bottle 8oz. [2]

This new P61 ball bag was designed to carry the unwrapped rounds from the pouch ready for the loading of the P53 Enfield. It was able to carry ten rounds; the wrapped rounds were taken from the pouch, unwrapped, and placed in the ball bag, which was worn on the snake hook waist belt on the right hip. From there each round would be taken out and loaded into the weapon. If the bag was a volunteer bag as issued by SIC&Co – as in the one pictured above – it would have an internal cap pocket which would hold the percussion caps. This must go to explain why the separate cap pocket – designed to be worn on the pouch belt – did not appear on any of the first SIC&Co invoices to the Confederacy, as the company copy of the regulation ball bag, but made for the volunteers, already had one on the inside.

SIC&Co ball bag showing the interior cap pouch. (Courtesy SCCRR & Museum)

This original Confederate used ball bag (right) was made by Alexander Ross & Co of Bermondsey, London, and is an exact copy of the sealed pattern 1861 ball bag that was regulation issue for British rifle regiments. Made from black waxed (rough out) leather, it has the tube inside for the oil bottle,

Regulation P61 "Ball Bag" from A Ross & Co. (Courtesy Atlanta History Center)

and does not feature an internal cap pocket. Since the adoption of the new pattern of sling mounted cap pocket, there was now no need for the new regular army pattern ball bag to have an internal cap pouch; only the volunteer bag now had this feature. The bag itself was designed to be fixed to the waist belt by a belt loop that measures some 3 ½ inches at the top and 2 ¾ inches at the bottom. It was fastened by a small brass finial on the underside of the bag, with another identical finial on the front to fasten the main flap.

Sealed patterns were supposed to be copied exactly by the various contractors that supplied the army, and makers like Ross & Co would have stuck rigidly to the official pattern or risk losing their contracts, even for the export market. S.Isaac Campbell & Co did not have this problem being banned as they were from making any sealed pattern equipage for the Army.

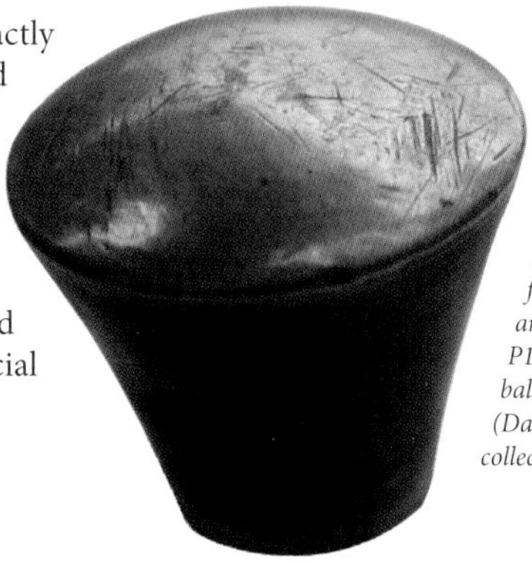

This British regulation Ross & Co ball bag is hand sewn and features superb craftsmanship, as an official

Brass finial from an original P1861 ball bag. (David Burt collection)

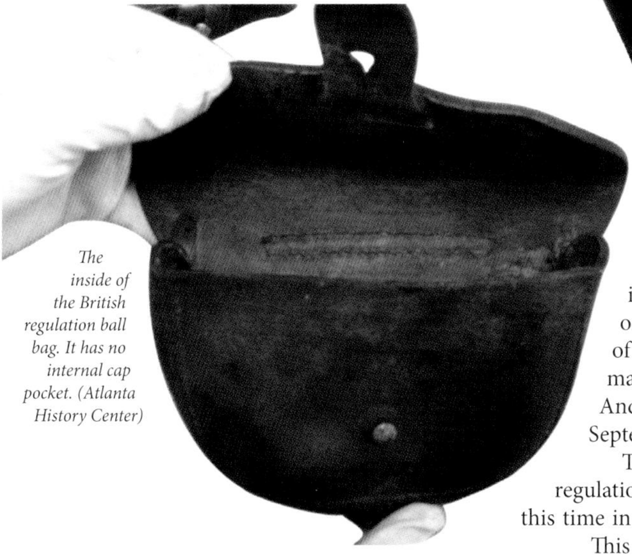

The inside of the British regulation ball bag. It has no internal cap pocket. (Atlanta History Center)

maker for the British Army would have to be. It has the *A Ross & Co C&M* (contractor & manufacter) *1861* on the inside of the flap. Judging by its 1861 stamp, this is probably one of the original £10,000 worth of accoutrements and other war materiel ordered by Major Edward Anderson from Ross & Co in September 1861.

The ball bag pictured below is a regulation copy of the P1861 ball bag, only this time in buff *waxed* (rough out) leather. This color of bag was issued to Guards and Line units in the British Army. The whiteners used in the manufacture of the ball bag were called "Paris whitening" or "Spanish whitening," which was made from a fine powder chalk. The yellow color of the buff as it is today is caused by the oil used in the currying process, which over time slowly turns a yellowish shade when it is not regularly whitened. This ball bag was used by an unknown Confederate soldier, and there are numerous mentions of 'buff' accoutrements in surviving invoices. One such invoice mentions: *buff gun slings, buff frogs, buff cap pockets, buff waist belts* and *buff pouch belts.* [3]

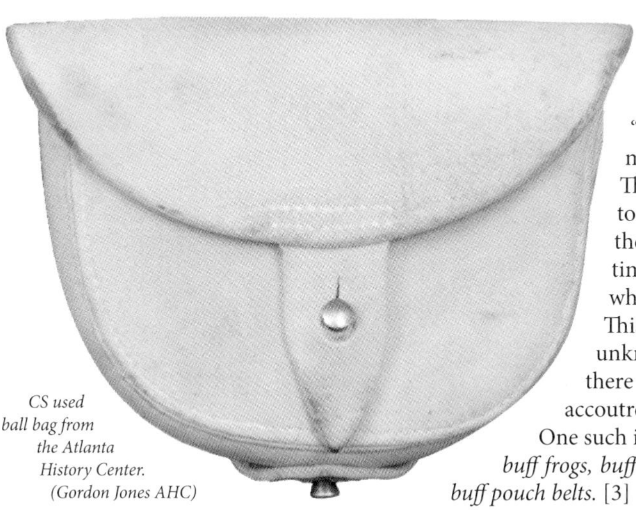

CS used ball bag from the Atlanta History Center. (Gordon Jones AHC)

The ball bag must have seen widespread use early in the war, as invoices show them being imported in great numbers in late '61-63. One such invoice by SIC&Co on December 23, 1861, saw 350 ball bags being sent aboard the steamers *Economist* and *Southwick*, and on December 31, 1861, another invoice saw 2,000 of them being shipped over by the company. [4]

A single surviving invoice from the second of *three* shipments of British equipment to Nashville lists 1,434 ball bags (816 of which had oil bottles). [5]

A Confederate-used P1861 Ball Bag complete with its snake hook waist belt. (Courtesy of the Military & Historical Image Bank)

The ball bag, however, proved not to be popular with the Confederate soldier, who – if issued British accoutrements – preferred to use the separate cap pocket and pouch to load his musket. It is hardly surprising the rank and file found the ball bag unpopular, as it has to be remembered that the British way of loading the P53 Enfield rifle musket differed from the American way. In the British way, the rounds to be used were taken directly from the ball bag and not the pouch, as American troops were used to.

In the summer of 1863 the Confederate Ordnance Bureau sent over 1,000 ball bags back to the Richmond Storehouse categorized as "scrap leather". [6] And in another separate invoice the Storehouse Keeper there, Colonel O. W. Edwards, sent on another "3,206 ball bags," again to be "taken up as scrap leather" on April 23, 1864, to Captain James Dinwiddie, who was a staff officer at the Richmond Arsenal. [7] These two large shipments of ball bags totalling well over 4,000 being returned to the Richmond Storehouse in 1863 and '64 – both identified as "scrap leather" – seem to be positive proof that they were issued to the troops, but they found them to be of very little use. This would make sense, as they would have been seen as surplus equipment to Confederate soldiers used to loading the rifle direct from the cartridge box and utilizing either a British or domestic cap pouch.

The cap pouch featured here is a standard Confederate box with a lead finial and the single belt loop at the back. It has, however, been reconstructed from a S. Isaac Campbell & Co accoutrement. It has a partially obscured SIC&Co cartouche located on the inside of the front flap by the latch tab; on the front bottom edge of the pouch can be seen pre-used stitch lines from its previous use.

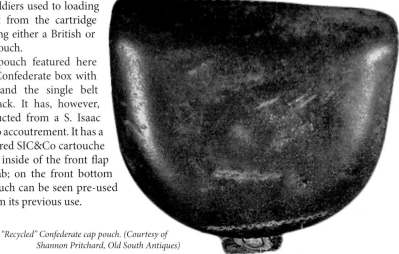

"Recycled" Confederate cap pouch. (Courtesy of Shannon Pritchard, Old South Antiques)

The SIC&Co cartouche located on the inside flap and partially obscured by the latch tab. (Courtesy Shannon Pritchard)

SIC&Co marked pouches and ball bags with this cartouche were the only items large enough to make cap pouches out of. It is unlikely it was made from a pouch, as they were being copied by C.S. arsenals' (See Confederate Copies of British Accoutrements), so the logical conclusion is that it was made from a former ball bag. The former accoutrement has been disassembled and re-made at a C.S. arsenal into this standard cap pouch. Given the fact that the troops could not take to the British ball bag because the loading method was alien to them and there exist invoices sending them back as *scrap leather*, could this cap pouch have been made from one of these ball bags?

By the middle of 1863 the ball bag had stopped being exported altogether, as domestic production of the cap pouch and the soldiers' reluctance to use the ball bag became all too apparent.

The P1860 Zinc Oil Bottle

This little oil bottle would be the one issued with the P1861 ball bag for export to the Confederacy. It was a standard issue implement used in the lubrication of the P53 Enfield, and it was first approved for use by the British Army on July 5, 1860.

An original P1860 Oil Bottle for the P53 Enfield. (David Burt)

The List of Changes read:

> 128 – *Oil Bottle, for fitting into the Ball Bag, Infantry –*
> *5 July 1860*
> *Specially provided for governing supply of 10,000 under*
> *contract*

This was amended in 1862:

> 568- *Zinc Oil Bottle, Seamless, for Infantry Ball Bags- 23 April*
> *1862*
> *Submitted by Mr A. Warner, 31 Threadneedle Street.* [1]

Consequently, the main type of oil bottle exported to the Confederacy would have been the bottle with the seam, rather than the seamless type.

The main body of the bottle was made from zinc with a brass cap, and fixed inside this cap was a steel applicator; the oil inside used in the cleaning and lubrication of the rifle was Rangoon oil.

So important was 'Rangoon' oil that a circular memorandum addressed to *Infantry at Home and Abroad* was issued on 23 July 1859 by G.A. Wetherall, Adjutant General, that read:

The steel applicator in the cap.
(Reproduction, David Burt Collection)

"The description of the best oil best suited for small arms is Rangoon oil, which is accordingly always to be used." [2]

This was backed up by Captain Martin Petrie in 1864, when he wrote:

"Rangoon oil is to be used in the ordinary cleansing and preservation of muskets, as it is considered preferable to any other descriptions of oil." [3]

The approximate size of the bottle was 2 ¾ inches in height with a diameter of 3 ¼ inches. The oil bottles were carried in a leather tube located in the right hand corner of the P1861 ball bag.

An original SIC&Co invoice for December 31, 1861, lists 2,000 oil bottles being sent in, and another dated December 23, 1861, shows another 75; on March 20, 1862, another 320 were exported by SIC&Co. [4] It is interesting to note too that oil bottles were sometimes issued 'loose', meaning they were imported on their own and not with the ball bag. In a surviving invoice from June 18, 1862, the Charleston Arsenal shipped 483 oil bottles to Atlanta. [5] Another surviving invoice reads:

An original frog with buckle attachment for the P56 sabre bayonet. (Courtesy Geoff Walden)

> 12th April 1862
> Captain R.M Cuyler C.S Arsenal, Macon, G.A to
> M. H Wright Nashville TN
> 138 Oil Bottles [6]

These 'loose' oil bottles were imported in large numbers on their own when the ball bag began to fall out of favor because they were easy to carry and use to keep the soldiers' rifle musket– irrespective of whether he was issued an Enfield rifle or not–in tip top condition. He would have been able to easily carry it in his knapsack or blanket roll.

The Pattern 1854 'Frog'

The 'Frog' was first introduced into the British army in 1850, along with the new waist belt that replaced the time honored cross belts that held the cartridge box and bayonet scabbard. [1] A new pattern frog – and one that would be exported to the Confederacy as part of the accoutrement set – was introduced in 1854, together with the new waist belt of that year. [2] The pattern 1854 frog can be easily identified from later models because it is the last style of frog to be completely hand sewn, as compared to the later 1866 style, which, although it was of the exact same design, would be the first type of frog to include rivets. [3]

It would be supplied in rough out whitened buff, which was regulation for Highland, Guards and Line regiments, and black leather. The black leather frog was the regulation for Rifle regiments, and the type of frog issued to the Rifles – because they carried the two band short Enfield with sabre bayonet – would include the buckle strap. [4]

The 'Frog' was simply the attachment that held the P53 bayonet and scabbard to the waist belt. The scabbard was fastened to it by passing the brass locket stud through the slit in the frog. The P-53 Enfield bayonet scabbards used a frog with no buckle attachment, as it was supposedly only the Enfield sabre bayonets, issued with the short Enfield P-56 and 60 rifles, that used the frog with a buckled strap. It is, however, sometimes seen in original pictures of Confederate soldiers that some Enfield P-53 bayonets and scabbards have the black leather buckle frog. Some British commercial manufacturers working for S. Isaac Campbell & Co also made the black leather frog with no strap simply because of the larger amount of three band Enfield rifles that were being exported and the greater need for this type of 'buckle-less' frog for the P-53 bayonet scabbards.

The frog was issued as part of the accoutrement set, and as such was imported in huge quantities, along with the other accoutrements by SIC&Co, Ross & Co, and other commercial makers because it could be quickly and easily manufactured. Strangely though, the scabbard itself was issued with the actual rifle and was not considered a part of the official accoutrement set.

Pictured here is a Confederate used P1854 whitened buff colored frog with its black leather scabbard. This particular one was made by the London firm S.W. Silver.

Stephen Winkworth of Silver & Co appears to have started life in 1838 as a clothier, with premises in Liverpool and London. By 1847 they described themselves as *Clothiers, Naval, Military and General Outfitters and Contractors* of 66-67 Cornhill Street and 4 Bishopgate Street, London, and St George's Crescent, Liverpool. They manufactured naval and military uniforms as well as equipment for the regular army like frogs, scabbards and knapsacks. [5]

Far from being a rare item, as previously presumed, 1,326 "buff frogs" were sent by Captain R.M. Cuyler, Ordnance Officer at Savannah, GA, to the Nashville Arsenal on November 25, 1861 as part of the shipment from the *SS Fingal*. Judging by its date, the one pictured above could well have been one of these first to arrive.

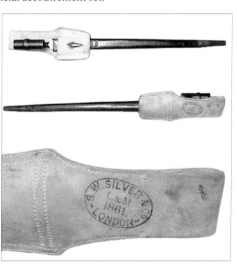

S.W. Silver frog and scabbard. (Courtesy Don Stoops Sharpsburg Arsenal)

The P1860 Pouch (Cartridge Box)

One of the most popular items of British military equipment issued to Confederate soldiers was the Pattern 1860 pouch (Cartridge Box).

In 1859, the List of Changes for the British Army reported a new type of pouch to be issued:

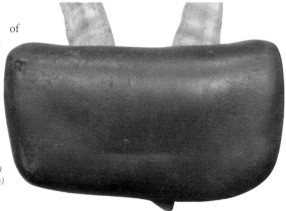

An original SIC&Co C.S. used P1860 Pouch. (Courtesy David Jarnagin)

No 60-Pouch, 60 Rounds, Obsolete Pattern – 23rd Nov 1859
Altered to hold 50 rounds, with receptacle for nipple wrench, cap pouch lined with fur, and tins with three compartments, to govern the alteration of the (60 round) pouches in store.

On 2 May 1860, the List of Changes for the British Army described a new cartridge box that had been proposed by the Adjutant General of the Army; it read:

No 127 Pouch, 50 Rounds, with Tin compartments for Infantry. [1]

This new pouch was just one of a new series of pouches issued to the British army in 1859/60. As well as being issued to the rank and file of infantry, new pouches were issued to the Rifles and Engineers, as well as the Militia. The dimensions of the new pouches were to be:

Serjeants, (All units) 7 x 3" Rank and File Infantry 7 x 3 1/4"

The new regulation infantry pouch was made from black bridle leather, which would be totally handsewn with white waxed thread. The outer flap was turned flesh side out to enable blackballing, and the latch tab was to be made of buff leather and *blind stitched* to the flap so it could not be seen from the outside. The regulation pouch had no provision for being worn on the waist belt and could only be carried by the shoulder strap. The reason for this is the regulation pouch was designed to carry the cartridges only, and was supposed to be worn slung out of the way of the ball bag, which was to carry them ready for use in action. The buckles which supported this strap were to be of the black japanned variety (a metal treatment that prevents rust and gave the metal a blue-black color).

The pouch was to have a cap pouch sewn on the front of the box under the main flap and a sturdy inner flap with rounded gores which had an implement compartment for musket tools, and it was to hold a five compartment tin for the ammunition. The tins of the regulation British cartridge box were to be at least three inches deep to allow for the increased height (+ ½") of the Enfield .577 cartridge. In a British-made cartridge the bullet is reversed and rammed along with the paper (which is lubricated). The Augusta Arsenal re-rolled imported English rounds to fit in domestic .58 cartridge box tins until late in the war, but many English cartridges were issued just as they came out of the shipping crate. A Union soldier recalled picking up a British made .577 Enfield cartridge from the battlefield at Stones River (Murfreesboro) in late December 1862; he wrote:

The rebels used English bullets almost entirely. I picked up a rebel cartridge, and on examining the cartridges found the makers' stamp on them; it was 'E. & A. Ludlow, Birmingham, England.' The balls are very pretty, being similar to the Minie ball, except at the base they are hollow for half an inch, in which is placed a wooden plug, so that at the explosion the wooden plug being driven into the ball, expands it, and prevents windage. [2]

The pouches imported by the Confederacy seem to have either been commercial copies of the regulation sealed pattern of the "Serjeants of Guards" pouch, only issued with the five compartment 50 round tin. This had the same dimensions as the "Rank and File" pouch, but lacked the external cap pouch; or copies of the "Rank and File" pouch as in the British regulations, but minus the external cap pouch. Confederate purchasing agents – most likely Huse and Anderson – clearly felt, probably also with a view to expediency, no need for any external cap pocket to be included on the pouch, as individual cap pockets designed to be worn on the pouch belt were already being imported, and they were also included in the majority of the S. Isaac Campbell & Co ball bags sent in so far. Again, as with the ball bag, differences between the English and American equipment and the different methods used to load the rifle were all too apparent. Tens of thousands of pouches, along with other accoutrements, would start to arrive in Confederate ports; among the initial shipments, at least 2,350 P60 pouches supplied by S. Isaac Campbell & Co were exported on board the steamers *Economist* and *Southwick*, which were invoiced for December 1861.

The commercial made copies of the P1860 pouches supplied by S. Isaac Campbell & Co for export to the Confederacy were rather crudely made with generally substandard workmanship as against regulation pouches. They included the single five compartment tin to hold ten rounds each; japanned tin buckles; they were hand sewn in white waxed thread, and had a fastening tab of white buff or black leather. Again, it did not have the external cap pouch or the implement pouch that the British Army regulations called for.

Side view of the SIC&Co pouch. The tin was too large for the box, as is clear from the damage done by pushing it into a box that was too small. (Courtesy David Jarnagin)

The most striking details, though, are in the use of the quality of leather and craftsmanship in the construction of the box, with the SIC&Co box being made from much poorer quality leather and finishing. In the privately owned pouch (above) it is also clear that the tin is too big for the box and having been forced in, the result is the stitching has come away in places. This pouch also utilizes a cloth sling instead of the leather one which would have been supplied with it.

The second SIC&Co P1860 pouch (pictured left) also carries the "S. Isaac Campbell & Co. 71 Jermyn St. London" stamping on the inside of the outer flap. The fastening tab is 'blind stitched' to the outer flap, so that the stitch lines are not seen from the outside; this is a feature which nearly all SIC&Co pouches have. The inner part of the flap on this second box has been finished with a sub-standard dye when compared to other British goods and is very plain to the eye. This comes at a time when Britain prided itself on having the best leather finishes around. This is surely a sign that these boxes were made by companies working for S. Isaac Campbell & Co that were used to supplying generally sub-standard equipment for the newly formed volunteers, and as such did not have to pass any rigorous government inspections. This would also be true of any equipment supplied to their Confederate customers who needed equipment in a hurry and were not particularly interested in the leather finish.

Second S. Isaac Campbell & Co pouch. (Courtesy Shannon Pritchard, Old South Antiques)

Indeed, the regulations for Volunteer regiments in 1859 called for a "Fifty-round pouch with cap pocket made from brown leather." So it is not inconceivable that some pouches and other accoutrements supplied by SIC&Co would have been manufactured from this color leather also.

On the flip side, the P1860 pouches supplied by the other London firm, Alexander Ross & Co, show superb craftsmanship as compared to the pouches supplied by SIC&Co. Alexander Ross & Co was formed in 1760 in Bermondsey, London, one of many tanneries in that area. So popular did Bermondsey become for the leather industry that the district became known by its nickname, "The Land of Leather," and by 1792 Bermondsey was processing a third of all England's leather (see Appendix H). Between July and September 1861, Major Edward C. Anderson, an assistant of Huse, visited Ross & Co, at their Grange Mill Tannery on numerous occasions to discuss orders and contracts, and by late 1861 was supplying accoutre-

The second SIC&CO pouch showing the five compartment tin. Notice the poor finish on the inside of the inner flap. (Courtesy Shannon Pritchard, Old South Antiques)

ments, including the P1860 pouch, in large numbers. On September 26th Anderson reported the purchase of "over £10,000" worth of goods through Ross & Co. [3]

Ross & Co, like many other contractors of the day, had two qualities when it came to the manufacture of pouches. The first rate one with the best quality leather and dyes was reserved for the British army, their main customer. The second quality pouch was reserved for any overseas orders. The quality of the boxes supplied to the Confederacy were still manufactured with outstanding

A. Ross & Co pouch with the outer flap lifted. Note the hemlock-dyed inner flap and the "star" shaped indents at each end of the flap. (David Burt Collection)

craftsmanship, but made from cheaper leather and dyes. The Ross pouch featured here is a prime example of a pouch made for the Confederacy, as it features a hemlock dyed inner flap which has changed color over time from black to brown. There exists another Ross pouch in a private collection which is entirely made from russet (hemlock dyed) leather. The color of the box, of course, would not be a problem for Huse and Anderson – they needed equipment and arms fast – and in quantity.

For their contracts with the Confederate government and the state of Georgia, thousands of pouches had to be made promptly. This led to a shortage of tanned leather at the tanneries, and it could take between six to nine months for the tanneries to supply more top quality leather. So using cheaper and more plentiful cuts of leather would be the only option until more top grade tanned leather became available. As with the pouches supplied by S. Isaac Campbell & Co, they did not have to pass any rigorous inspections where government inspectors could reject any items that were poorly made or did not conform to the correct pattern.

The Ross & Co P1860 pouch pictured here was offered for sale by a military antiques dealer; it is stamped on the inside of the outer flap by the latch tab 'A ROSS & Co C&M 1861', with a line under the *o* in *Co*. It does feature the hemlock dyed inner flap as previously discussed, but features top quality craftsmanship as compared to the rather shoddily made article provided by SIC&Co. Again, there are differences between this and the regulation pouches which were common with private commercial makers. The exterior cap pouch was again missing from the box, and there was no internal receptacle pouch on the underside of the inner flap.

The Ross & Co "C&M 1861" stamp between the buff tab and the outer flap. (David Burt Collection)

The pouches themselves were constructed using a time consuming and complicated procedure. To begin with, the cut pieces of leather for the pouch itself were tacked to a wooden block; this procedure was known in the trade as 'blocking'. In the 1860s leather was expensive compared to labor, and this is one of the reasons the British boxes were comprised of so many pieces. The nails are used to attach the different parts of leather to the block, where they are glued together, with the most common glues used being hide or fish glue. After about a day the glue would be dry, and the box was then hand punched with an awl prior to being sewn by hand. The "star" shaped indents so often seen on the completed pouches are formed when the tack holes made when attaching the various pieces of leather to the wooden block are counter punched in order to close the hole in the leather. This process would have been done in order to prevent moisture from entering into the leather and damaging it.

The one thing the Confederate agents did not consider when they ordered the P1860 in numbers was that it was not meant to be opened and closed with every round loaded as in the American way of loading the rifle musket; it was solely meant to transport the cartridges. As a result it was difficult to open and shut, but this did not prevent thousands of Confederate soldiers from using it during the conflict, as the many photographs and surviving examples testify. It was in fact – when you consider the photographic evidence – the second most popular item of British equipment (behind the snake hook waist belt) issued to Confederate troops during the war.

An A. Ross & Co Confederate-used P1860 Pouch. Notice no stitch marks attaching the tab to the flap. It has been "blind" stitched to the flap. (David Burt Collection)

Side view of the Ross pouch. Note the two "star" shaped indents on the leather where the piece of leather was nailed to the wooden block while the glue dried prior to being hand sewn. (David Burt Collection)

The P1859 Serjeant's Pouch

Written in the "Abstract of Summary" letter by Colonel J. Gorgas on February 3, 1863 is the mention of "650 sergeant's accoutrements" being purchased by Major Caleb Huse from England. [4]

The List of Changes for the British Army note in 1859:

> Pattern of 31st August 1859
> 26. Black leather pouch with fur cap pocket attached, for serjeants of Infantry, Rifles, Engineers and Militia, to hold 20 rounds. [5]

Sergeants in the British army were typically second in command of a troop or platoon of up to 35 soldiers, with the important responsibility of advising and assisting junior officers. Therefore, the sergeant would be busy issuing orders and supervising the other ranks in the unit whilst in action, and would not therefore require the amount of ammunition that the ordinary private would typically use. The sergeant's pouch held a three compartment tin, with one compartment having a hinged lid to carry any necessary items. It was to hold 20 rounds of ammunition as compared with the 50 rounds for the normal private, as well as the addition of an internal percussion cap pouch on the right front of the main box underneath the outer flap which would carry 45 caps.

Pictured here is the body of an unfortunate Confederate soldier taken on the Rose Farm area of the Gettysburg Battlefield shortly after Lee's retreat. Right above the trigger guard of the rifle can clearly be seen an opened cartridge box with a cap pouch attached to it. This is clearly evidence of the sergeant's pouch being used at the mid-war point.

Note the cap pouch clearly visible on the cartridge box, above the rifle trigger guard. (Courtesy Library of Congress)

This regulation British P 59 Serjeant's (the British spelling) pouch still bears its old original museum tag written in ink, with the words "Confederate Cartridge Box." It was originally displayed at Lee's Headquarters Museum in Gettysburg before being sold by an online auction site to a private buyer. The pouch shows period use but is in fine, pliable condition; it has underneath the exterior flap a cap pocket with animal fur lining. It is sewn to the pouch along its top and it is wired to the pouch at the base, and it features a receptacle on the interior flap for the nipple wrench. This receptacle is an extra piece of leather sewn under the inner flap with the tab cut into the flap, which could be lifted to insert the musket tool.

Pattern 1859 Sergeant's Pouch. (Courtesy Heritage Auction Galleries)

Note how the tin is not flush with the top of the box. (Heritage Auction Galleries)

As previously discussed, the serjeant's pouch was supposed to have a three compartment tin to hold 20 rounds of ammunition, but this particular pouch has the regulation five-part tin inserted instead. Upon careful inspection it can be seen that the tin is not flush with the top of the box (left).

It is jutting out of the top of the box by about ¼ of an inch. This is because the original three-compartment tin has been replaced by this regulation 50 round tin. The size of the regulation P1860 pouch was some 7 inches across by 3 ¼ inches in height, but the serjeant pouch measured 7 inches across but only 3 inches in height, [6] hence the regulation tin was too big for this pouch. Evidently someone, likely at the issuing Confederate Depot, substituted the 20 round serjeant's tin for the regular British army fifty-round tin so it could carry extra ammunition.

English Pouch found on the Gettysburg battlefield. (Courtesy Milwaukee Public Museum)

The exact same thing is true of this second P1859 British serjeant's pouch that was also recovered from the Gettysburg battlefield. The soldier that carried this particular pouch has cut off the outer flap so that it would be quicker and easier to draw and load the cartridges from the box. Yet again, the original three-part tin has been replaced by a British P60 five-part version that has been forced into the box. It can be seen upon examination that the bottom of the left hand corner is rounded where the tin does not fit properly inside the box.

Thousands of replacement British army pouch tins had been exported to the Confederacy by Caleb Huse, with some 10,000 more ready for shipment from London by February 1863. [7] These were likely to be used in the copies of the P1860 pouches the Confederates were planning to manufacture: (See *Confederate Copies of British Accoutrements*). This is clear evidence that, far from being issued to sergeants in the Confederate armies, as these particular pouches were used for in the British army at least some – if not the majority – were turned into the more favored fifty-round pouches to be issued to the Confederate rank and file.

The P1856 Knapsack

In 1805, the 'Trotter' frame knapsack became the regulation British Army knapsack; it measured some 18 x 13 x 3 inches. John Trotter had been running his business from Oxford Street and Soho Square in London for over 30 years. By the early 1800s his company had become the

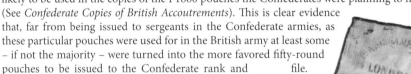

The "Dogan" P1856 Knapsack, marked S. Isaac Campbell & Co. (Courtesy SCCRR & Museum)

major equipment supplier to the British Army. The original frame knapsack he personally designed had boards just at the sides of the main compartment only.

In 1823 the 1st box knapsack was introduced, and it had boards at the top, bottom and sides; it was made of canvas or linen. This new style knapsack would itself undergo another six modifications over the years as follows:

1824 2nd pattern 'box' knapsack approved with improvements to the 1823 version.

1827 3rd pattern 'box' knapsack approved, this was smaller and lighter than the previous two patterns.

1829 4th pattern 'box' knapsack introduced

1840 5th pattern 'box' knapsack – This version had the breast strap removed.

1854 final pattern 'box' knapsack introduced; measuring some 15 x 12 x 3 inches, it was much smaller in size and capacity. The main flap and interior were lined in linen.

1856 A wooden reinforcement and guard strap added to the top of the pack and the Y straps made separate. [1]

Contrary to popular belief, this new P1856 knapsack bore absolutely no resemblance to the original 'Trotter' pack, due to the considerable improvements made over the years. It was commercial copies of the new regulation P1856 knapsack, produced by companies such as A. Ross & Co and companies working for S. Isaac Campbell & Co, that were exported for the Confederate market.

Undoubtedly, the biggest supplier of the knapsack was S. Isaac Campbell & Co, with nearly 5,000 shipped over by the firm during the first few months of the war alone. [2] This original Confederate used P1856 knapsack provided by SIC&Co (pictured) belonged to Private William Dogan of Co E, 5th South Carolina Infantry.

It is made of black painted canvas with black waxed interior and exterior leather straps and reinforced black leather corners, which were made from bridle, or *smooth out* leather. The shoulder straps fastened using brass 'J' hooks and brass hoops; it was designed to be issued with a wooden frame, and it is stencilled on the inside of the flap S. ISAAC CAMPBELL & CO, London in large black lettering.

Pictured on the following page is an original invoice from SIC&Co dated March 20, 1862, for knapsacks. [3] The knapsacks were packed together and imported complete with "knapsack straps, mess tin straps, mess tins and mess tin covers and coat straps." What is interesting to note on this invoice

The "Dogan" knapsack with exterior flap down (SCCRR & Museum, David Burt)

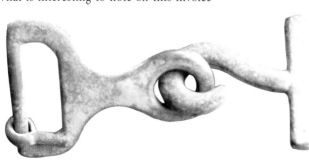

Original British knapsack hooks excavated at Cedar Creek, VA. (David Burt collection)

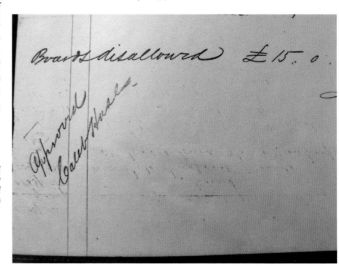

(David Burt)

is that the boards were "deducted," meaning they were not sent with the knapsacks (see below). The same is true of all the knapsack invoices examined, with boards "disallowed, cancelled or deducted," meaning that the majority of knapsacks exported by SIC&Co and issued to Confederate troops in the field were in a soft pack style and not the rigid packs with the boards inside as they were supposed to be.

Further invoices by SIC&Co in the McRae papers show knapsacks being ordered as early as August 12, 1861, with the 2,000 in the invoice above being shipped on board the steamer *Economist*. The first heavy shipment of knapsacks came on board the steamer *Fingal*, with a big portion of these from A. Ross & Co. An invoice for November 1861 discusses some of the knapsacks from the initial *Fingal* shipment; it reads:

Knapsack invoice showing "disallowed" boards. Note Caleb Huse's signature and the word "approved." (David Burt)

Invoice of Stores turned over 25th Day of November 1861 by Captain R.M Cuyler, Ordnance Officerat the Macon Arsenal (Ga.) to M.H Wright at Nashville, TN.

816 Knapsacks and Straps
816 Mess Tins & Covers [4]

After this there are numerous invoices for knapsacks with dates from late December '61 up to late '62. Huse himself wrote to Gorgas from Liverpool on April 1, 1862 that the SS *Minna* carried some "5,900 knapsacks and boards." [5] The biggest single shipment of knapsacks were shipped on board the *SS Melita*, which were then run into Charleston, SC, on board the lighter, speedier blockade runners *Minho* and *Leopard* in late July 1862. These shipments included 70 cases of knapsacks and 24 cases of mess tins. [6]

Among the many items that purchasing agent in England Major E.C. Anderson ordered from A. Ross & Co were commercial copies of the regulation P1856 knapsack. As usual, the Ross model was made of better materials and craftsmanship as compared with the SIC&Co variant. An original A. Ross & Co pack in a private collection also differs in other ways from the SIC&Co pack: the internal buckles are iron that have been hot dipped in tin, and the pack has rough out corner reinforcements that have been blackballed smooth. The interior straps are made of whitened buff leather, and the exterior straps are all buff blackened with the exception of the two straps that hold down the flap, which are 'waxed' vegetable tanned leather (Leather finish on the flesh or rough side). [7]

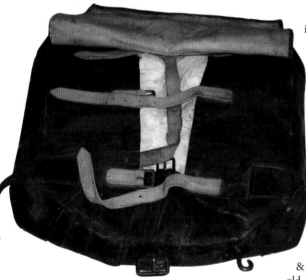

The inside of the Ross & Co knapsack. Note the interior straps of whitened buff leather. (David Burt, Courtesy Atlanta History Center)

The pack measures 14 x 16 x 4 inches and it is WD marked, meaning it had passed the rigid British Army inspection and was accepted for army use. But the fact was that no Confederate agent could deal directly with the government for official War Department surplus. Although official government marked (WD) items were not supposed to be supplied under the neutrality laws, the fact is that some British government marked equipment did make its way to the Confederacy during the conflict, mainly obsolete firearms and old P1842 pattern bayonet scabbards. The London gun maker J.E. Barnett & Sons were known to have bought old obsolete Pattern 51 muskets from the British War Department and then replaced worn, damaged and missing parts, which they then sold on to the Confederates.

Officially any 'surplus' or condemned equipment was marked with two broad arrows facing point to point to show that the piece was now 'Out of service'; it could then be sold on to whoever wanted to purchase it. This knapsack does not show these particular marks, which means it is more likely a surplus or obsolete knapsack that has been bought back from government or other stores and reworked for the Confederate market.

Another virtually identical Ross & Co pack is exhibited at the Atlanta History Center and is made the same way, but there is no WD stamp present. Again, it is made of superior materials and exhibits superb craftsmanship. The corners of this pack are made from enamelled buff leather. This is a highly finished blackened buff leather which closely resembles smooth out bridle leather. The exterior straps are all blackened buff leather with the exception of the two straps that hold down the flap, which are made of waxed leather. As in the previous pack, the interior straps were made from whitened buff leather. The 'Y' straps are waxed tanned leather with *A. Ross & Co C&M 1861* stamped into the bottom of the buckle strap. The pack has the Ross stamp on the inner flap, which is a circle with A. Ross & Co Grange Mills London stamped in black ink.

Both of these Ross knapsacks seem to have been extensively re-worked, and are most likely surplus or outdated knapsacks that have been substantially altered to mimic the official pattern 1856 knapsack in order to help fill the early orders for equipment that both Huse and Anderson had placed with Ross & Co, both for the central government and the state of Georgia. In order to meet these huge targets, Ross & Co also had to sub-contract to outside firms in the making and re-working of the packs and other equipment. Lots of pouches, ball bags, knapsacks and other items of British origin do not bear any makers' marks, almost certainly because they were made by outside contractors, or 'middlemen', as they became to be known, working to supply accoutrements for both SIC&Co and Ross.

What is interesting to know is that both the aforementioned Ross & Co knapsacks were issued complete *with* their boards. These boards simply clip together on the

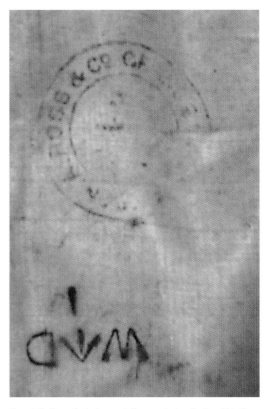

Ross & Co Stamp in the knapsack from a private collection. Note the "WD." (Courtesy Cody Mobley)

inside of the pack, making it a rigid box style knapsack, as it was designed to be. (The boards were disallowed or cancelled by Huse on the knapsacks supplied by SIC&Co on the majority of their invoices.) However, a good deal of knapsacks supplied to Confederate troops came complete with the boards as issued by C.S. Ordnance depots. Surviving invoices from Ordnance officers to units in the field mention around 3,500 packs issued without boards and some 2,500 knapsacks with the boards being issued (see Appendices D & F). Judging by the evidence from surviving S. Isaac Campbell & Co invoices and surviving relics, it has to be reasonable to presume that the knapsacks issued with the boards included were made by Ross & Co or their sub-contractors.

By February 3, 1863, the *Abstract of Summary* letter written by J. Gorgas had reported that 34,655 "*knapsacks complete*" (meaning the knapsack had with it a mess tin, cover and all straps) had arrived safely from England to the Confederacy. When you look at the total of accoutrement sets also imported (34,731) you will see that there was one knapsack for nearly every set of accoutrements. [8]

Commercial copies of the British P1856 knapsack by both Ross & Co and S. Isaac Campbell & Co saw major service in all the Confederate armies, particularly in the early to mid-war period, and would have served the troops in the major battles of 1862, including Shiloh and Sharpsburg. The "English" knapsack was still being distributed and issued as late as 1864. One such ordnance invoice from the Richmond Arsenal's military storekeeper, Captain O.W. Edwards, lists "50 English box knapsacks" [9] being issued to the 1st Corps, Army of Northern Virginia, on April 28, 1864, just prior to the Battle of the Wilderness. Infantry units were not the only ones to be issued the P1856 knapsack. The Confederate States Marine Corps was fully equipped with packs following the 1,000 that were ordered by Secretary of the Navy Mallory in September 1861, and Artillery units were also regularly issued them, with "166 knapsacks and mess tins" issued to the Virginia Heavy Artillery on

June 2, 1863. [10] Added to these other units were the 1st Regiment of Engineers who were formed in late 1863 as combat engineers to construct defenses and roads. The knapsack (pictured) was issued to Private John T. Gibson of Company I, 1st Engineer Regiment after his enlistment in February 1864. On April 8, 1864, Company K of the 1st Engineers were issued with further British arms and accoutrements (see Appendix D). [11]

Today there are at least twelve of these imported British knapsacks that still exist in museums and private collections across America, indicating just how numerous and popular the P56 knapsack was with Confederate soldiers. These include:

1) Wisconsin Veteran's Museum
2) Augusta History Museum
3) South Carolina Confederate Relic Room & Museum, Columbia, SC
4) Museum of the Confederacy, Richmond, VA
5) Stone Mountain
6) Atlanta History Center
7) Gettysburg National Military Park (x 2)
8) North Carolina Museum of History
9) Pamplin Park, Petersburg, VA
10) Chimborazo Hospital (NPS System), Richmond National Battlefield Park
11) Jefferson Barracks Historic Park, Missouri
12) An A. Ross & Co knapsack in a private collection

The P1856 British Knapsack of John Thomas Gibson of the 1st Confederate Engineers Regiment. Gibson enlisted on February 25, 1864 in Richmond, and surrendered at Appomattox Court House, VA, on April 9, 1865. (Courtesy of the Military & Historical Image Bank)

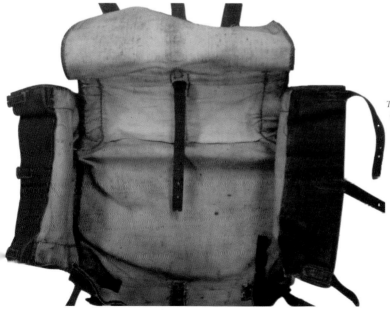

The interior of an S. Isaac Campbell & Co knapsack. (Courtesy Wade Rogers)

The Pattern 1854 Mess Tins and Covers

The British pattern mess tin (above) belonged to Lt. William Jesse Taylor of Co K, 26th S.C. Infantry. The mess tin was first introduced into the British Army in 1813 to replace the tin plate; it was modified in 1850, and again in 1854, by taking away the ring on the top of the lid. It was this P1854 version that was exported to the Confederacy complete with the P1856 knapsack.

The mess tin was constructed of hot dipped or rolled tin plate and was a distinct 'D' shape, unlike the later patterns, which had more rounded edges, and it was comprised of the lid, tray and pan. The pan was 4 1/8" in height; the interior tray, which had an interior handle, some two inches; and the lid, which doubled as a plate, was 6/8 of an inch in height. The total height of the whole mess tin was some 4 ½ inches. A British Army regulation tin had the top turned over, and the edge is rolled and wired to form a stop for the lid. The two side seams are hooked

P1854 Mess Tin. Note the "D" shape of the tins. (SCCRR& Museum, Columbia, SC, courtesy Mike Nicholls)

together and crimped, and two brackets of cast iron or white metal are riveted to each side to support a bail handle of brass wire. [1]

There is evidence that, just before the Wilderness campaign of spring 1864, the Army of Northern Virginia's troops were fully supplied with mess tins, covers, and corresponding knapsacks, as they were being sold to officers as surplus. Ordnance Stores sent to the A.N.V. Ordnance Train on April 27, 1864 had "1000 mess tins and covers to be sold to officers only at £1.50 each." [2] "Mess tins and covers" seemed to be very popular private purchases for Confederate officers, and they were bought from depots in places such as Richmond, Macon, Charleston, and Selma. [3]

Rear view of the English mess tin belonging to Lt. William Jesse Taylor, Co K, 26th S.C. Infantry. (Courtesy Mike Nicholls)

The Mess Tin Cover

Mess tin covers were supplied with linen or canvas covers until 1838, when the covers were changed to black painted canvas with the buff straps changed to black leather, and it was to have between one and four leather keepers. (C&M July 24, 1838). [4] This original in the collection of the Gettysburg National Military Park, and found on the Battlefield, is made from black painted canvas and measures 7 ½ inches in length by 5 ½ inches in height and is 4 ¾ inches deep. It has a four flap closure on the flat side secured by two short leather straps and two small zinc buttons which are 11/16th of an inch in diameter. Two ¾ inch by 2 ⅜ inch long black leather belt loops are sewn to the top and front of the cover for attaching to the knapsack. The mess tin was placed inside the cover, and it was designed to be fastened from the back and strapped to the top of the P1856 knapsack, rather than on a harness attached to the back of the pack as it had been in the previous 1854 model.

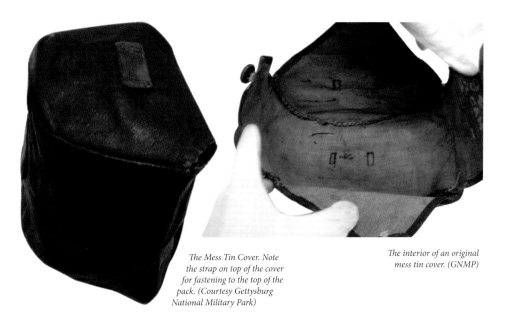

The Mess Tin Cover. Note the strap on top of the cover for fastening to the top of the pack. (Courtesy Gettysburg National Military Park)

The interior of an original mess tin cover. (GNMP)

Cover showing the leather belt loops on the front and top for attaching to the knapsack. (GNMP)

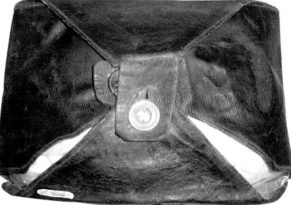

The rear of the cover showing the zinc buttons and leather fastening straps. (GNMP)

Confederate Copies of British Accoutrements

This British equipment was issued to all the main Confederate armies from the outset of the war until at least late 1863, by which time the domestic arsenals began to produce enough equipment of their own. It is interesting to note that accoutrements from England began to tail off by late 1863, and more and more bulk leather was imported to supply the Confederate arsenals that were springing up all over the South.

A typical example was the December 1862 arrival of the SS *Justitia* from Liverpool, which brought in the biggest cargo of supplies from S. Isaac Campbell & Co to date. The invoice spanned some 36 pages, and included large amounts of bulk leather and furnishings, including the following items:

> 300 pouch middlings;
> 500 knapsack sling middlings;
> waist belt furniture;
> 642 lbs cut leather for knapsack trimmings,
> buff pouch billets,
> sets of accoutrement furniture (buckles etc)
> 300 belt middlings,
> 150 middlings for frogs,
> 150 middlings for gun slings and
> 10,000 fifty round pouch tins. [1]

By the end of November 1862, S. Isaac Campbell & Co had already supplied the Confederacy with "10,000 sets knapsack furniture, 10,000 sets accoutrement furniture, 6,000 sets waist belt furniture and 11,600 gun sling buckles." [2]

The Gorgas "Summary of Statement" letter also revealed that "Supplies in London ready for Shipment, 10,000 pouch tins, prepared for accoutrements." [3]

The mass importation of all these items is a clear indication that the Confederate arsenals were beginning not only to manufacture domestically made equipage from imported leather, but were in fact actively making copies of English accoutrements. The most popular English items copied according to these invoices seem to have been the pouch, waist belt, cap pouch, and knapsack.

Pictured (right) is a Confederate made copy of the British pattern 1860 pouch. It has been manufactured from black smooth out bridle leather and features a five tin compartment. This box appears to have been copied from the more numerous pouches supplied by S. Isaac Campbell & Co, which had a slightly longer outer flap than the ones provided by Ross & Co. The only other noticeable change is that the latch tab is squared off, rather than coming to a pointed end as in all British pouches. What is also interesting to note in the *Justitia* invoices are the mentions of "waxed pouch backs and black grain hides for pouch covers." [4]

Confederate copy of the British Pattern 1860 pouch. (Courtesy of the Military & Historical Image Bank)

Featured (right) is a Confederate copy of the British P56/57 cap pouch with some distinct modifications. The British cap pouch had a single belt loop on a slant and was designed to be worn on the pouch belt. The Confederates, however, tended to wear them on the waist belt at a slant instead, so when the Confederates copied it, they simply changed the slant design to a standard vertical configuration with the addition of two belt loops at the rear. Like the English box, this box does not have end flaps, nor did it have a wool strip sewn to the inner back.

Confederate copy of the British cap pouch, minus the angled sleeve so it could fit onto a belt. (Courtesy Shannon Pritchard Old South Antiques)

The box's front, back, and closure tab are made from a single piece of russet leather. The inner flap is also made from the same russet leather. [5] Again mentioned in the *Justitia* invoices are the purchase of "20 brown hides for pockets." [6]

Given the evidence of the S. Isaac Campbell & Co invoices for the imports of accoutrement furniture and the special types of leather and trimmings for all the different British accoutrements – plus surviving examples of equipment – there can be no doubt that the C.S. arsenals had started to copy British army equipment from late 1862 onwards. The most popular of the items copied seem to be the P1860 pouch, cap pocket (minus the angled sleeve), and the knapsack. This would seem to explain why the amount of imported accoutrements dried up, as more and more leather and furnishings came into the Southern arsenal system to make both the copied and standard domestic equipment.

CHAPTER TWO:
Early Confederate Purchases

Huse Anderson & Bulloch

When the Confederate States seceded from the Union in 1860-61 it was short of just about everything a nation needed to wage war, particularly arms and munitions. To try and solve their immediate needs, while the South started to set up its own manufactories the newly appointed Colonel Josiah Gorgas of the Ordnance Department needed a man to act immediately as purchasing agent in Europe. The man he chose was a man in whom Gorgas had total confidence, one Captain Caleb Huse. Joining him would be Major Edward C. Anderson, who would aid Huse in purchasing goods for the army, and Captain James Dunwoody Bulloch, principal agent for the Navy Department.

Caleb Huse graduated from West Point in 1851 and later served as instructor of chemistry there, and in 1860 became Superintendent and Commandant at the University of Alabama. He resigned from the Union army on February 25, 1861, and was commissioned a Captain in the Confederate States Army.

Huse arrived in Liverpool, England, on May 10, 1861, to begin his role as purchasing agent for the Confederate Ordnance Department, responsible for the purchase of arms and equipment for the Confederacy. Britain was officially neutral, which meant Huse could not buy directly from the official government armories or storehouses, but he could buy from commercial manufacturers. He travelled from Liverpool to London and quickly made contact with the commission house of *S. Isaac Campbell & Co, Army Contractors, Outfitters & Accoutrement Makers* of 71 Jermyn Street, who had, up until 1858, been the official supplier of all military equipment to the British army. The company had strong connections with all the commercial manufacturers of arms and equipage in England and had its own factory in Northampton, and therefore could purchase and supply all the war materiel Huse needed without him having to scour the markets himself, a deal which suited Huse perfectly. The company had been banned from making and supplying equipment to the British Army in 1858 for an allegation of bribery at the Weedon Bec storehouse, in which Samuel Isaac (the owner) was accused of paying a bribe of £500 to the storekeeper there. The allegation was never proved, but Isaac was stripped of his army contracts on the grounds of improper gratuity. [1] To get around the ban in 1859 the Isaac brothers, Samuel and Saul, used their positions as Captains in the volunteers to win contracts to supply these newly formed units with equipment. The equipment provided to the volunteers did not have to undergo any rigorous examinations by regimental boards of survey that regular army equipment supplied by contractors working for the War Office did, and neither did it have to stand up to any prolonged usage in the field.

In June 1861, Huse received from S. Isaac Campbell & Co a pricing invoice of the items of equipment he needed for the Confederacy. He then proceeded to order one each of all the items requested for inspection by him, which would then be forwarded to the Confederate government as an example of the patterns he was purchasing. These included all the sealed patterns of British accoutrements that were needed, and once they had been approved by Huse he started to order in bulk. These 'sealed patterns' were approved when an example of each item would be deposited with the appropriate Committee, signed, sealed, and certified as being the sealed pattern, against which all items worn in the future would be compared. At future inspections of each regiment, any item showing variations from the norm would be amended or scrapped.

Although the sealed patterns provided for Huse's and the C.S. government's inspection were of obviously good quality, most of the equipment supplied by SIC&Co to the Confederacy would be made generally of inferior leather and poor craftsmanship. Arms and equipment provided by the firm usually included obsolete pattern muskets from the Crimean war, plus lots of volunteer accoutrements. Although these accoutrements were copied from the official sealed patterns adopted for certain volunteer units – the ball bag and pouch in particular – they differed from the regulation British army patterns. Quality, though, at this moment in time was not Huse's main concern – quantity was.

Arriving to assist Huse on June 21, 1861, was Major Edward C. Anderson. Anderson was a well-to-do planter from Savannah, Georgia, who had previously been in Richmond buying heavy ordnance from the Tredegar Iron Works for the state of Georgia. Georgia, by this time under its Governor Joseph E. Brown, was frantically trying to arm and equip itself away from the central Confederate government. Brown was fanatical in adhering to the doctrine of state sovereignty, and as a result was in constant conflict with the Confederate government. But he was also an efficient administrator, and was determined to serve the interests of his state as he saw fit, and money was appropriated to purchase arms and equipment in England. The man who would act as Brown's agent in England was Charles Green, an English-born owner of a Savannah commission house who was dispatched to England in the summer of 1861 to liaise with Anderson to procure arms and equipment for the state.

On August 1, 1861, Green met Anderson in Liverpool and informed him that he had been appointed by Governor Brown the agent for the state of Georgia, as well as his official role for the C.S. government, and he had been sent over $100,000 to be expended "in the purchase of arms and war materiel for the state." [2] The next day Brown sent a memorandum to Anderson with a list of articles he wished to be purchased, mainly the Enfield rifle and accoutrements. On August 6, 1861 Anderson called on A. Ross & Co of Bermondsey, London, to make contracts both for Georgia and the main Confederate government, where he began to order "leather and equipments of various descriptions." [3] This firm was an official supplier to the British army, and supplied accoutrements and other equipment made to the highest quality from the official army patterns. On 21 August 1861 Green gave Anderson another £5,000 from Governor Brown for further arms and equipment, of which most of this was deposited with the firm Sinclair, Hamilton & Co for the purchase of arms. A good number of Enfield rifles for the state of Georgia were purchased from J.E. Barnett & Sons of Minories, London, and through S. Isaac Campbell & Co, with one invoice for "1,000 Long Enfield Rifles" dated February 7, 1862, marked "JEB G" (Joseph E. Brown Georgia) for shipment on board the *SS Minna*. [4]

Finally, on September 4th a last payment of £11,500 was given to Anderson by Governor Brown, through Green, and at the end of that month Anderson paid Ross & Co over £10,000 for knapsacks, accoutrements, and other goods for both Georgia and the Confederate government. In addition to the remittances from Georgia, Huse and Anderson were now armed with two drafts totalling some $496,000 from the Confederate government, [5] and tens of thousands of pounds (£) worth of Enfield rifles and other arms were purchased through the various commercial gun makers in both London and Birmingham, plus thousands of pounds worth of war materiel through SIC&Co, for which they charged a 2 ½ per cent commission.

The first agent to arrive in England for the Navy Department was one Captain James Dunwoody Bulloch. Born in Savannah, Georgia, on June 25, 1823, he was a naval man through and through. He had served for fourteen years with the United States Navy as a Captain before joining a private shipping company. Bulloch arrived in Liverpool on June 4, 1861, with his primary mission to purchase ships, or to have them built for use by the newly formed Confederate States Navy. His first job, though, was to purchase arms, uniforms and equipment for the Navy Department, which in effect was starting from absolutely nothing. Stephen R. Mallory, Secretary of the Navy, wrote to Bulloch on May 9, 1861 with a list of items he wished to be purchased in England; amongst these were:

1,000 navy pistols, revolvers, with 100,000 rounds of fixed ammunition and 500,000 percussion caps; 1,000 navy carbines with 100,000 rounds of fixed ammunition and 500,000 percussion caps, and also 1,000 navy cutlasses. [6]

Captain James D. Bulloch

On August 13, 1861, Bulloch wrote back to Mallory:

> The sea-service rifles and the cutlasses could not be ready-made. I contracted for them through an agent and they will all be ready in about three weeks. The cutlasses are identical with those used in the British Navy and can be shipped upon the end of the rifle as a bayonet. Revolvers were not to be had on any terms. I therefore contracted with a large factory for 1,000, as per order; these, I hope, will be ready for shipment soon. Every article is of the very best quality, and was selected only after comparison with its corresponding pattern in the British service. [7]

Mallory wrote to Bulloch again on September 26, 1861, which included the following:

> Wants for the Marine Corps 1,000 waist belts, black leather (such as in British service) with cartridge box, cap box, and bayonet scabbard, attached by means of slides; 1,000 knapsacks, such as used in British service, with straps to connect with the waist belt. [8]

Records of Quartermaster Major Algernon S. Taylor of the Marine Corps attest to most of this equipment's safe arrival, and show items of equipment to have been issued commonly to the Marines from the Richmond Depot, including "waist belts, bayonet scabbards for Enfield rifles, bayonets, cap pouches, cartridge boxes and sword bayonet frogs." [9]

In mid-1861, as Huse, Anderson and Bulloch were busy purchasing arms and equipment for the Confederate government, Navy, and the state of Georgia, other state governors were equally strong supporters of state sovereignty, as Brown sent agents to England to start to purchase arms and munitions. These included Louisiana, Mississippi and South Carolina. Louisiana had an agent named Tilton in London with some £300,000 at his disposal from state governor Thomas Overton Moore to outfit her state troops. Mississippi also had purchasing agents in England from before the beginning of the war. Evidence of their successful purchasing came from one Charles Helm, Confederate Consul in Havana, Cuba, who wrote from there on November 9, 1861, that "There are 1,800 Enfield rifles with accoutrements and cartridges in store here belonging to the State of Mississippi." [10] South Carolina Governor F.W. Pickens, being governor of the first state to secede and being equally fanatic of states' rights and sovereignty as Brown of Georgia, became determined to conceal from the Confederate government in Richmondwhat imports his state had managed to procure from England. He wrote in October 1861 "Keep them in a secret…until the hard fact of the winter, and when we know where they may be needed most." [11] Even after outfitting her troops, the amount of British arms and equipment on hand at the Charleston and Columbia arsenals in South Carolina on October 1, 1863, totalled:

> 2,553 Enfield Rifles
> 374 Enfield Rifle Cartridge Boxes
> 142 Moulds, English, Enfield Rifle
> 55 Screw Drivers, Enfield
> 224,898 Cartridges 57 Enfield
> 892 Enfield Bayonets
> 1006 Knapsacks
> 1067 Knapsack Straps [12]

To ship all these vitally needed arms and equipment to the Confederacy and state governments, Anderson Bulloch and Huse purchased the steamer *Fingal* for £17,500 on September 11, 1861. She was a brand new 800 ton iron built vessel, and she sailed laden with some "9,620 Enfields," including 1,100 bought by Georgia and 1,000 by the state of Louisiana on October 14, 1861. She also carried a big shipment of accoutrements, knapsacks, mess tins and other war materiel. She arrived safely in Savannah, Georgia, on November 14th with Major Anderson on board, his mission completed. Before her another steamer, the *Bermuda*, successfully docked in Savannah, GA, on September 18, 1861, with the initial shipment of a least 3,500 Enfield and Austrian rifles and accoutrements. Other significant early purchases of accoutrements, arms and munitions were shipped on board the steamers *Economist* and *Southwick*, which departed in December '61, as well as the *Gladiator*, which sailed from London on November 7, 1861, with another huge shipment. F.H. Morse, the U.S. Consul in London, wrote on November 8, 1861, that "The Gladiator is deeply loaded and has on board 20,240 Enfield rifles, cartridges, caps etc." [13] In addition to these arms, the *Gladiator* was also loaded with thousands of sets of accoutrements, knapsacks, mess tins, ammunition, etc. After her arrival in Nassau, New Providence, in December '61, her weight and subsequent slow speed meant she became trapped when a Union gunboat – tipped off of her arrival there – blockaded the harbor, and any attempt to make a run for it became impossible. After several weeks, just when her Captain decided to head back to England, the *Gladiator's* cargo was transshipped on board the lighter, faster steamers *Kate* and *Cecile*, which were then to make for the unguarded port of New Smyrna, Florida. The *Kate* was loaded with part of the *Gladiator's* cargo which consisted of "6,000 Enfield rifles, 94 boxes of Mess tins, knapsacks and pouches, (Enfield cartridge boxes) 514 boxes of Enfield cartridges, and 90 cases of percussion caps." [14] She safely arrived in New Smyrna on January 31, 1862. The *Cecile* followed several weeks later with the remainder of the cargo, which landed intact on March 2, 1862.

More ships chartered by S. Isaac Campbell & Co in running the Union blockade included the *Sea Queen*, *Sir William Peel*, *Springbok*, *Stephen Hart*, and the *Harriet Pinckney*. Another steamer to bring in arms, munitions, and other war materiels was the *SS Minna*. She served as a transport between Liverpool and Nassau, in the Bahamas, and set sail in March 1862. Her cargo consisted of "5,700 rifles, 5,900 knapsacks, 5,690 sets of accoutrements, 1,840 gun slings, 992 sabre belts and 1,850 sabres." [15] Amongst this cargo S. Isaac Campbell & Co shipped the following items: "1,000 long Enfield rifles and bayonets, 900 knapsacks, straps, mess tins and covers, 320 sets of accoutrements, and 1,400 cavalry swords." [16]

Another major shipment of British equipment came in on board the *SS Melita*, which sailed from London in April 1862. She carried some "4,000 rifles, 70 cases of knapsacks, 20 cases of mess tins, 5 cases of gun slings and 73 cases of accoutrements." [17] These were – as in the case of the *Gladiator* – transported to the Bahamas and then ran the blockade on smaller faster vessels, which included the *Leopard*, *Minho* and *Herald*.

The *Herald* arrived in Charleston on July 3, 1862, with a transshipment from the *Melita*. She carried from the islands "40 cases of rifles, 9 cases of Knapsacks and accoutrements, 33 cases of knapsacks and mess tins," and another "case of accoutrements and waist belts." [18]

By the beginning of 1863 Huse, now acting alone for the Quartermaster and Ordnance Departments since Anderson's departure on the *Fingal*, had gone on to purchase over £1,068,000 worth of military supplies for the Confederacy from Britain, with some £582,700 worth of goods purchased through S. Isaac Campbell & Co alone. [19]

A letter dated February 3, 1863, by the Chief of Ordnance Colonel Josiah Gorgas titled "Abstract of summary showing quantity and value of army supplies purchased and shipped by Maj. C. Huse on account Confederate States Government" showed that, by this time, Huse had purchased and shipped to the Confederacy:

> 34,731 sets accoutrements,
> 34,655 knapsacks, complete,
> 81,406 bayonet scabbards,
> 40,240 gun slings,
> 4,000 canteen straps and
> 650 sergeants accoutrements costing £54,873, 16s 3d.

Total numbers of arms shipped:

> 131,129 stands of arms as follows:
> 70,980 long Enfield rifles,
> 9,715 short Enfield rifles,
> 354 carbine Enfield rifles,
> 21,400 British muskets,
> 20 small bore Enfield rifles,
> 2,020 Brunswick rifles at a cost including cases, moulds, kegs, screw drivers &c of £417,263,9s 11d. [20]

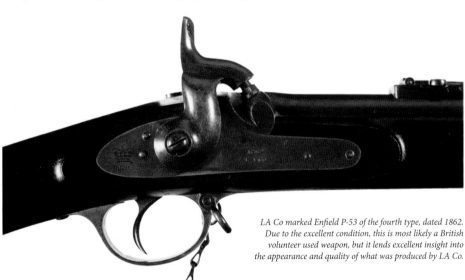

An original SIC&Co invoice for accoutrements bought by Caleb Huse from Samuel Isaac

LA Co marked Enfield P-53 of the fourth type, dated 1862. Due to the excellent condition, this is most likely a British volunteer used weapon, but it lends excellent insight into the appearance and quality of what was produced by LA Co.

The above statement showed that imports of the Enfield rifle, both the *long* three band P53 and the two band *short* P56 and 60, were more than double the imported accoutrements at the mid-war point. Only the imports of bayonet scabbards kept pace with the Enfield rifles, the scabbards themselves not being part of the official 'accoutrement set'. Another interesting detail is that there were only enough gun slings for half the amount of Enfield weapons imported.

Pictured is an original invoice from S. Isaac Campbell & Co for accoutrements sold to the Confederate Government dated December 23, 1861, purchased through them by Huse for shipment on the *Economist* and *Southwick*. It shows all the different pieces of equipment that made up the official 'accoutrement set', which was the *Waist Belt, Ball Bag, Pouch*, (Cartridge Box) *Pouch Belt*, and *Frog and Oil Bottles*. The total cost for 350 of these on this invoice was £231.2s.6d.

Sinclair, Hamilton & Co.

Sinclair, Hamilton & Co. was a London Commission House like S. Isaac Campbell & Company, both of which worked primarily on behalf of Confederate buyers in the U.S. Civil War. Upon arriving in London in May 1861, buyer Caleb Huse set about to procure as many military arms as he could find for the Confederate government. Also in London at the time were buyers from various Northern and Southern states, representatives of the U.S. government, and speculators seeking to profit from the sudden shortage of arms due to the outbreak of the U.S. Civil War. The first matter Huse attended to was to determine exactly who had a supply of military arms ready to sell. He learned that the Liege gun makers in Belgium were tied up with orders for the immediate future, hence, "…it was deemed best not to give any further attention in that direction for a few months." [21] His next stop was to meet with "a merchant of the highest respectability," Archibald Hamilton, Chairman of the London Armoury Company and a man well connected within the English gun trade.

The first attempts by Huse to enter into a contract with Hamilton and London Armoury were unsuccessful, as LA Co was finishing up a War Department order (which the government refused to postpone) and was already committed to fill orders for Massachusetts, whose buyers had arrived just ahead of Huse. There was no inventory on hand ready to buy at the moment. However, Hamilton, as representative for the commission house of Sinclair, Hamilton & Company, had another offer. Huse notes that:

> He was willing to undertake to obtain as many rifles as possible for us in consideration of receiving a commission of 2 ½ per cent, on the amount of the purchases. As the only possible chance of getting any arms was to purchase them from the small manufacturers scattered over England, but principally working in London and Birmingham, and as the agents purchasing for the United States and for the individual Northern States were men quite well informed concerning the trade, we did not hesitate to make the arrangement. [22]

A commission house such as Sinclair, Hamilton & Co charges a "fee" to act on behalf of the buyer and, in other conditions, the seller. Their services are not without value. The Confederate government was not recognized in the international community, which made it difficult to secure credit or enter contracts with multiple small manufacturers, who usually insisted on a sizeable down payment up front. In addition, time was of the essence and Huse was operating in a foreign country. He noted that:

> Sinclair, Hamilton & Co. at once entered upon the business, and in everything they have done we have reason to be more than satisfied. Without their assistance we would be in the hands of a class of contractors who are bound only when they are obliged to be. Sinclair, Hamilton & Co. has nearly exhausted the amount deposited, and an additional $125,000 has been placed to their credit. We submit with this report a statement from them of the number of arms already obtained and of the number they expect to have ready in time for another shipment. [23]

It appears Caleb Huse was able to secure a few thousand arms from LA Co through Archibald Hamilton sooner than expected. These were among the first Enfield long rifles to be shipped from London Armoury in July 1861 and loaded aboard the blockade runner *Bermuda*. The cargo of the

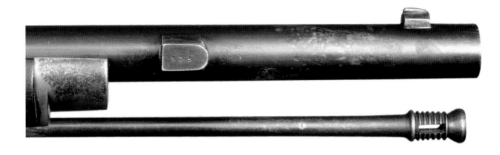

Inspection and acceptance stamps for the firm of Sinclair, Hamilton & Co, which consist of the initials S H and C under a crown.

Bermuda also included food, blankets, dry goods, and drugs which were brokered through Sinclair, Hamilton & Co. [24]

Alexander Sinclair and Archibald Hamilton began their career as merchants in the 1840s with premises located at 17 St. Helen's Place, London. Sinclair had passed away, strangely enough while winding up the estate of his brother back in Scotland in the mid-1850s. **Alexander Sinclair had moved from Scotland some years before and became a merchant in London:**

> ...head of the well-known firm of Sinclair, Hamilton, & Co., engaged in the Cape Hope (South African) trade. His eldest son is Mr. Robert Sinclair, long the esteemed Greenock manager of the locomotive department of the Glasgow and Greenock Railway. Alexander, came to Greenock to wind up his brother's estate, and while so engaged his own death took place, and his remains now rest in the lair belonging to his brother-in-law, John Davidson, in Innerkip Street Burying Ground. Strange, that after spending a long life of active usefulness elsewhere, he should have revisited his native town to die! A tablet erected over his grave bears testimony to the benevolent character of this excellent man. [25]

It is interesting to note that Alexander Sinclair's eldest son Robert did not follow his father in S.H. & Co, as was traditional at the time, or join the firm later after his father unexpectedly passed away, as did Hamilton's son, John J. Hamilton. Perhaps Robert Sinclair just preferred living in Scotland; if not his reasons are not recorded.

At the time of the U.S. Civil War Sinclair, Hamilton & Co was being run by Archibald Hamilton. Commission houses not only procured military arms and war material, they also got involved in shipping the goods, which was extremely profitable. S. Isaac, Campbell & Co was well known as one of the most enterprising owners of blockade runners until the Confederacy ceased to do business with them in 1864. On May 21, 1862, Archibald Hamilton became the registered owner of the *Agrippina*, a 258 ton merchant sailing ship known as a bark or barque. It was soon loaded with coal, wool cloth, gun powder and heavy artillery. The ownership documentation was a ruse, "the bark is owned by the Confederate government and nominally held by Sinclair, Hamilton & Co of London and sails under the

British flag." [8] The financing for the *Agrippina* was purportedly arranged through Fraser, Trenholm & Company of Liverpool on behalf of the Confederate government. [26] No surprise there.

Shipping direct to the Confederate ports on a bark was risky, because the wind powered sailing vessels could not out-run the warships that the U.S. Navy sent after them. S. Isaac, Campbell and Co learned this the hard way when their bark *Springbok*, which was flying under a British flag in 1861, was taken by the U.S. Navy as a prize of war. Hence, it soon became standard practice to ship goods from England to a neutral port either at or near a British possession, or at least in British waters. Once anchored the cargo was loaded onto speedier blockade runners. One incident similar to the capture of the *Springbok* involved Sinclair, Hamilton & Co in October 1863. The *USS Vanderbilt* went in search of the *CSS Alabama* and its Captain (Raphael Semmes), but instead found the bark *Saxon* flying the British flag and boarded it "on suspicions of being engaged in the contraband trade to the ports of the Southern Confederacy." [27] The ship had just unloaded 250 tons of coal onto Penguin Island, a British possession off the coast of South Africa. An officer from the *USS Vanderbilt* shot and killed the first mate on the *Saxon*, which was then claimed as a prize of war and taken to New York. The matter caused a diplomatic stir, as might be imagined. Sinclair, Hamilton & Co were the London agents for the *Saxon*, which was registered to South African owners in Cape Town. The bickering went on for some months about whether or not Penguin Island was a British possession, if the capture was justified, and so on. The correspondence back and forth fills several volumes. [28] The Prize Court in New York was unimpressed. The fact is, when the *USS Vanderbilt* crew boarded the *Saxon* they found on board (besides coal) a large quantity of recently captured goods from Yankee merchant vessels.

Confederate buyers in London said of Archibald Hamilton that he was capable of the most gracious hospitality as long as it was outside of business. Major Anderson was a guest of Hamilton at his country house in Kent on September 15, 1861, and commented on the 'princely treatment' he received that weekend, including lavish dinners and expensive bottles of wine. However, when it was time to settle on contract terms he noted, "Mr. Hamilton is the businessman in the London Armoury contracts and in trade haggles over the ha'penny." [29] A year after the U.S. Civil War ended, Archibald Hamilton voluntarily liquidated London Armoury Company to its creditors. It is often stated more or less *de-facto* that it was due to the collapse of the Confederacy. While the loss of the Confederate business was a setback, it did not bankrupt LA Co or Sinclair, Hamilton & Co. According to Caleb Huse:

> our payments for London Armoury are made by cheques drawn on Fraser, Trenholm & Company...when the end came and some of the largest sellers were ruined, I never heard one word of complaint of their being over-reached or treated in any way unfairly. [30]

The remnants of LA Co reorganized as London Small Arms Company in Tower Hamlets, which continued to produce military weapons well into the 20th century.

Archibald Hamilton passed away in 1880 at his country house in Kent. His son, John James Hamilton, continued in the trade as Sinclair, Hamilton & Company at 17 St Helen's Place, which was still listed by Lloyd's Shipping Register in 1902. [31]

CHAPTER THREE
The English Gun Trade

T he Confederate States seceded from the Union ill-equipped to fight a prolonged war–or any other type of war for that matter. Out of necessity, the South quickly adopted a strategy of importing huge numbers of small arms (as well as other provisions) with which to field an army. The majority of the small arms were imported from England. The best and most widely available commercial military arm was the Enfield rifle musket, Pattern 1853. The period term for this arm in the gun trade was "Enfield long rifle." There were also several patterns of two-band "Enfield short rifles", one of which was known as the Army or Sergeant's rifle; another was the Naval Rifle. Some barrels were five grooved, while others had three and so on. The shipping manifests, contracts and other records of the time do not always distinguish between the long and short rifles, both of which were in use. While the overwhelming majority of Confederate contracts were for the Enfield long rifle, there were also a number of short rifles in use. To prevent further confusion over which names to use we will apply the period term "Enfield rifle" inclusively, and specify the "long" and "short" versions only when the record itself makes that distinction. Feel free to disagree if you like, but this was the Victorian-era parlance in use by the English gun trade. In the four years following the first shots fired at Fort Sumter in April 1861, an enormous number of Enfield rifles would be purchased by Confederate agents for the armies of the Southern states. Perhaps more surprising is the number (428,292) purchased by Union agents in about half the time, since the Federal orders terminated in mid-1863. [1] The U.S. Civil War-era was a great time to be in the English gun trade.

The Beginnings

We will begin by setting the stage, historically speaking, when Queen Victoria opened "The Great Exhibition of the Works of Industry of All Nations (Crystal Palace)" in 1851 to "exhibit" to the rest of the world the industrial, military and economic superiority of Great Britain in the mid-19th century. In modern history we look back at the London "Crystal Palace" event as an enduring symbol of the Industrial Revolution in Britain during the Victorian era. However, it was here that the American system of arms manufacture by machinery was first displayed to a broader European audience. The beginning of mass production represented a paradigm shift in European military arms making. The exhibition marked the introduction of the methods of manufacture with machinery which would come to be widely adopted in the years afterwards. The Great Exhibition of 1851 led directly to an English commission investigating the use of machinery for the production of military arms in 1853. [2] This was one factor which led to a change in how the Government procured small arms and the subsequent modernization of the Royal Small Arms Manufactory at Enfield Lock in 1854. The commercial gun makers of London and Birmingham felt the pressure on their purses, and by the late 1850s (post-Sepoy Rebellion) they noticed a remarkable reduction in their government work. By that time the Royal Small Arms Manufactory was turning out around 2,000 Enfield rifles per week—sometimes more—and the pinch was being felt across the Gun Quarter. This was compounded by a workers' strike in Birmingham during 1859 (over wages), which was subsequently settled through arbitration. However, there were nine weeks of lost production time, and the War Department viewed the strike as evidence that they made the right move. [3] It was becoming clear that while strikes in the gun trade were somewhat uncommon, they did seem to coincide with the issuance of large government contracts or rumors of war. The government had no intention of going back to doing business in the gun trade the old way.

The method of production by hand work prevailed in both London and Birmingham much as it had for hundreds of years, with the exception being London Armoury Co. The manufacturing processes employed in the gun trade were somewhat complicated and depended a great deal on the skill of the individual worker. London Armoury Company was the first commercial firm to grasp the potential of mass production technology and purchased American gun making machinery for their new factory in Bermondsey. [4] They were producing parts interchangeable Enfield rifles on government contract by 1860. The locks are marked LA Co (versus the earlier *London Armoury*) with the date. The parts interchangeable LACs were a unique minority of the total production of London and Birmingham, and as such will be discussed in greater detail later in the monograph.

The military gun manufacturing processes of Birmingham and London were somewhat distinct, and the difference merits some discussion. To begin with, London gun makers were part of the Livery system, meaning workers were members of centuries old trade guilds. Generally speaking, children left school at the age of 14 and went out to work. If the parents could afford to do without the child's wage, the child would be apprenticed in a craft, such as gun making. In London and other major cities this meant working for seven years for a reduced wage. At the age of 21 the apprenticeship phase ended with the presentation of a "proof piece" to the Company to prove that the necessary skill set had been mastered. The apprentice then had to work as a journeyman for two more years before he could be called a Master gun maker, and thereby be granted permission to open his own business by the Worshipful Company of Gun-makers. At this stage he would register his "mark", and in theory all his work would be stamped with it. Birmingham makers were not required to mark their work and most did not, preferring to remain anonymous. In addition, Birmingham firms were less strident about apprenticeships. Another difference was that the London gun makers were mostly centralized in a small geographic area proximate to the Tower, where work was inspected and final deliveries made. And of course, London had the first gun barrel proof house in England dating from 1637.

Gun Manufacturing in the 19th Century
Birmingham Small Arms Trade

In England during the mid-19th century, the War Department had very limited or no government owned modern weapons making capability. Instead, they depended on the Birmingham and London commercial gun makers to produce weapons for the armed forces as needed on a contractual basis. In late 1853, with hostilities brewing with Russia, the War Department contracted with four reputable Birmingham gun makers to produce the improved long rifle design called the Pattern of 1853, or P53. The so-called "old four" or "original four" firms were Tipping & Lawden (Fig 1), Swinburn, Thomas Turner, and Hollis & Sheath (Fig 2). These four gun makers were responsible for furnishing twenty thousand finished P53 long rifles with bayonets and implements that had passed a government inspection by the dates specified in the contract at a rate of a thousand per week. The four gun makers "set up" or assembled the weapons from parts provided by individual businesses employing craftsmen subdivided into a number of specialties. For example, for the initial War Department contract barrels were made by Ezra Millward, William Deakin, Henry Clive, Beasley & Farmer, and others. The locks were produced primarily in neighboring areas, such as Wolverhampton, Wednesbury, and Darlaston. The lock makers included William Corbet, J. Brazier, John Duce, and J. & E. Partridge. Rammers were made by Thomas & Charles Gilbert, James Francis, James Grice, and R. & W. Aston, who also contracted to make bayonets, wood screws, and barrel bands. Further, bayonets were also made by Salter, G.W. & E. Roe, William Deakin, and others. [5] There was some initial confusion, and a lack of standardization led to delays. Even though the first contract was relatively small, the four firms defaulted at the deadline for their weekly quota set to begin in February 1854 and remained behind schedule. The last deliveries on that contract were not made until March 1855, and only then because a few additional firms stepped in to meet the shortfall. This raised some concerns within the War Department about the reliability supply chain. The Select Committee of Small Arms was formed to look into the matter and report to Parliament.

Although final deliveries were still running behind with the first contract, in December 1854 a second larger contract for 27,400 additional P53s was made. Fourteen more firms were added to the original four for purposes of filling the new orders, setting prices, and regulating labor costs. [6] In January 1855 there was a third contract for an additional 10,000 more. The partnering Birmingham gun makers formed an association which was subsequently called Birmingham Small Arms Trade. The members were by no means all of the gun makers in Birmingham. [7] A commercial directory from the time period lists over five hundred "master gun-smiths" or gun makers, each operating independently. The firms in Birmingham worked with roughly 7,500 independent craftsmen hand-making parts or factory workers fitting the parts and finishing the guns. The "outworkers" numbered about 3,500 and the "setters-up" (factory workers) close to 4,000. The gun makers comprising the

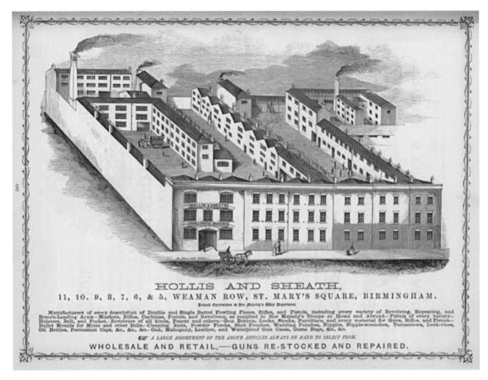

HOLLIS AND SHEATH,
11, 10. 9, 8, 7, 6, & 5, WEAMAN ROW, ST. MARY'S SQUARE, BIRMINGHAM.

WHOLESALE AND RETAIL,—GUNS RE-STOCKED AND REPAIRED.

Fig. [2] another member of the "original four" was Hollis & Sheath, Maker to Her Majesty's War Department. Isaac Brenthall Sheath and Isaac Hollis (originally of Hollis Bros.) became partners in 1844, and by the time of the formation of the Birmingham Small Arms Trade were large wholesale gunmakers. The famous gunmaker William Tranter was both a business partner and former apprentice of Hollis. The image above lends some insight into the large scale of these factories. When Sheath passed away in 1861, the firm reorganized as Isaac Hollis & Sons. (Image used by permission of revolutionaryplayers.uk.org)

BSAT stock roundel stamped on the rear stock flat during the U.S. Civil War, drawn by Craig L Barry.

Birmingham Small Arms Trade were predominantly large factories, long standing in the gun trade with over-lapping family connections and well capitalized. The Chairman of this new syndicate, John D. Goodman (Cooper & Goodman), believed that adding the additional fourteen firms would provide the stability needed to complete new government orders promptly without the chaos associated with the initial contract of a year prior.

Some of the known master gun makers identified with Birmingham Small Arms Trade–in addition to the old four–were W.L. Sargant, Joseph Bourne, Cooper & Goodman, W. Scott & Sons, Bentley & Playfair, Joseph Smith, R. & W. Aston, Pryse & Redman, King & Phillips, E. & G. Hackett, Cook & Son, Benjamin Woodward & Son, Thomas Moxham, and Joseph Wilson. [8] The War Department business was not all sent to Birmingham. London gun makers were involved as "setters up" in additional contracts as well, beginning in May 1854, providing a much smaller number of finished arms by November 1854.

Ironically, in the newly formed Birmingham Small Arms Trade it seemed that with the greater number of gun makers came even greater confusion. The additional fourteen firms (and original four) fell behind on filling the new War Department contracts almost immediately. Deliveries eventually

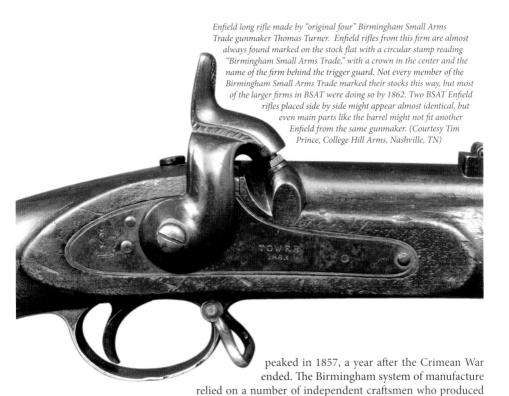

Enfield long rifle made by "original four" Birmingham Small Arms Trade gunmaker Thomas Turner. Enfield rifles from this firm are almost always found marked on the stock flat with a circular stamp reading "Birmingham Small Arms Trade," with a crown in the center and the name of the firm behind the trigger guard. Not every member of the Birmingham Small Arms Trade marked their stocks this way, but most of the larger firms in BSAT were doing so by 1862. Two BSAT Enfield rifles placed side by side might appear almost identical, but even main parts like the barrel might not fit another Enfield from the same gunmaker. (Courtesy Tim Prince, College Hill Arms, Nashville, TN)

peaked in 1857, a year after the Crimean War ended. The Birmingham system of manufacture relied on a number of independent craftsmen who produced most of the needed parts by hand. [9] The rifles from Birmingham Small Arms Trade were subject to an inspection with gauges at the Tower. A hand-made military arm, even one that passes inspection with gauges at the factory, is not necessarily parts interchangeable to the standards of machine made arms. The War Department insisted on parts interchangeability, and tight tolerances and rejections from inspectors at the Tower were common. Passing of a government inspection with gauges is the meaning of "TOWER" engraved on the lock plate of commercial military arms accepted by the War Department. [10]

The Birmingham Small Arms Trade and their time honored system of manufacture by hand again failed to live up to the expectations of the War Department. To meet their immediate needs during the Crimean War, the War Department had to take the extreme step of looking to Belgium and France for arms, and even placed an order with an American firm (Robbins & Lawrence of Windsor, Vermont) for an additional twenty-five thousand Enfield rifles. Realizing the serious implications of the predicament, the Select Committee on Small Arms initiated discussions about refurbishment and modernizing the Royal Small Arms Manufactory (Factory) at Enfield Lock with an eye toward manufacturing their own military small arms by machinery on the "American Plan."[11] The effect of this chilling news on the Birmingham gun makers resulted in well-founded concern, as their main customer was about to become their main competitor. However, in the mid-1850s it was still widely believed that the manufacture of military weapons by machine was only working out in America because they lacked the skilled craftsmen of the English trade associations, a system which had been in place for hundreds of years. It was still far from certain that gun making on the "American Plan" could be done as well or for less cost than by hand, especially considering the massive initial investment necessary for the new factory and machinery. At least this was the sentiment expressed by the Chairman of the Birmingham Small Arms Trade and others called before Parliament to testify in 1854. [12] The testimony during the Parliamentary sessions was contentious. For one thing, a prior attempt at government arm making at Enfield in 1812 was less than successful. In addition, a great number of jobs were at stake in Birmingham, as well as the independent way of life to which workers in the gun trade were accustomed. The War Department argued that the master gun makers in Birmingham were too dependent on the whims of skilled labor in the gun trade, "held hostage" in other words.

It is important to keep in mind that one main reason for the formation of Birmingham Small Arms Trade in 1854 was to control prices for labor and materials and address those issues. While production loss due to strikes was uncommon, labor disputes were another story. There is no doubt that one main feature of the Birmingham Small Arms Trade was to keep a check on rising wages and commit the output of individual craftsmen to their firms. Birmingham gun makers were well aware their labor costs were 20% higher than in Belgium (Liege). [13] Prior to Birmingham Small Arms Trade, gun makers were too numerous and independent to act in concert on such matters. When a contract was granted to a gun maker, workers saw that as an opportunity to demand a raise in payments or threaten to strike. When such an impasse was reached arbitrator(s) that both sides agreed upon would be appointed to resolve the matter. The following example occurred in 1852, when gun makers Joseph Bourne and Westley Richards were selected to arbitrate a labor/management dispute between 'stockers and finishers' and several factory owners over a War Department contract:

> The following may be taken as a fair practical example of the benefits likely to arise from a thoroughly organized plan of arbitration between employers and workmen. It was mentioned, in April, 1852, that the differences which, for some weeks, existed between the master gun-makers and operative stockers and finishers of Birmingham, had at length been satisfactorily arranged, and that, in consequence, the Government contracts for a supply of 23,000 Minie rifles (Pattern of 1851) would be immediately commenced. This result was effected by Mr. Westly Richards and Mr. Joseph Bourne, whom both parties agreed to appoint as arbitrators; their decision being that the prices paid by the contractors to the men should be for finishing, 12s.; stocking, 3s. Id.; making for both branches 15s.Id.; being 5d.less than the demand made by the men, and 1s. 9d more than the terms offered by the masters; the latter to be liable for all risks over which the stockers and finishers have no control. [14]

Industry leaders in the Gun Quarter like Joseph Bourne would later join the Birmingham Small Arms Trade, while other well known gun makers like Westley Richards and W. Greener remained independent of the group. Smaller gun makers bore the brunt of the economic impact from Birmingham Small Arms Trade. Their advantages caused some smaller Birmingham firms to dissolve or forced them into receivership. The well regarded firm Moore & Harris is an example, which was sold at auction to W. Scott when it failed in 1864. [15] Overall, labor relations with the Birmingham Small Arms Trade were amicable. The gun makers paid top wages, and although a downturn in 1859 resulted in a nine week strike – settled (again) by arbitration – complete labor stoppages were often threatened but rarely carried out.

In the end though, the War Department received approval and bought U.S. made machinery from Ames Mfg in the mid-1850s. They refurbished the Royal Small Arms Manufactory to produce parts interchangeable Enfield long rifles and short rifles, and hired American James H. Burton (of expanding minie ball fame), previously Superintendent of Harper's Ferry Armory. His task was to put together the Enfield operation and train a work force to use the new technology. By 1858 the government factory was turning out completed, parts interchangeable Enfield rifles in large quantity. The production of Royal Small Arms Manufactory was reserved for outfitting the British Army and was not sold overseas to either the U.S. or CS. The Enfield rifles manufactured by the government are marked ENFIELD with the year on the lock plate, V-R under the crown behind the hammer, and will have government acceptance and proof marks. These arms were both better and cheaper. The Birmingham Small Arms Trade had long argued that making guns by hand was less expensive than manufacture by machine. [16] However, in a report to Parliament, the cost of a completed Enfield rifle from the commercial gun trade is stated as follows, compared to the Royal Small Arms Manufactory:

> The cost of non-interchangeable long Enfield rifles with bayonets, under a contract made in 1859, was £2 J 8s 6d each to which must be added the cost of the stock 2s 6d, and viewing expenses 3s bringing the total cost to £3 4s each. It is stated that the average cost

of the long Enfield rifles made at the Government factory, including an allowance of 5 per cent, on the cost of buildings and machinery, for depreciation, has averaged about £2 each. In 1859 a contract was entered into for short Enfield rifles, which, complete, and including stocks and viewing expenses, cost £4 14s each. The cost of subsequently producing the same weapon at Enfield is stated to be £2 14s each. [17]

The reported costs per finished weapon at Royal Small Arms Manufactory varied just slightly from year to year, depending on materials, overhead, production, and other variables, but the point made here about cost savings was beyond dispute. As early as 1859, it was no longer seriously debatable whether manufacturing Enfield rifles by machinery resulted in a military arm that was both "better", meaning parts interchangeable, or whether it was less expensive to produce. The improved quality and lower cost was a simple matter of fact. And as such, the Birmingham Small Arms Trade appeared in danger of extinction.

Feeling the icy hand of evolution tightening around their neck, John Goodman, still Chairman of Birmingham Small Arms Trade, proposed a new business venture to manufacture military arms by machine to better compete with the government facility at Enfield. In June 1861, Goodman raised £ 24,500 in capital and purchased land to begin construction on a new factory at Small Heath. The venture was called *Birmingham Small Arms Company*, and while some of the same gun makers were involved in both, these were entirely separate ventures. Confusion exists, perhaps because the names are very similar. However, Birmingham Small Arms Trade was a cooperative association made up and administered by the large gun makers themselves under Director John D. Goodman. The BSAT maintained offices on Steelhouse Lane, while BSA Co offices were on Armoury Road, near the factory. The newly elected Board of Directors of BSA Co included John D. Goodman, Chairman; J.F. Swinburn, Vice Chairman; Isaac Hollis; Joseph Wilson; Edward Gem; Charles Pryse; Charles Playfair; Sir John Ratcliff; and Samuel Buckley. There are some recognizable names of gun makers from Birmingham Small Arms Trade here and some names which are not. For example, BSA Co board members Sir John Ratcliff, Edward Gem, and Samuel Buckley had no known connection to the gun trade. They were merely investors. [18]

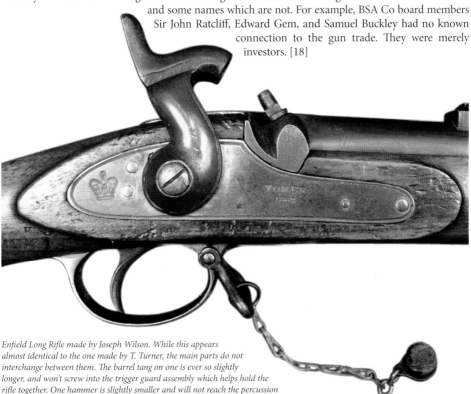

Enfield Long Rifle made by Joseph Wilson. While this appears almost identical to the one made by T. Turner, the main parts do not interchange between them. The barrel tang on one is ever so slightly longer, and won't screw into the trigger guard assembly which helps hold the rifle together. One hammer is slightly smaller and will not reach the percussion cone on the other rifle, and so on. (Courtesy of Tim Prince)

Oddly enough, neither the Government manufactory at Enfield nor the 1861 ground breaking for the new BSA Company factory at Small Heath proved the death knell for the Birmingham Small Arms Trade. Two unforeseen developments intervened to save it, at least in the short run. In 1859, the Second Volunteer Movement in England provided new civilian markets for military arms. The real bonanza came two years later in 1861, and the apex of the Birmingham Small Arms Trade arrived with the outbreak of the U.S. Civil War. Buyers for individual states, as well as both U.S. and Covernments, were soon in Birmingham (and London) to contract for military arms and equipment on a massive scale. The U.S. Consul in London, F.H. Morse, wrote to Secretary of State Wm. Seward in 1861:

> At Birmingham several persons, all pretending to be purchasing for the U. S. Government, are bidding against each other, and have run up the price of rifles, which receive only a nominal inspection and some none at all, from 60s up to 75s and 80s (sterling) each. The Confederates are getting the same guns at Birmingham, but not enough to disturb the market…The price has been run up. [19]

Indeed, prices had been run up. Marcellus Hartley, founder of Schuyler, Hartley & Graham of New York, was in Birmingham in August 1862 on behalf of the U.S. Government to purchase Enfield rifles from Birmingham Small Arms Trade. He refers to them as the "*combination of Birmingham manufacturers that produces 3,000 rifles per week.*" However, discussions with the manager in charge, "Swinburne" (sic)—probably John F. Swinburn—did not yield any arms from "the Birmingham combination" for the price previously agreed and Hartley withdrew. He later learned that Birmingham Small Arms Trade was filling contracts with the Confederacy and other Union buyers at the same time, and the lot of rifles which he was there to purchase went to them. Hartley left Birmingham frustrated, and continued on to London before he ended his trip in Belgium. He could not get an immediate answer from London Armoury Company on a new Enfield long rifle contract, so while in town he visited some other gun makers in the area. Hartley recalled:

> When I went to London to see what I could do with the wealthy manufacturers, I found that Swinburne (sic) from the Small Arms Trade, had telegraphed to London in advance asking the refusal of all their arms at 60s/ for one week. They, understanding his tricks, showed me the telegrams, knowing at once what his object has been and is.

Hartley also learned that Birmingham Small Arms Trade pushed for higher prices by telling prospective buyers "*that any arms not made by them or coming through them are the rejects.*" He concluded that, as a result, he "*had not had a very agreeable task among these Englishmen. Birmingham Small Arms (Trade) has been deceiving us…the manufacturers are a slippery set.*" Hartley subsequently arrived in Belgium and found the gun makers at Liege conducted their business in the same duplicitous manner as those with whom he dealt in Birmingham. He was, however, able to procure a large number of P53 Enfield rifles intended for the Confederacy by employing the same tactics used against him at BSAT. And wise enough now to not trust the Belgians, Hartley remained at Liege until the rifles were inspected, boxed, and shipped to New York. [20]

About those glory days of easy money for the Birmingham Small Arms Trade, Chairman John Dent Goodman admits:

> The first shot was fired at Fort Sumter on the 12th April, 1861. On the 9th May following five purchasers of arms, some commissioned by different Northern States, others private speculators, arrived in Birmingham. Each had so well-kept secret the object of his mission, that when they found themselves all engaged in Birmingham on the same errand they suspected each other of purchasing for the enemy, and their anxiety was increased accordingly to secure the few thousand arms that were then in store in Birmingham. The few in hand were at once shipped off, and large orders were given, which continued to occupy the trade at their full power till March, 1863. [21]

The first three years of the 1860s proved to be the last of the huge military contracts for Birmingham Small Arms Trade. War Department contracts were hardly missed, which is well and good, because by 1863 Royal Small Arms was turning out 2,000 finished arms per week. So flush with cash were the workers with Birmingham Small Arms Trade it was said that, "profligate gun makers and barrel makers on wages of £20 and £50 a week were taking cabs to work and 'lighting cigars in public houses with £5 notes.'" [22] Goodman recalled later:

The trade worked at its full power, straining every nerve until I find by the return from the Birmingham Proof-house, that in one month, the month of October, (1862) 60,345 rifle barrels were proved, being very few short of 2,000 per day from Birmingham alone, a number altogether unprecedented in the history of the trade. At that time the supplies produced in America at the Springfield Armory and elsewhere began to tell upon the demand. We still find, however, that the numbers were 40,000 to 50,000 per month, till March, 1863; they then fell to 14,000 per month, till in September, 1863, the Northern demand ceased altogether. Without notice the orders were suspended, and guns that had been sent over were often returned to this

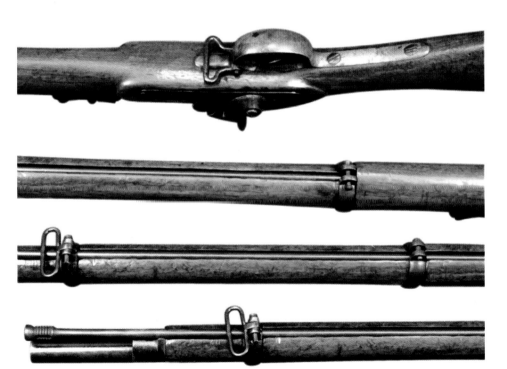

Note the slight shrinkage of wood at the butt plate by the toe.

country. The United States Government found at that time their factories equal to supply the whole demand. [23]

After September 1863, the sole American customer was the Southern Confederacy and some of the individual Southern states. Their representatives stepped in and procured the excess capacity at very reasonable terms. These Tower-marked P53 Enfield rifles from Birmingham Small Arms Trade were some of the last of the hand made military arms in history. BSA Company at Small Heath did not supply any machine made Enfield rifles to America during the Civil War. Their first commercial contract was with the Turkish government for 20,000 short rifles in 1866. By the 1870s, virtually every European country was making military arms with machinery on the so-called "American Plan."

For his part, Chairman John Goodman kept the proverbial "stiff upper lip" about the end of military gun making by hand. He opined that it would free up the Birmingham Small Arms Trade gun makers to better supply the civilian "sporting gun" market. Ironically, some individual gun makers who stuck with hand made sporting guns were still in business well into the twentieth century. Birmingham Small Arms Trade officially dissolved in 1878, by which time the BSA Co at Small Heath was manufacturing bicycles. [24]

The Birmingham System of Manufacture

Where and how were all those hundreds of thousands of Enfield rifles made? The city of Birmingham had an area called the Gun Quarter, which was centered between the foot of Steelhouse Lane and Aston Ward. It was bounded by the Jewelry Quarter, Business Quarter and Retail Quarter. There were a mixture of factories of moderate size, as well as small factories and workshops which were rented out to individual out-workers or small makers. It was a cramped section of early Victorian tenement buildings pushed in between buildings of an earlier time and function. The largest buildings were occupied by members of Birmingham Small Arms Trade. Some smaller gun makers, such as Moore & Harris on Loveday Street or John Poole, who was located on a mixed commercial block of Price Street, were alongside some of the big factories. [25] It was an interesting place. The older section of Price Street went back to the eighteenth century and "...in its fifty-nine houses and seven courts there were shopkeepers, two cow keepers, a kettle and tea urn manufacturer, a coal dealer, a marine store dealer, an earthenware dealer, a bone button maker and two beer retailers to name but a few." We can take from this that (obviously) not every business in the Gun Quarter was directly associated with gun making. There were workshops for twenty-two tradesmen associated with the gun trade in the older section of Price Street. On the other hand, the newer section developed strictly as a result of the expanding gun trade. Gun makers and the various trades occupied every single one of the twenty-eight buildings there, and mingled in with the various factories were smaller workshops. In the middle of the nineteenth century it was common practice in the Birmingham Gun Quarter for masters to pay wages at the Bulls Head Pub at 1 Price Street. Money in hand (wages) inevitably led to a few drinks, followed by brawling on the sawdust covered floor. "At this time there was a strong Catholic community in the Gun Quarter and often rather than summon the law, the proprietor (of Bulls Head pub) would call on the local priest to sort out the fighters while the fiddler continued on with his playing." [26] A local 19th century pundit noted that "both high life and low life blackguards Brums engaged in occasional barroom fisticuffs...ever since the traditional Sunday dog fights fell out of favour."

How were the grade two/hand made commercial Enfield rifles made in Birmingham different from London? John D Goodman (Cooper & Goodman) notes of the English gun trade, "The chief branches are as follows:—Stock, barrel, lock, furniture, and oddwork making; and for military guns there are in addition,—bayonet, sight, and rammer making." The general branches to which Mr. Goodman refers are common to both London and Birmingham, but the difference is in the specific system of manufacture employed. [27] In London, the factory often contained most of the shops, with the outworkers employed there, and at London Armoury the entire P53 is essentially produced under one roof, start to finish. By way of contrast, in Birmingham the numerous parts of the gun are produced by distinct trades, of which there are more than sixty. Workers in the gun trade primarily operated as individual craftsmen with assistants. Lacking the livery system, Birmingham gun trade apprenticeships were shorter in duration and not as common. The workshops that employ material makers are generally at separate premises from the main factory. An individual outworker, such as an engraver, may do work for several masters. The parts are made up piecework, then collected by the manufacturer, known as the "gun-maker." They are then assembled at the factory, or "set up." Payments were calculated by that method (piecework) as well. Gun maker John D. Goodman (Cooper & Goodman) continued:

> No very correct estimate can be given of the rate of wages earned by the workmen in the gun trade. With very few exceptions the work is paid for by the piece, and the rate varies considerably with the demand. During the past ten years there is little doubt but that the wages earned in this trade have probably exceeded those in any other. Several branches require very high skill, and the remuneration is in proportion... [28]

Stock Making

Beginning with the stock, the primary wood used for the commercial Enfield rifle was walnut. Goodman notes that "...domestic beech-wood is employed for African markets, and for the lower description of sporting guns; its liability to expand and shrink with changes of the atmosphere renders it unfit for any but guns of the cheapest description." Where did the walnut come from? England could not grow enough walnut trees domestically for the enormous needs of their commercial gun trade. As a result, most walnut gunstocks were imported (with few exceptions) from Italy and Germany. The stocks were shipped to Birmingham, cut from the plank into the rough form of the gun. Goodman continues, "One Birmingham contractor, to meet the demand occasioned by the Crimean war, established saw mills in Turin (Italy) and since that period has converted into gunstocks nearly 100,000 walnut trees." [29] The mysteriously unnamed owner of the saw mill operation in Turin was a founding member of Birmingham Small Arms Trade, W. Scott & Son. William Scott moved to Birmingham from London. In 1859, the firm changed names to W. Scott & Son and moved to quarters on Princip Street. The firm was finally William Scott & Sons, the plural "Sons" being added post-1869. Trading ceased in 1875. The Turin saw mill employed about 100 men until 1877, when it was sold by W. Scott & Sons to a local businessman, Mr. Ferrato, who continued the gunstock cutting operation. [30] The W. Scott & Son(s) firm should not be confused with W. & C. Scott, which is William and Charles Scott, an entirely different gun maker. The firm of "W. & C. Scott" (William & Charles) was also based in Birmingham during the same time period. They began in business about 1842, and were purchased in their entirety by revolver maker P. Webley & Sons in 1897, becoming Webley and Scott. As previously stated, though similar in name, these are two completely different firms.

On average, about thirty gunstocks can be cut from a single walnut tree. If so, then about 3 million gunstocks were exported from Turin by W. Scott & Son to Birmingham (and London), beginning with the Crimean War up until the end of the U.S. Civil War (1865). As stated, the stocks arrived in Birmingham "cut in the rough form of the gun." The stockers, along with screwers and finishers, were employed in the largest numbers. The rough stock was first given to a stocker to cut the barrel channel and lock mortise. He then roughly formed the stock and fit the lock to the lock mortise and the barrel to the channel. The screwer removed lets in the stock and installed the furniture, then further finished the stock. The finisher took the barrel out and sent it for browning, the lock was sent out for engraving, and so on. More importantly, when the parts came back the finisher put the whole gun together, doing the final fitting of those parts. 75% of those employed were in "setting up" work in one of these three areas. "The many tasks here are also subdivided," according to one periodical of the time. "Since the outworking is performed in different workshops, the gun trade employs a large number of young boys as couriers to take the parts to the other various stages and bring them back to the finishers." [31]

The stocks were sanded again, then finished with boiled linseed oil. This was the standard stock finish for military arms of the time period, as it both protected the wood and was water resistant. Tung oil gives a similar result in terms of appearance with the added benefit of being waterproof, but it was not in use before World War I, at least in the Western world. Stocks stamped with the Birmingham Small Arms Trade roundel on the flat all display an interesting characteristic, where the brass butt plate extends perhaps a fraction of an inch below the toe of the stock. This is not found on gunstocks finished in London as a general rule. Wood shrinks with loss of moisture. This characteristic may be due to how the stocks were cut at the Scott & Son saw mill in Turin, all of which were likely to have been exported to Birmingham. Or most likely, it could be a side effect of how the gunstocks were seasoned. Shrinkage will generally follow the grain and is due to a reduction in moisture. Wood that is allowed to dry and season gradually is stronger and displays less shrinkage than wood which is artificially dried, as is often the case with gunstocks. In the U.S. Civil War era, walnut gunstocks were sometimes placed in a desiccating chamber where hot air at fluctuating volume is blown across the wood. "In this fashion," according to an article from 1859, "can a year of seasoning thus be saved… the walnut-wood is as good, after this process, as if the seasoning had been accomplished by time and exposure, and works more smoothly under the cutting instruments of the stock-machinery." [32]

Barrel Making

Goodman testified before Parliament in 1865, "No (gun) barrels are made in England, except in Birmingham, and its immediate neighbourhood." This statement seems contradicted by the following, which clearly describes gun barrel making by the so-called "Burton Method" at Royal Small Arms Manufactory in London on April 16, 1859:

> The first state of the barrel is that of a slab of iron which weighs 10 1/4 pounds. This is welded and finished in a building separated from the main building. The first process causes this plate or slab to become a tube; it is then drawn out to the required length, *the bore being kept hollow by means of a rod of iron*; the breech-piece is welded on by means of a nervously excitable steam-hammer, which strikes a series of blows with uncommon rapidity. The boring is then proceeded with, many and various instruments being used. The outside is next turned, and any extra parts are taken off. The viewing then takes place. [33]

What Goodman likely means are the barrels for the London and Birmingham commercial gun trade, exempt for London Armoury Company. The thought process was that LA Co was copying Royal Small Arms Manufactory rifles exactly as possible, which means gun barrels were parts interchangeable with Government Enfield rifles. If so, technically (and in a legal sense) Goodman is correct. He should know, as he was a litigant on the matter of barrels some years before. In the case of Goodman v. Spencer, April 23, 1857 (*Court of Common Pleas of Great Britain, Volume 2*), see the following:

> To this plea…in support of the demurrer (a)—The question presented for the consideration of the court upon this demurrer, is, whether the Gun-Makers' Company in London and also the Gun-Makers' Company at Birmingham are bound respectively to receive for definitive proof gun-barrels which have been provisionally proved at the other place. It appears that all barrels are manufactured at Birmingham, and that, previously to the 53 G. 3, c. 115 (1813), the only proof-house was that of the Gun-Makers' Company in London. That act established a proof-house at Birmingham, for the proof of barrels there. It being found that that statute was extensively evaded, another act was passed,—55 G. 3, c. 59,—to amend the former act."

Birmingham barrels were made starting with a slab of iron 12 x 5 inches and 1/2 inch thick. "A rolled barrel is merely a strip of iron folded up lengthwise like a pea-shooter, and welded along the joint. The fore-part of the barrel, however, being less thick than the breech end, these barrels are usually made of two lengths or tubes." The strips, or plates of iron were heated and beaten in a groove until they formed a half tube. They are then heated again and closed with the edges overlapping. The edges were then welded on a mandrill, and when a certain number of pieces were prepared workmen welded together the two pieces of each barrel. The end of the breech part was opened a little on the beam of the anvil, the end of the forepart was introduced, and the joint was completed. The iron was first turned in a pair of grooved rolls until the edges met.

The process of machine making gun barrels by means of grooved rolls is credited to a Birmingham manufacturer named Henry Osborne in 1812. Goodman notes of the invention that:

It was on the occasion of a strike of the barrel welders that he was led to make the experiment. He was not allowed to introduce his system without opposition, for no sooner were his rolls set to work than twelve hundred barrel welders, each armed with his forge hammer, proceeded to the private residence of Mr. Osborne, in the Stratford Road, threatening its destruction. The military was called out before the disturbance could be quelled, and for many days afterwards a guard was placed over the mill in which the work was carried on.

It was the first major technological breakthrough in English barrel making and it was too good to be ignored, even in the Luddite era. In the 1850s, a man named John Fritz developed an improved version with a third roller on top. This permitted the work piece to be passed back to the boss roller which started the process, between the top and the middle rollers, thus greatly reducing the time and labor involved in rolling out the gun barrel to full length, but the concept was the same. The work was physically challenging and the skill required was great, hence the wages were better. Goodman notes:

> A judgment can be formed of the delicacy of workmanship required…when it is understood that a military barrel has to be bored with such truth that it must receive a plug measuring 577-thousandths of an inch, and is condemned as useless if it takes one of 580. A workman in this branch, with full employment has frequently been known to earn £5 to £6 a week.

Some of the better known Birmingham contract barrel makers that supplied P-53 barrels to the Crown included Beasley & Farmer, John Clive, William Millward, Ezra Millward, William Deakin & Son, Joseph Turner, and Henry Clive. The first contracts were for 3,000 barrels from each and date from October 1853, Ordnance Department order O/411. These were essentially the same barrel makers who provided the P-51 barrels on earlier British government contracts, as well as subsequent government contracts. [34]

Ezra Millward was a commercial barrel maker who leased a facility called Benton's Mill during the early 19th century. Benton's Mill, also called Nechells Park or Park Mill, stood on the south side of Plume Street, near its junction with Long Acre in Birmingham. The mill is believed to have been built by two men (Aston and Nechells) in 1532, but it changed hands and was known as Benton's Mill by 1758. During the early 19th century the Benton family leased the mill to Ezra Millward, who maintained a barrel making operation there through the U.S. Civil War period. By 1900 the mill had apparently become part of the Plume Works' industrial premises. The remains of the mill were demolished in 1941. [35]

What of the London gun making firms (other than Royal Small Arms Manufactory and LA Co) and barrel making? According to W. Greener, the last commercial London barrel making operation ceased in the 1840s, and the last practitioner in the business was a Mr. Fullard, "…but with his death barrel welding ceased in the metropolis (London)." [36] By 1893, roll welded gun barrel making was a lost craft in England, though still performed at Liege (Belgium) for a while longer, since they were slower to mechanize. Lastly, it bears mention that what was meant by "all gun barrels made in Birmingham" was a barrel in the state of a rough, unfinished tube. The rest of the barrel finishing work was done at the factory, either in London or Birmingham. Perhaps the most correct statement that can be made is that gun barrel manufacture in England during the 1860s was conducted mostly at Birmingham, LA Co, and Royal Small Arms Manufactory, with very few barrels made elsewhere.

Barrel Boring

When a barrel is rolled and welded it is taken to the boring-bench and secured on a sort of carriage that can travel the length of the tube. A boring bit of proper size is fixed into a revolving spindle, and the point introduced into the front of the barrel. The bit is worked forward until it has passed the length of the tube. During this operation a stream of water plays on the barrel to keep it cool. Bits of larger size are then used till all the blacks and scales are bored out and the tube rendered of the proper gauge.

The Ordnance standard for the Enfield is "25" gauge or .577 caliber. Another common gauge is "24" or .58, the Springfield Armory standard. From the boring-bench the barrel passes to the grindstone. The stones are of very large size and revolve at a terrific rate, and the workmen have a method of allowing the barrel to turn in their hands at half the rate of the stone. According to the *Encyclopedia Britannica* 1853-60, "By this means they produce a fine surface, and remarkable accuracy of form. Best barrels are turned after being ground; inferior barrels are struck up with a large smooth or fine cut file. They are then tapped in a temporary way, the proof-plug screwed in, and in that form they are sent to the proof-house." [37] When barrels are turned they are fixed in the lathe—usually self-acting—by means of plugs or mandrills, made perfectly true, and of various diameters, to fit different bores. These are placed on the centers of the lathe, and a carrier is fastened on the plug that projects from the breech end of the barrel. The leading screw that travels the slide-rest is then set at the angle to which the barrel is to be turned, and the tool proceeds until the whole exterior of the tube is finished. Greenwood & Batley of Leeds produced rifling and barrel manufacturing machinery of this sort.

Barrel Browning

Virtually all Enfield rifle barrels were "…browned to prevent them rusting." Some Civil War soldiers removed the finish in the field, but with few exceptions the barrels left the factory browned. There are several methods of browning, and each gun maker has little modifications of his own. The following is the recipe for the wash with which many barrels are stained:

> 1 oz. muriate tincture of steel, 1/4 oz. strong nitric acid,1 oz. spirits of wine, 1/4 oz. blue-stone, 1/4 oz. muriate of mercury, 1 quart of water. These are well mixed and allowed to stand a month to amalgamate. The oil or grease is carefully removed from the barrels by lime, and the mixture is laid on lightly with a rag or sponge every two hours, and scratched off with a steel scratch brush every morning until the barrels are dark enough. The acid is then quenched by pouring boiling water on the barrels. Inferior barrels are stained by a different process. Muriate of mercury is dissolved in a glassful of spirits of wine, and this solution is mixed with a pint of water. Some of the mixture is then poured on a small quantity of whitening, and laid on the barrel with a sponge; as soon as dry it is brushed off, and a fresh coat laid on. This is continued till the colour is dark enough, which is generally in about two days. Hot water is then applied, and the barrels are suddenly immersed in cold water to heighten the colour. Another method, called smoke-brown—although the colour produced was a greyish black—was also employed, and is strongly recommended in Mr Greener's Treatise on the Gun; but it is apt to injure the barrels unless performed with the utmost dexterity and care. It has therefore fallen out of use, except for a few rifle barrels. [38]

Although the barrels turned a bluish-black from this process, in the Gun Trade the term in use for the process was "browning." It was hazardous work, and the use of mercury in the process unintentionally resulted in a shorter life expectancy for barrel browners.

In finishing an Enfield rifle, all iron parts are not browned. Barrel bands are heat blued. The hammers and lock plates are "case-hardened" by the bone and charcoal method. That is to say, the parts are superheated to 1700 degrees or so (Fahrenheit) with dried animal bones and leather to add carbon to the iron. The swirling colors on the surface of case-hardened parts are due to the quenching process, and from the introduction of air bubbles and attendant oily residue in the cooling tanks. The coloration occurs naturally and it was not added for aesthetics, though it is pleasing to the eye. Not all the small parts are case hardened; for example, if barrel bands were hardened to that level they would break apart from the pressure of barrel expansion during live fire with black powder, and if the percussion cone were case hardened the force of repeated strikes from the hammer (which is case-hardened) would eventually crack the nipple off at the base and potentially leave the threaded end stuck in the bolster. This happened with some Enfield rifles issued to the 35th Massachusetts infantry just prior to Antietam in 1862. [39] The instructions in *The Army Manual* state that once an iron part is case hardened, the process is not to be done to the same part again.

Black Country Iron

According to Goodman, Birmingham produced the best barrels because they had the best iron, "… *superior for gun barrel making to any other.*" For many years, Springfield Armory (U.S.) got iron for its barrels from Sheffield, though this ended early in the Civil War. American iron masters and armorers referred to this as "gun iron", meaning merely high-quality iron suitable for gun barrels and similar work. The best "gun iron" from England came from a particular iron works in Wednesbury. The product was known as "Marshall" iron. Note the following:

> There is another Staffordshire speciality in Iron making, which would be understood better if we say Marshall and Mills, of the Monway Works, Wednesbury. These gentlemen, many years since, succeeded in making the best gun-barrel Iron in the world, and have for years supplied the Iron to the Birmingham gun makers, also to the British and American Governments, the quality of their Iron being approved and sanctioned by both Governments. The price they obtain now would be about £33 10s. per ton. The firm was dissolved, by mutual consent some years since, Mr. Mills having grown-up sons whom he wished to introduce. Mr. John Marshall remained at the Monway Works, which has eleven puddling furnaces and two charcoal fires, and carries on the original business. Henry Mills and Sons erected the Victoria Works at Walsall, a modern unique concern, which Mr. Mills carries on in connection with his sons, making also, the same specialities which gave so much celebrity to the firm of Marshall and Mills. [40]

It appears that, with some degree of certainty, the overwhelming majority of military gun barrels on commercial Enfield rifles supplied to Confederate troops in the U.S. Civil War were of Black Country roll-welded iron, and those barrels were produced in and around Birmingham, whether the rest of the weapon was or not.

Iron vs. Steel Barrels

The making of roll welded gun barrels must be done with high quality iron. The difficulty of obtaining iron of this quality in other countries led to the substitution of steel for some military rifle barrels; this was the case for some gun makers during the 1860s in America, as well as Europe (Austria and Prussia). Colt Mfg (U.S.) used steel barrels for their Special Model 1861 contract rifle musket. Whitney used steel barrels for their U.S. 1841 contract work. Remington also used primarily steel barrels as well. Steel is a form of iron containing from up to 1% carbon. If a piece of steel with carbon content of more than about 0.6% is heated to a suitable level, usually over 1,000 degrees Fahrenheit, and then suddenly quenched in a cool fluid, it will become hardened. It is usually then reheated or "drawn" to a lower heat and then quenched again. This hardening ability was the defining characteristic of steel during the last half of the 19th century "Steel was obtained by re-carbonizing wrought iron – that is, by putting back at least some of the carbon that the forge had taken such pains to remove," explains Jim Westberg. [41] When steel is used the process of manufacture is somewhat different; a solid bar of steel is tilted to the required size and the bore afterwards drilled out. Steel becomes weaker when hammered or roll welded, quite the opposite of iron. Steel gun barrels were not used by the English commercial gun trade to produce Enfield rifles during the U.S. Civil War era. However steel was in use in England, as the Colt factory revolvers manufactured in London during the mid-1850s were made with steel barrels.

Lock Makers

Next in importance to the barrel of the Enfield rifle is the percussion lock. The gun lock had undergone many successive improvements, finally reaching a state of simplicity, excellence, and efficiency with the percussion lock. The percussion lock ignites the charge by means of a hammer striking a copper cap containing a small charge of detonating powder. The springs of English gun locks were superior to those made anywhere else in Europe. W. Greener and Isaac Hollis once filed a lawsuit against a fellow gun maker who was caught forging their marks on a Belgian-made percussion lock. Greener was less perturbed by the loss of potential profits and more upset by the potential impact to the firm's reputation "…when in two or three years the mainsprings of the Belgian lock turn too soft to explode the cap." It was considered such a well-known trait of Belgian springs that Greener (and Isaac Hollis) won damages against the other firm.

The Encyclopedia Britannica 8th Edition (1853 to 1860) states:

> The percussion-lock had so completely superseded the flint that the latter was obsolete; and, though still used, flintlocks were no longer manufactured. It is unnecessary, therefore, to describe more than the percussion-lock which is ingenious and consists of the separate pieces technically called the *works*. A, the lock-plate ; B, the tumbler; C, the bridle; D, the swivel; E, the main-spring; making. F, the sear, on the projecting branch of which the trigger acts; G, the sear-spring, which resists the pull of the finger, and keeps the sear in the notch of half-bend or full bend. The works, however, may be partially reversed so as to place the lock in the hand of the stock, in which case the lock is termed *back-actioned*. The *back-actioned* lock was popular some years ago (in Belgium and France) but the general opinion of (English) makers seems to have decided so completely in favour of the bar-lock, that no other is now made in the ordinary way of business."
>
> "Very common locks, such as those applied to the old muskets, were made with a hook instead of a swivel (*tumbler link*—Editor). Such locks have a dull, heavy action, and never work with the lively motion of the swivel-locks. The swivel, although apparently a mere means of connecting the main-spring with the tumbler, is a very important part of the mechanism. If well hung, it has the effect of making the heaviest pull or greatest force of the main-spring—not when the hammer is on full-bend, as might be supposed from the circumstance that the more a spring is bent the greater its force—but when the hammer is down on the nipple. This, in fact, is one of the principal tests of a well-made lock; and an experienced finger will at once detect a bad lock, from the mere circumstance that the pull increases instead of decreases as the hammer is drawn up. For military purposes it has not been customary to use the swivel-lock, except for the most recently-made rifles (*like the long and short Enfield*—Editor); but it is poor economy on the part of the government to arm a soldier with an inferior weapon, when the extra cost would not amount to more than a couple of shillings for each musket or rifle. [42]

The Directory for Birmingham lists a handful of lock makers (as distinct from lock forgers and filers). The majority are from the nearby West Midlands region, Wolverhampton, Darlaston, and Wednesbury. Contemporary documentation has shown that lock makers in the County of Staffordshire provided a large percentage of the locks required by the gun trade, including the military locks required in England by Ordnance, as well as some that were sold to foreign gun makers. What follows is a partial list of known lock makers registered in England during the U.S. Civil War era and the approximate dates they were in business: [43]

Back action lock. (Photo used with the permission of Jim Westberg)

Archer, John, Darlaston (Staffs.) GL Maker, 1854-1864
Bailey, T. Birmingham GL Maker, 1861-1863
Brazier, James Wolverhampton (Staffs.), GL Maker, 1845-1862
Brazier, Joseph & Son Wolverhampton (Staffs.), GL Maker, 1849-1977
Brazier, Thomas, Wolverhampton, GL Maker 1838-1881
Brazier, Wm, Wolverhampton GL Maker, 1851-1877

Bridgewater, J. Staffordshire GL Maker 1855-?
Burns, Charles Willenhall GL Maker, 1855-1868
Burns, Jonah Willenhall GL Maker, 1864-1868
Butler, Ellen Darlaston (Staffs.) GL Maker, 1864-1867
Corbett, William Darlaston GL Maker, 1854-1865
Crisp, Robert D. Birmingham GL Maker, 1857-1861
Duce, John Taylor Wednesbury (Staffs.), Ordnance and GL Maker, 1854-1876
Dudhill, Adam Darlaston GL Maker, 1855-1865
Dudhill, Ambrose Darlaston (Staffs.), GL Maker, 1854-1868
Eccleston, J. Birmingham GL Maker, 1848-1863
Evans, Hiram Birmingham GL Maker, 1855-1868
Evans, James Birmingham GL Maker, 1857-1868
Frazier, T. Birmingham GL Maker, 1863 -1865
Golcher, George, Sr. Darlaston (Staffs.), GL Maker, 1853-1896
Grainger, James, Wolverhampton GL Maker, 1853-1874
Grainger, John, Wolverhampton, GL Maker 1861-1935
Griffiths, Gideon Wednesbury (Staffs.), GL Maker, 1854-1867
Homer, Richard Wolverhampton GL Maker, 1838-1865
Law, John, Wolverhampton GL Maker 1837-1887
Newton, John Wolverhampton GL Maker 1841-1861
Page, H. Birmingham GL Maker, 1859-1861
Partridge, David, Wolverhampton GL Maker 1861-?
Partridge, Job & Enoch Darlaston (Staffs.), GL Maker, 1853-1865
Read, M. Darlaston (Staffs.), GL Maker, 1864
Roberts, John West Bromwich GL Maker, 1855-1865
Robinson, Joseph West Bromwich (Staffs.), GL Maker, 1827-1872
Smith Cornelius Wednesbury GL Maker, 1854-1865
Smith, George, Wolverhampton GL Maker, 1851-1885
Smith, Joseph Birmingham GL Maker, 1851-1895
Southall, J. Birmingham GL Maker, 1863-1865
Speares, John Birmingham GL Maker, 1855-1865
Stanton, John Wolverhampton (Staffs.), GL Maker, 1855-1900
Stanton, Geo. Wolverhampton GL Maker, 1845-1870
Stanway, J. Darlaston GL Maker, 1864-1865
Steatham, Joseph Wednesbury (Staffs.), GL Maker, 1854-1880
Styke, Edward, Wolverhampton, GL Maker 1864
Terry, James Whitechapel (London) GL Maker, 1862-66
Turner, Thomas Wednesbury GL Maker, 1838-1865
Watson, James Wednesbury GL Maker, 1854-1872
Whitehouse, John Darlaston GL Maker, 1858-1879
Wilson, Frederick Handsworth (Staffs.), GL Maker, 1855-1868
Yates, George Birmingham GL Maker, 1861

A word or two about lock makers in the West Midlands seems in order. It is not documented exactly why so many lock makers came to set up shop there. In the earliest days of the gun trade neighboring villages also had a number of gun lock makers whose names would eventually appear in the West Midlands (mostly the Wolverhampton directory) during the U.S. Civil War era. The parish records of both All Saints and the later Roman Catholic St. George's churches contain the surnames of many of the families who would become known as gun lock makers of Wolverhampton, including Newton, Homer, Brazier, Stanton, Law, Partridge, and Grainger. Proximity to both coal and iron ore obviously played a role. The lock making business was usually comprised of a master and one or two craftsmen in training. The employees were generally divided into specific functions, such as forgers, filers, pin (screw) makers, and mainspring makers. Some were engaged as outworkers in their own small workshops, and a few undertook the manufacture of a variety of gun components, such as gun sights, trigger guards, butt plates, etc. "The work was labour-intensive," writes C.V. Clark, "with the smiths working at forging hearths, benches, vices and foot-treadle lathes. The hammer, chisel and file were his principal hand-tools, with simple dies, jigs and implements made in-house specifically for particular operations. The assembling, spring making, hardening and tempering and regulating/ finishing required considerable skill..." [44] The trade continued on the common practice of employing family members; usually a father apprenticing his son either to himself or a relative, with the accepted presumption

Lock marked by Joseph Brazier/Ashes. (Photo used by permission of Jim Westburg)

that the family business would be passed down through successive generations.

There are some names in this list familiar to students of the U.S. Civil War Enfield, possibly none more famous than Joseph Brazier of Wolverhampton. Joseph supplied locks which carry the "Joseph Brazier/ Ashes" and "IB" marks. "Ashes" indicates the name of his shop "Ashes Works" on Great Brick Kiln Street in Wolverhampton. Some of these locks are found on rifles used during the American Civil War. The greatly prized Joseph Whitworth .451 long range target rifles are often found with J. Brazier marked locks "of the Enfield pattern", which were noted for workmanship "comparable to a fine Swiss watch."

Furniture and Oddwork

The portions of a gun, other than the barrel, the lock, and the stock, are termed "gun furniture." They consist of the heel or butt plate, which covers the rear of the stock; the trigger plate; the trigger-guard; the hammers; the screw escutcheons (washers) and bolt which fasten the barrel into the stock channel; the cap or tip of the stock; the tops, worms, and caps of the ramrod; and the oddwork necessary to put the gun together. The oddwork consists of small parts like pins (screws) and sling swivels, but may also include implements like nipple keys (cone wrench), turn screws (screw driver), lock (mainspring) vices, etc.

The London System of Manufacture

Because a London address was considered important to carry status in the gun trade, it was a well-established practice by the time of the U.S. Civil War for Birmingham gun makers to have London subsidiaries. Birmingham gun makers, such as W. & C. Scott, Needham, Isaac Hollis, W. Greener, Robert Hughes, James Tolley, Callisher & Terry, Charles Osbourne, John Wilkes, and Westley Richards (to name a few) all had some form of London operations. In fact, Westley Richards is so closely associated with London that many forget that the firm was a Birmingham enterprise.

There was a fair amount of regional overlap within the gun trade but very little cooperation. What is the source of the rivalry between the gun makers of London and Birmingham? In brief and to oversimplify, it seems to have begun in the early 1600s when King James I granted a charter to London gun makers to operate as a virtual monopoly in exchange for fees which were paid to the King for the right to produce firearms. The first barrel testing facility for firearms was the London Proof House, chartered in 1637. The evidence suggests that the London firms could not entirely supply all the arms needed for the defense of the Realm. Eventually, guns and gun parts were smuggled into London to satisfy this demand. However, it was also suspected that these parts were being made in Birmingham, in effect circumventing the fee paid to the King. In late 1687, during the reign of King James II, it was reported that complete firearms were being produced in Birmingham, lock stock, and barrel. Investigating the rumor, King James II sent his agents to Birmingham, and the reports were of course found to be correct. Timing, as they say, is everything, and also at this time England was at war with Holland, and the King was pleased that another acceptable domestic source of firearms had been found to arm its soldiers. "Sir Richard Newdigate (Warwickshire) advised the King that his constituents were capable of satisfying his needs," writes Wm. Greener. "He was furnished with two sample muskets (to copy) and they were dispatched

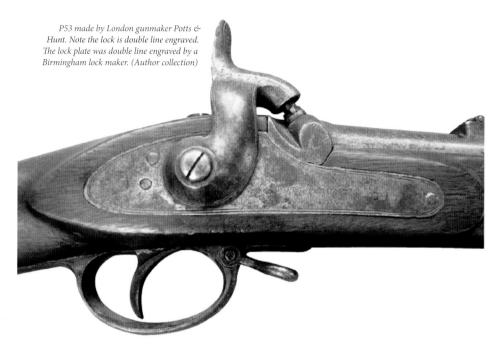

P53 made by London gunmaker Potts & Hunt. Note the lock is double line engraved. The lock plate was double line engraved by a Birmingham lock maker. (Author collection)

instantly to his Birmingham constituents." [45] Subsequently, a contract was offered in 1689 to five Birmingham gun makers for 200 muskets per month and the rest is history. This new contract with "upstart Birmingham" did not go unobserved by the Worshipful Company of Gun-makers in London. The result was resentment, rivalry, and competition that continued in the English gun trade for the next two hundred years, only abating to direct mutual animosity at their common enemy in the Belgium (Liege) Gun Trade.

Whatever the case, the fact is the vast majority of parts used in the English Gun Trade, including locks, forgings, and barrels (in an unfinished state) would eventually come from Birmingham, even those found on Enfield rifles produced by "London" gun makers. See the following comments from W. Greener, who is (as usual) not shy with his opinions about the subject:

> I am unfortunately too much in on the secret: I know too well where and how the vast majority of London guns are made. Why keep up a distinction that does not exist? Why call a gun London-made because the seller rents a shop and calls himself a gun maker? Why not at once say, "Our manufactory is in Birmingham, as we find we can make both better and cheaper there." This is truth, and ought to be told. It is now the extreme of folly to say, "These are Brummagem (slang: Birmingham) guns" (and) that term only applies to the "rubbish" and the low priced article, which no honest man has hardihood enough to brand with his own name…it is in fact, slanderous. [46]

No secret, there were many London gun makers who felt they deserved a premium price for their "quality" work and belittled the efforts of Birmingham gun makers, knowing full well that the weapon was either produced entirely in Birmingham, or else finished and "set-up" in London from Birmingham parts. Either way, to W. Greener the final product was a "Birmingham gun", regardless of where it was sold or who sold it. It appears W. Greener exaggerates to make his point, and this does not quite reach the legal definition of "slander." There could be a grain of truth in here about the superiority of London guns. There was a quality piece to the finishing process. If we examine the regional production practices in the commercial English Gun Trade more closely (excluding LA Co, of course) a clearer picture emerges of the London gun makers. It has been noted that when Confederate buyer Caleb Huse arrived in London in mid-May 1861 he set about to secure as many serviceable arms as he could find, enlisting the help of the Commission House(s) of Sinclair, Hamilton & Co and S. Isaac, Campbell & Co. The story of the London Commission House(s) is an important one for any student of the Civil War Enfield and will be covered in greater detail. The London firms documented to have supplied Enfield rifles to the Confederacy through Sinclair, Hamilton include Parker, Field & Sons, E.P. Bond, Barnett, LA Co, Potts & Hunt, Wilkinson, R. Pritchett, Lancaster, and E. Yeomans & Sons. The first 6,500 Enfields received in the Confederacy were aboard the steamship *Bermuda* and "most were London guns, from Barnett and LA Co." [47]

The London gun makers may have been among the first to supply the Confederacy with Enfield rifles, but as time went on a much wider variety of gun making firms both large and small, from London and Birmingham, would do business freely with both sides right up until mid-1863, when the Union cancelled all unfilled orders. Afterwards, the Confederates were the sole American customer of the English Gun Trade, and the evidence from surviving shipping manifests suggests they picked up the newly available capacity. Birmingham gun maker John D. Goodman (Cooper & Goodman) offers further insight, stating that Birmingham produces 85% of the Enfield rifle parts made in England, while a little more than two-thirds of them are actually manufactured, or "set up", in Birmingham factories. He adds that "…from the proof house returns I obtain the following numbers, showing the extent of the (total) supply of arms from this country." [48]

Let's presume for a moment that whether or not the total figures Mr. Goodman gives are exact to the number—he is, after all, going by the number of barrels proofed, not finished rifles set-up, crated, and shipped—the ratio of production capacity between the Birmingham and London gun makers seems to be at around 70-30, a figure which does not change appreciably throughout the period. [49] Since most professional researchers and historians are probably comfortable with that output ratio, the question then is how a London P53 built from parts made in Birmingham differs from a Birmingham Small Arms Trade P53 "set-up" from essentially the same parts? What are the possible variables at work here?

While most London and all Birmingham produced weapons which were "grade two, hand-made" (non-interchangeable parts), in London it was customary for the workers employed in "set-up" to be working on premises. Gun makers in London were part of the Livery (Trade Guild) system, which required lengthy apprenticeships prior to setting up shop. It is likely that the quality difference (if there was one) occurred in "how" London P53s were set-up more so than any difference in the quality of the component parts.

It is also probable that, since many of the so-called "best guns" for the civilian trade were traditionally made in London, the workmanship of the commercial military gun makers benefitted from a "halo effect." [50] In the end, whether "set-up" in London or Birmingham, the hand-made commercial Enfield rifle still had to go "through the hands of ten or twelve different (gun) makers and an inspection was necessary at each stage of the process." There were some minor quality differences; for example, we do know that walnut gunstocks arrived unfinished in a rough form that had to be seasoned, shaped, sanded, and oiled by the stockers in London. We know the surviving gunstocks on London gun maker Enfields appear to be better seasoned than those from Birmingham, as there is less evidence of noticeable wood shrinkage at the toe where it meets the butt plate (see explanation in section on *Stock Makers*). We know that barrel finishing, final lock fitting, and filing were done on premises during set-up at the factory in London, all processes considered to require a higher level of skill, and so on. So what made London guns better overall? The biggest single quality advantage for London (more so than potentially better rifles hand manufactured in-house) was the substantial number supplied to the Confederates by London Armoury Co. The London Armoury Enfields were all superior first class/parts interchangeable military rifles. None of the Birmingham made Enfield rifles used in the U.S. Civil War was first class/parts interchangeable guns. Since there were zero from Birmingham statistically speaking (because of LA Co), a much higher percentage of "best grade" military weapons were made in London.

Were the Birmingham Enfields poor quality? Obviously, given the numbers of handmade rifles involved, there would be a greater variation in quality. Looking at surviving records from early in the war, there were some legitimate complaints registered about the Birmingham rifles issued to the Union troops which are curiously missing from Confederate accounts of the same time period. [51] These statements are interpreted by historians as evidence of the poorer quality of Birmingham guns. We know early in the war buyers from the Union purchased Enfield rifles that were refurbished or repaired arms from the Crimean War contracts sold back into the Gun Trade in 1861. There were also some numbers of Birmingham guns that were rubbish, as well as a few London guns (Barnett) which were found to be made up from previously condemned parts. [52] What we can say is that the output from London that went to the Confederates was enthusiastically received for a variety of reasons. In contrast, there was less enthusiasm expressed by Union troops for most of the foreign arms they were issued, including grade two Enfield rifles. See the following excerpt dated October 21, 1861:

> The muskets were delivered to the men, and this furnished another excuse for a hearty growl from the 1st Mainers." Had we not been promised a new blue uniform and Springfield muskets?" To be sure we had the blue uniform and a good outfit in every way, "but look at these Enfield muskets," said they, "with their blued barrels and wood that no man can name!" They were not a bad weapon, however, differing little from the Springfield, in actual efficiency, weight, length, and caliber, but far behind in point of workmanship. [53]

It was not uncommon in the Union army to be promised new U.S. 1861 rifle muskets as an inducement to re-enlist. Another factor affecting the diminished perception of quality is that Enfield rifles made in Belgium (and elsewhere on the continent) were marked and sold as Birmingham guns.

CHAPTER FOUR
History of Some Larger Birmingham Gun Makers

Tipping & Lawden

Tipping and Lawden was another of the so-called original four "contractors for arms to Her Majesty's War Department" for the first Enfield long rifles produced. During the mid-19th century the firm was among the top gun makers in England. Typical of these firms, they produced a wide variety of firearms for both the civilian and commercial markets. A period advertisement for the firm reads as follows:

Maker's mark behind the trigger guard plate.

> TIPPING AND LAWDEN,
> 40/41, CONSTITUTION-HILL,
> MERCHANTS, GUN MAKERS, and others visiting Birmingham to purchase, are assured that every article sold by T. and L. is of the very best manufacture, and warranted sound; every material used being made entirely under their own inspection.
> FOWLING PIECES OF EVERY DESCRIPTION.
> Rifle Guns.
> DUELLING, HOLSTER, POCKET, AND OTHER PISTOLS, Air Guns, Staff Guns, Air Canes, &c.
>
> Gun Makers supplied with every variety of Material, Implements, Gun and Pistol Cases, &c. [1]

The founder was named Thomas Tipping. He was born in 1789 in Birmingham. In 1811 he married Mary, and in 1812 they had a daughter named Mary Ann. In 1820, Thomas established his business as a gun maker in Legge Street, Birmingham. In 1827 he moved to their premises on 40 Constitution Hill. About this time his father, also named Thomas Tipping, was involved in the development of an oval lathe. The cutting of ovals has always been a challenge for woodworkers. A business journal published many years later (1877) recalled:

> There is a belief here in Birmingham that the oval lathe was invented in Birmingham by a clever mechanic named Tipping, father of the late Mr. Tipping, gun manufacturer (of the firm of Tipping & Lawden), of this town…I have heard this from good authority—from a man who worked at an oval lathe more than sixty years ago when, if I understood him right, they had just come out. It would take some years after the invention to get the lathe fully into work. [2]

The trade of "mechanic" in Birmingham referred to "men of science—inventors." It was a gentlemanly pursuit. One trade journal was called "English Mechanic and World of Science."

Thomas Tipping's daughter Mary Ann married a gun maker, Caleb Lawden, in about 1830, and in 1833 they had a son, Thomas Tipping-Lawden. In 1837, Thomas Tipping made son-in-law Caleb Lawden a partner in the business, which was renamed Tipping & Lawden. A retail shop was then opened in London. In the 1841 census Thomas and Mary were living at Hockley, in Birmingham; Thomas described his occupation as "gun maker." However, Caleb and Mary Ann are not recorded in Birmingham, and it is possible Caleb Lawden may have been running the T & L retail shop in London, which would be a likely explanation. It has been reported that between 1845 and 1847 founder

Tipping & Lawden

Thomas Tipping retired and the firm was taken over by his son-in-law Caleb and grandson, Thomas Tipping-Lawden. In the census of 1851, Caleb and Mary Ann Lawden were listed in Hampstead Road, Handsworth, in the West Midlands, with son Thomas Tipping-Lawden aged 18 residing, and listed as "gun maker." The Tipping & Lawden firm during the U.S. Civil War era was actually a father and son venture. A glance at the number of father and son firms in the English Gun Trade suggests a good many were multi-generation family businesses of the same sort. [3]

The Tipping & Lawden firm had a reputation for "best guns" alongside gun makers such as Greener and Hollis. One observer of the craftsmanship in England on the eve of the Great Exhibition of 1851 noted, "…of course, our remarks have reference exclusively to the highest class of sword-makers, such as Reeves, Grieves, & Co., who employ the best hands and turn out the best work; just as much so as Westley Richards, or *Tipping and Lawden* do in the manufacture of guns." There was a booth at the Great Exhibition of 1851 at Crystal Place (London) for **Tipping and Lawden, Birmingham—Manufacturers**. Their exhibit consisted of the following items:

> * Specimens of iron and steel in various stages of preparation, to show the manufacture of gun barrels:- Horse-nail stubs. Scrap steel, a mixture in a partially welded state.

> * Specimens, showing a twisted stub-barrel in the various stages of manufacture, from the first process. The stubs and scrap-steel are first welded into a rod, which is afterwards rolled out into a flat bar; it is then coiled round a mandrill and welded into a barrel; it is afterwards ground and filed, and finally brought to a finished state.

> * Lengths, showing the various stages of manufacture of Damascus and laminated steel barrels. Double gun, the barrels made of twisted stubs.

> * Several guns, of varied construction, and one entirely in pieces, to show all the parts of a gun separately, especially the internal work of the stock.

> * Double and single rifle guns. Single and double guns; varieties both of fowling- pieces and military guns.

> * Air-gun; barrel of best twisted stubs, with improved roller breech, the butt made of twisted stubs.

> * Air-cane, twisted stubs, with improved roller action, pump, etc., complete.

> * Small walking-stick air-cane, with rifled barrel, of improved construction. Air-cane lock.

> * Six-barreled revolving pistols, ivory stock, silver inlaid; walnut stock, silver inlaid; and chequered stock.

> * Various pistols. [4]

Business was increasing every year, and in 1852 the factory in Birmingham was enlarged to occupy premises # 41, as well as # 40 Constitution Hill. Tipping & Lawden was one of four firms selected by Ordnance to "set up" the first Crimean War-era Enfield long rifles in late 1853. The "original four", which also included Swinburn & Son, Hollis & Sheath, and Thomas Turner failed to deliver on that contract due to a shortfall of rear ladder sights. Tipping & Lawden were also among the founding members of the Birmingham Small Arms Trade for the ensuing Ordnance contracts in 1854 and several more that followed. After the Crimean War (which was brief) orders fell off, as Ordnance began modernizing their own manufactory (Royal Small Arms) to make Enfield rifles by machinery, parts interchangeable. The Gun Trade missed this turning point and returned to complaining about the ever-increasing output from the continental gun makers at Liege (Belgium). One gun maker opined that:

Birmingham has suffered in her gun trade of late years from the competition with Belgium; Liege has, in fact, become the continental storehouse for fire-arms, and this is mainly owing to the fact that labour is cheaper with the Liegois than with us; and that therefore in the manufacture of low-priced articles, in which the cost of labour forms the chief element of expense, we cannot successfully compete with them. Further, the Belgian makers are not put to the expense of proving their weapons, which alone would give them a considerable advantage in a market where cheapness carries the day. In point of quality and workmanship, the Belgian weapons will not stand comparison with those of our own makers. Messrs. Tipping and Lawden, Constitution Hill, (whose works I have been over), Messrs. Hollis and Co., St. Mary's Square, and Mr Westley Richards, High Street, are among the principal manufacturers. [5]

They should have been keeping an eye on what was happening at Royal Small Arms Manufactory instead.

The London retail shop moved to 17 Woodstock Street. Founder Thomas Tipping of Hockley Hill, Birmingham, passed away in 1854, according to the obituaries, at age 65. Tipping had been out of the day to day running of the business for the better part of a decade by that point. On February 13, 1861, Caleb Lawden and T. Jones registered patent No. 368 for a percussion and pin-fire breech-loader mechanism. In the 1861 census Thomas Tipping-Lawden was recorded living at Northfield, Worcestershire, with his wife Kate, two daughters, Mary E (1857) and Kate J (1858), and one son, Alfred T. Lawden (1860); no extra credit for predicting the initial "T" is for "Tipping". Despite the name and heritage, Alfred Tipping-Lawden eschewed the family business entirely and studied law.

In 1862, Caleb Lawden patented a new drop-down barrel breech-loader and a cane gun. The firm was also known for the Sharps four barreled rim-fire pepperbox "protector" pistol, which they made beginning in 1860 under license. Pocket-size pepperboxes made under the Sharps patent by Tipping & Lawden in Birmingham were becoming outdated, but were still popular. Obviously, Colt and Remington dominated the revolver market during the U.S. Civil War (and some time afterwards), but pepperboxes were still in fairly wide use. These belt pistols were mostly made for the civilian self-defense market, but were also used as private purchase arms for cavalry. They were also carried for personal use by infantry troops in a semi-permanent camp scenario or on leave. A report by the U.S. Ordnance Bureau, listing firearms that had been used regularly by the U.S. Army (but not necessarily issued), mentions "revolving pistols—pepperbox—percussion." [6] There is anecdotal evidence of a Union soldier away from camp looking for edible enemies of the Union ("foraging") when he stumbled into a Confederate picket. The Confederate's musket failed or missed, and at least one of the pepperbox's four shots didn't, since the Union soldier lived to tell the tale back in camp. How could the picket miss with a musket at the effective range of a pepperbox? Mark Twain tells another anecdote about a hapless traveler in 1861 demonstrating the use of his pepperbox. The man took aim and hit a mule thirty yards to the right of the target. Those pistols were best for very close work. [7]

The T & L firm also made single-shot rim-fire rifled carbines under the Sharps patent. Christian Sharps was issued a total of fifteen firearms-related patents. Although it was not the first breech-loading rifle, Sharps' carbine was the first to be accepted widely, and with the onset of the U.S. Civil War it was produced in large quantities. The Sharps carbine was very widely used by the Union cavalry. It was so successful that it was copied and manufactured in reasonable numbers (4,900) by the Confederate government to arm its mounted troops. [8] The Confederate version was unreliable to the point that Robert E. Lee noted of the CS-Richmond produced Sharps "...it was so defective as to be demoralizing to our men." A late war account of the last days of the Confederacy recalls weapons imported via Matamoros, Mexico, into Southern depots, "...they now possessed six thousand Enfield rifles, four Colt revolvers for every man and the Sharps Carbine." [9] It is unknown how many or to what extent the Tipping & Lawden version of the Sharps carbine may have been in use, but they were certainly being manufactured and were available for export during the time period.

During the U.S. Civil War-era, Tipping & Lawden also had a retail outlet for their shotguns in New York City (Manhattan), but the firm is not listed in any of the city business directories under that name. It is possible their shotguns were imported and sold by a large New York sporting goods retailer like Schuyler, Hartley & Graham. One advertisement for Schuyler, Hartley & Graham in the

Sportsmen's Gazette listed shotguns, "...by W. & C. Scott, Westley Richards and other celebrated makers." Tipping & Lawden would certainly fall into the latter category of "other celebrated maker." Like many firms in the English Gun Trade, they were manufacturers, but also sold to retailers as well as retailed guns themselves. In 1871, John Thomas was employed by the firm Tipping & Lawden as works manager. Previously, on March 13, 1869, he had patented a center-fire self-extracting revolver (patent No.779), which Tipping & Lawden made, so there was that evidence of a past business relationship. There was a food chain of sorts in the English Gun Trade, with larger more aggressive firms taking over smaller ones. In addition to his responsibilities with the T & L firm, Caleb Lawden served as director of Birmingham Financial Company, Ltd (a bank) as late as 1868. Lending houses apparently had the same dog eat dog business plan as the gun makers, and during 1862 Birmingham Financial absorbed Midland Financial Company, an institution about half its size, which then became Birmingham & Midland Bank. Caleb Lawden shows up in the court records on behalf of the B & M bank on bankruptcies and foreclosures. Interestingly, gun maker John D. Goodman, Chairman of BSAT, later became the Chairman of Birmingham & Midland in 1879.

John Thomas took out another patent (No. 3091) for a "wedge-bolt" hammer gun action which was made by the firm. In 1877, another patent by John Thomas and Thomas Tipping-Lawden covered a very similar hammerless action. It was the last for the firm. Compared to other firms, Tipping and Lawden were not as aggressive in patenting new designs. It is possible that Caleb Lawden was devoting most of his time to the bank or passed away about the time John Thomas joined the firm in 1871. The death of Caleb Lawden is not recorded, but he is not listed again by the census afterwards in Birmingham. Tipping & Lawden survived the loss of Ordnance work in the 1850s and large scale commercial military work after the mid-1860s. However, in 1877 the firm was sold to P. Webley & Son.

John Thomas left the firm – whether voluntarily or not is unknown – to establish his own business as a "birding gun maker and general machinist to the trade." The London retail shop under the T. & L. name may have stayed open until P. Webley & Son opened their premises at 60 Queen Victoria Street later in the 1880s. In the 1881 census Thomas Tipping-Lawden and his wife, Kate, were recorded at "The Uplands," Handsworth. Thomas now described himself as a retired gun maker and farmer of 300 acres, employing five men, two women, and three boys. Also living with them was his mother, Mary Ann, and his son, Alfred Tipping Lawden, probably nearing completion of his legal studies. To become a solicitor in England, one must first complete a law degree and then work three additional years as a clerk in a law firm. Alfred was still listed in practice at 40 Bedford Row at the end of the 19th century. He shared offices at that time with four other solicitors and an accountant. [10] The surviving courthouse records reflect a successful legal career, mostly handling property disputes, divorces, and run of the mill cases. Interestingly, he varied on the practice of using his middle name professionally, appearing in documents as Alfred T. Lawden sometimes and others as Alfred Tipping-Lawden.

There was a Richard Tipping of Great Hampton Street, Birmingham, who does not appear to have been related to the firm. He was listed as a gun maker and went bankrupt on August 18, 1837. There is no evidence that gun maker Richard Tipping had been in business with Thomas Tipping from any of the surviving records. [11]

Isaac Hollis & Sons (formerly Hollis & Sheath)

The English Gun Trade has families that overlap and intertwine over the course of the decades—in some cases centuries — while they are in the trade. There are many cases where nephews share the same names as uncles, eldest sons with fathers, etc. The Barnett family is a great example of this. The reconstruction of the Isaac Hollis story is somewhat complicated because it was a family with several branches in the Birmingham Gun Trade. The seminal gun maker William Hollis was born in 1777 and established his business in 1807 at St Mary's Row; he was recorded there until 1811. He most likely had at least one brother, Richard Hollis, in the firm. There was a nephew who was also named Richard Hollis (1829-1853). Around 1814, William and his brother moved to 73 Bath Street and did business as Richard & William Hollis at Bath Street until 1829. In 1838 the firm became William Hollis & Sons, but it reverted back to a sole proprietorship as William Hollis in 1839 when sons Frederick and Isaac formed Hollis Bros & Company. When William Hollis died in 1856 at the age of 79 he claimed to be the oldest manufacturer and contractor in Birmingham. [1]

Hollis & Sheath

In 1829, William's brother Richard Hollis opened his own premises at 3 Lench Street. In 1833, Richard also occupied 20 St Mary's Row, but for a short time only. In 1847, Richard moved from Lench Street to go to 79 Weaman Street, and it appears that he teamed up with Christopher Hollis, who was possibly a brother or son; the record is not clear from there. This firm is no longer recorded after 1853.

The firm of Hollis Brothers & Co started trading from 11 Weaman Row in 1839. The partners were Isaac Hollis and Frederick Hollis. The well-known pistol maker William Tranter—also a member of Birmingham Small Arms Trade—at the age of 14 was apprenticed to the firm of Hollis Bros. & Co. Tranter left Hollis Bros. in 1839. He was also in partnership with John Hollis at 10-11 Weaman Row between 1844 and 1849, and then with Isaac Brentnall Sheath from 1845. The firm of Hollis & Sheath, a partnership of John Hollis and Isaac Brentnall Sheath, formed in Birmingham, England, in 1844 at 10-11 Weamon Row through 1850, then 49 Whittall Street through 1853, and finally at 5-11 Weaman Row from 1853-1861. The firm stopped trading as Hollis Bros in 1848, some years after the death of Frederick Hollis. The Hollis & Sheath Company was the name of the firm when it was involved in the setting up of the first contracts for Ordnance for the Enfield pattern 1853, and later as founding members of the Birmingham Small Arms Trade. Around 1861 the firm became Isaac Hollis & Sons and claimed establishment from 1814; however, their immediate predecessor was the firm Hollis & Sheath. Isaac Hollis & Sons were recorded in 1861 through 1900, after which time the firm became Hollis, Bentley & Playfair. [2]

When the first Ordnance Department contract for Enfield long rifles was placed with Birmingham gun makers in October 1853, the responsibility for "setting up", or assembling the weapons, fell to four firms, one of which was Hollis & Sheath. [3] They were supplied by names familiar to students of the Civil War Enfield. [4] We have previously examined in detail the outworker system of manufacture of Birmingham in use by gun makers. The piecemeal system resulted in delays when a lack of standardization with the component parts led to problems in manufacturing the

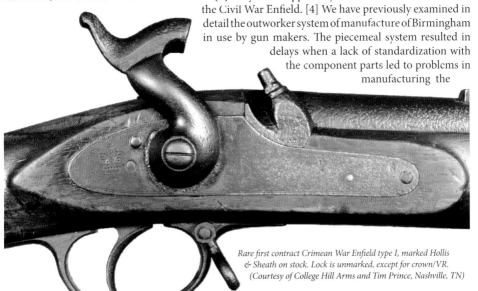

Rare first contract Crimean War Enfield type I, marked Hollis & Sheath on stock. Lock is unmarked, except for crown/VR. (Courtesy of College Hill Arms and Tim Prince, Nashville, TN)

arms. [5] Even with sealed patterns and government inspections at the "Tower", the tolerances were sloppy and much work had to be rejected.

Ironically, the original four firms selected as "setters up" (including Hollis & Sheath) had to default on their obligation due to a lack of enough rear ladder sights, and other makers found it hard to finish the orders, including Deane, Adams & Deane and Wm Tranter. [6] Hollis was not strictly dependent on military arms, as an advertisement from the late 1860s suggests that if it shoots, Isaac Hollis could probably make it for you:

> ISAAC HOLLIS & SONS (late Hollis & Sheath) Manufacturers of Every Description of Breech or Muzzle Loading Sporting & Military Guns, Rifles, Pistols, Revolvers &c., A Large Finished Stock always on hand of Breech-Loading Double Guns and Double Rifles for Central Fire or Pin Cartridges; Muzzle-Loading Single and Double guns, at all prices from the lowest; Military Rifles of all kinds, Long and Short Enfield, Cavalry and Artillery; Pistols &c.; Breech-Loading Military and Sporting Rifles on 'Snider's,' 'Chassepot's,' "Major Fosbery's," 'Green's,' and other Patented Systems; Gun Cases and Implements, Portable Leather Cases, Holsters &c. Manufactory 5 to 11 Weaman Row, Birmingham, established 1814. [7]

You can tell a good deal about a business from the court records of the time period and what activities landed them before a judge. Samuel and Saul Isaac, of the commission house of SIC & Co, were in court quite often. The assassination attempt on Emperor Napoleon in January 1858 by two Italian revolutionaries (Pierri & Orsini) involved bomb components made in England. The two would-be assassins were armed with Adams revolvers made by Hollis & Sheath. France began threatening overtures to invade "Perfidious Albion" in retribution, which directly led to the 2nd formation of the British Volunteers to address the so-called "Crisis of 1858." Fortunately for militarily disaster-prone French, cooler heads prevailed. At the trial in April 1858 of the conspirators, gun maker Isaac Hollis was called to give testimony, which takes an amusing turn under cross examination, as follows:

> Examined by the **Attorney-General**—State your name and occupation.
>
> *Isaac Hollis* — I am a manufacturer of guns and pistols at Birmingham. On the 29th of October last (1857) two persons came to me and purchased two revolvers. I have since seen both those persons in prison at Paris. The Director of the prison, or the Governor, I do not know his name, pointed out two persons to me; they were *Pierri* and *Orsini*. They purchased two revolvers, each with five chambers. This is one of them *(looking at one produced by* Estien*)*, the numbers are 5,609 and 5,561. This is the other *(looking at it)*. Each of them had a case or box with implements complete. Those are the cases *(those produced by Estien)*; the price was 95*. each, including the boxes, all complete. *Orsini* paid, and we sent them to the hotel in Worcester Street in our town, to Mr. *Pierri*. *Orsini* then wore a beard that had disappeared when I saw him in Paris in prison.
>
> (Cross-examined by **James**)
>
> **James**— Revolvers lately have come a good deal into use, have they not?
>
> *Hollis*— They have.
>
> **James**— Are they used more than other pistols, should you say?
>
> *Hollis*— I should say so, now much more than ever.
>
> **James**— They were used, as we know, a good deal in the Russian War; almost every officer in the army is now provided with them
>
> *Hollis* —I believe they are.
>
> **James**— How many may you make in the course of a year?
>
> *Hollis*— I could not tell you, some hundreds.
>
> **James**— It (the revolver) is an American invention, is it not?
>
> *Hollis*— Not at all…
>
> **James**— I thought they took the credit of it.
>
> *Hollis*— Not at all, these are **Adam's patent**. [8]

Hollis & Sheath .38 caliber revolver.

Speaking of the British Volunteers, the following is advice on arms from a manual intended for the formation of new Volunteer units; note the advice about "Tower rejects," as plenty of those saw service across the pond in the U.S. Civil War:

> The SHORT ENFIELD is a particularly handy and convenient arm, and is highly effective for every purpose required by a corps. The bore, of course, is precisely the same as for the long Enfield; the same ammunition serving for each. The sword bayonet is precisely of the form we have engraved under the head of the Pritchett artillery carbine. The length of the barrel is 33 inches ; of the entire gun 48 inches; and with sword bayonet, exactly the length of the long Enfield and bayonet, viz., 5 feet ll inches. The weight of the barrel is 3 lbs. 12 oz., and of the entire arm with sword-bayonet 10 lbs. 3 oz.
>
> The short Enfield, so called, is supplied by most gun-makers ; but as so many of them thus supplied are not of regulation weight, calibre, and measure, it is of the utmost importance to use every care and precaution in selecting not only the gun, but the maker from whom it is had. By far the greater part of those supplied by ordinary gun-makers, or rather dealers, are what are technically termed "Tower rejects," *. e.g:, they have been rejected by the authorities from some cause or other and are then sold (by the dealers) as perfect guns. We have, of course, not tested every make of the Enfield, but we have no hesitation in saying that if a corps wishes to be really well supplied with an arm which shall be a credit to them, and one on which they may thoroughly depend for good workmanship, accuracy, and every essential for a first-rate arm, they cannot do better than place their orders in the hands of such men as Mr. R. T. Pritchett, of 86, St. James's Street, London, the inventor of the universally-approved Pritchett bullet; Mr. G. H. Daw, 9, Threadneedle street, London, the maker of the Jacob rifle; or in course of preparation by Messrs. Hollis and Sheath, whose character as manufacturers stands high as it is a respectable house. In such hands you may rely on being supplied with good regulation arms. [9]

Isaac Hollis & Sons became volume producers of military guns and inexpensive trade guns, but they also made quality sporting guns for the South African as well as the Asian/Indian markets, the Australian and New Zealand markets, and the domestic English civilian market. In 1861 Isaac Hollis, by now at least 66 years old, patented a trigger guard (No. 1082), and he patented another in 1868 (No. 4922) when he was over 73. Other patents for the firm include Patent No. 386 of 21 February 1855 and 3,036 of 22 December 1856 for F. Prince's Percussion Breech-loading arms. This license was taken over by the London Armoury Co., Ltd. in 1861, probably at the time Hollis and Sheath were reorganized into Isaac Hollis and Sons. Isaac Brentnall Sheath was granted British Patent No 996 in April 1853 for a percussion revolver. Isaac Hollis was granted British Patent No. 1083 of 1 May 1861 for a Trigger Guard Construction, also registered Design No. 4922 on May 18, 1868, for a Trigger Guard design, so presumably, while Isaac Sheath was no longer a named partner after 1861, he was still affiliated with the firm in 1868. [10]

Another court case which caused a lot of comment in the Gun Trade concerned a rival firm charged with conspiracy to defraud J. Hollis & Greener by stamping the firm's names on sporting guns which they sold as genuine articles. Both Greener and Hollis sued and recovered damages. [11]

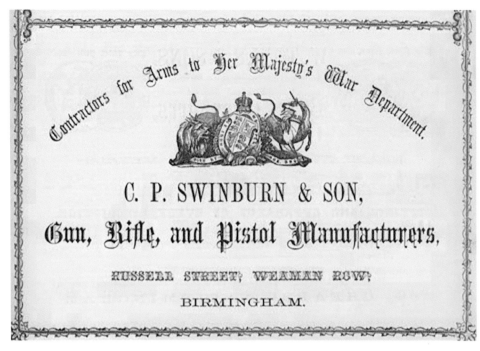

Advertisement for Swinburn.

Charles Philips Swinburn & Son and T. Turner, Birmingham

"Swinburn & Son" was established by Charles Phillips Swinburn in 1834. The firm did business for three years as Swinburn & Waterhouse until 1837 at 22 Hill Street. He advertised as "C.P. Swinburn, successor to J. Field, 15 Newtown Row, Gun and Pistol maker to Her Majesty's Honourable Board of Ordnance, No. 17 Russell Street." It appears evident that Charles Swinburn's son, John Field Swinburn, is named after the "J. Field" listed in the advertisement. There is but a single "John Field" found in Birmingham operating as a gun and pistol manufacturer at 15 Newtown Row in 1830, but he is not listed afterwards. There is in the same directory a listing for one Thomas Waterhouse, gun and pistol maker, who is very likely to have been Swinburn's first partner. Perhaps Swinburn apprenticed with John Field who then passed away? Whatever the case, Charles Swinburn felt enough gratitude to name his only son after the man, and the partnership with Thomas Waterhouse did not last but three years. [1]

In 1838 Swinburn moved to Weaman Row, St Mary's, and also had premises at 16-17 Russell Street, doing business as "C.P. Swinburn." [2] In 1850 the firm became C.P. Swinburn & Son, with Charles' son John Field Swinburn in charge until 1883. In the 1851 Birmingham census, the firm reports "employment of 150 hands." This was considered a large number of employees for one firm. John Field Swinburn kept a close working relationship with the famous Birmingham gun maker Thomas Turner.

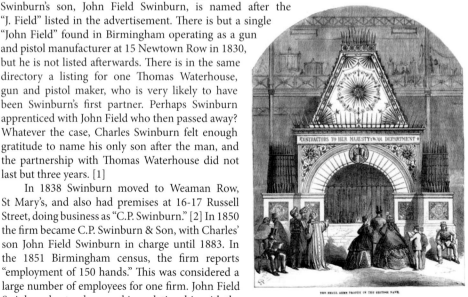

Birmingham Small Arms Trade entry in the Exhibition of 1862. (Craig Barry)

Thomas Turner and John Field Swinburn shared several patents together. The first was patent #1881 in August 1853, for "improvements to long range sights" and later another for breech loaders. [3] John Field Swinburn was a founding member of Birmingham Small Arms Trade and was one of its major shareholders.

Thomas Turner was one of the most successful and innovative gun and barrel makers and designers in England during the mid-19th century. Born in 1805, Thomas Turner had a very long, successful career in Birmingham as a gun maker, with the firm operating in the trade from 1834-1890, though he himself retired in 1873. His son, also named Thomas, took over the Fisher Street address at that time. The Turner gun business continued on well into the 20th century. Thomas Turner is notable for a line of very successful small bore (.451) target rifles that were believed to be as accurate as the Whitworth & Kerr rifles. In fact, some had small bore Whitworth target barrels rifled by Turner. Turner received multiple English patents, including one for rifling that (supposedly) would not foul; his patent on the small bore rifling reads as follows:

> The natural expansion of the ball in front of the charge, so impinges the barrel through the part that usually becomes foul, that all fouling left from the preceding charge is carried away by the one following. I effect this improved system of rifling by so fashioning the rod that regulates the cutter that according to the amount of inclination to be imparted to the rifling towards the breech so is the rod more or less twisted, the spiral of the twist increasing as the rifling deepens, and in rifling that portion from the apex of the incline to the muzzle, the rod that regulates the cutter (before referred to) is twisted in the reverse direction, the twist or spiral being perfectly regular, by which means the rifling through that portion is left perfectly parallel. [4]

Along with John Field Swinburn, Turner was a founding member of the Birmingham Small Arms Trade, which was located at Steelhouse lane in Birmingham from 1854-1878. BSAT was made up from the prominent Birmingham gun makers that were on the Ordnance Department's list of approved contractors. The group was formed during the Crimean War to fill contracts for P53 military arms, a chaotic effort at which the BSAT failed, causing the War Department to make up the shortfall buying from Belgium. This was an extreme measure, and the lesson led the government to re-tool and open the Royal Small Arms Manufactory. Fortunately for BSAT, the U.S. Civil War rolled around and business was conducted on favorable terms with both the U.S. and CS governments.

BSAT was the first attempt at organization of what had always been independent (competing) gun makers in the Birmingham/Midlands region, and their clout ran a number of smaller firms into receivership. Most of the BSAT gun makers later launched the Birmingham Small Arms Company, Ltd, in 1861 at Small Heath, with the goal of producing military small arms on the interchangeable parts principle, as was accomplished by the Royal Small Arms Factory at Enfield Lock (RSAF) and the nearby London Armoury Company. Thomas Tuner was the 2nd largest shareholder in the BSA Co enterprise, with 95 shares of its stock. Only John Field Swinburn held more shares, with 110. Thomas Turner was one of the so-called "original four contractors" to the British War Department in 1854, which also included his old friend Swinburn, plus Hollis & Sheath and Tipping & Lawden. [5] Turner was involved with the manufacture of almost every pattern of mid-19th century British military arm.

John Dent Goodman, Chairman of Birmingham Small Arms Trade.

He was an innovator who often built the prototypes in his own workshop. [6] He also served a term as Master of the Birmingham Proof House.

These principle Birmingham gun makers contributed to the trophy: Messrs. Bentley and Playfair, Cook and Son, John D. Goodman, Hollis, W. L. Sargant, W. Scott and Son, Joseph Smith, C.P. Swinburn and Son, Tipping and Lawden, W. Tranter, Thomas Turner, James Webley, Joseph Wilson, and B. Woodward and Sons.(Source: Cassell's Illustrated Observer of 1862)

Cooper & Goodman

From published articles such as this obituary (below), as well as his writings about the gun trade in S. Timmins' (ed.) *Birmingham and the Midlands Hardware District* (1866), quite a bit is known about the important role of John D. Goodman.

Pepperbox pistol made by JR Cooper.
(Courtesy of Victoria Museum)

EXCERPT OF OBITUARY OF JOHN GOODMAN:

In the person of Mr John Dent Goodman, the city of Birmingham has lost of its most prominent citizens and the gun trade one of its most admired leaders. He has been 45 years as the head of the largest arms manufacturing concern in the gun trade, his chairmanship of the Birmingham Small Arms Company entitling him to this distinction. Both in character and in appearance he was a true type of the English gentleman. Thoroughly straightforward and so kindly disposed to all, these virtues, combined with his ability, won for him the respect of everyone

…Mr. Goodman's connection with the gun trade was of long standing. In 1838, while in the employ of a firm of merchants, he entered into partnership with Mr. J. R. Cooper, and, subsequently, with that gentleman's brother, Mr. Charles Cooper, the business being carried on at first under the name of J. R. Cooper & Co., and afterwards under that of Cooper and Goodman, until 1886. From an early period he took the lead in matters connected with the trade. At the meeting held on March 15, 1855, to arrange for the promotion of the Act of Parliament establishing the Birmingham Proof House, he presided, and on March 10, 1856, at the first meeting of the trade held under the Act, he was appointed chairman for the year.

The year 1855 also saw the origin of the Birmingham Small Arms Company, with which through all of its vicissitudes, Mr. Goodman remained prominently associated. On the breaking out of the Crimean War, the Government being urgently in need of arms, called upon fourteen firms in Birmingham to furnish a supply. These firms subsequently became an association under the title of "The Birmingham Military Arms Trade," with Mr. Goodman as chairman…Mr. Goodman was naturally regarded as the chief authority on the Birmingham gun trade. [1]

The comparatively less often mentioned partner was founder Joseph Rock Cooper. He is first recorded in business in 1838 with brother Charles Henry Cooper at 24 Legge Street, where he kept premises until 1853. Along with Joseph Bentley of Birmingham (later Bentley and Playfair), Joseph R. Cooper was regarded as the principal designer and manufacturer of British pepperbox revolvers in the 1840s. [2] In the 1849 Birmingham City Directory, Cooper is listed as: Cooper J. R. &Co., gun and pistol manufacturers 24, Legge Street. [3]

Another earlier listing for J.R. Cooper is most likely his residence called "Park Cottage" in Aston, and the second directory listing was his known place of business at that time.

Joseph Cooper was one of the Exhibitors at the Great Exhibition of 1851, where he showed "… six barreled revolving pistol, central fire [i.e. Pepperbox] with a safety bolt and a 12 barrel revolving pistol. One side of the stock removed to show the working parts of the lock." [4] In December 1855, Joseph R. Cooper was awarded another patent along with fellow gun maker Westley Richards, "…for improvements to breech-loading firearms." [5] About this time the firm, by then known as Cooper and Goodman, built a large factory on Woodcock Street near the Gun Quarter.

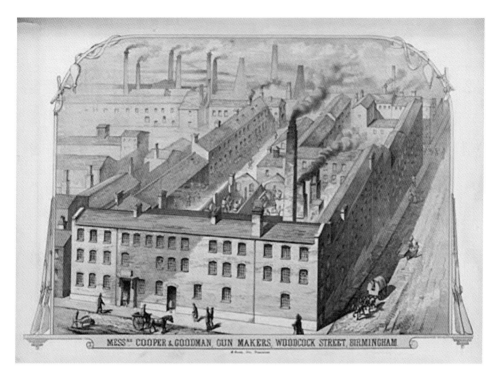

Cooper & Goodman factory.

The firm was involved in litigation relatively infrequently, considering their involvement in all matters of Birmingham business and politics. The one noteworthy case with lasting implications arose from the Gun Barrel Proof Act of 1855. The case was *Goodman v. Spencer* (1857), and it resolved the matter of how to handle gun barrel proof marks when the "provisional" proof was done at Birmingham and the "definitive" proof performed at London. [6] The reason this was a significant issue is that the overwhelming majority of gun barrels were produced in Birmingham and the proof house received a fee for each barrel inspected. The case was resolved in the form of a judgment for the defendant (Spencer), and as history has shown there are no known examples of any barrels stamped with both London and Birmingham proof marks. In other words, commercial barrel proof marks are either from The London Gun-makers Company or the Birmingham proof house, not a mixture of both.

J.R. Cooper was also involved not only as a gun maker, but also as a barrel maker. There are at least some surviving P-53 Enfield Rifles with Civil War provenance with barrels that are marked as such (JR COOPER) on the bottom.

Not as much is known about the other brother in the firm, Charles Henry Cooper. As stated in the above obituary, John Goodman entered the firm first as a partner with only Joseph R. Cooper in 1838, and it states '*subsequently*' (i.e., later) as partner with the other brother Charles. The reasons for this are lost to history, but several explanations are possible. It could be a mere formality, because the firm was doing business under the name "J.R. Cooper" as opposed to "Cooper Bros." Or it may be because Charles was only a limited partner in the enterprise. When Birmingham Small Arms Trade was formed, the first stockholders included J.R. Cooper (48 shares) and J.D. Goodman (47 shares), but there is no mention of any shares held by Charles H. Cooper, or any involvement with the startup of Birmingham Small Arms Trade for that matter. While J.R. Cooper had a long list of patents for new firearm designs, Charles does not show up in any of the scientific journals as having designed or patented anything during the years the Cooper & Goodman firm was active. It appears Charles may have held responsibilities along the lines of a "factory manager," keeping the manufacturing operations going while John D. Goodman served as Chairman of BSAT beginning in 1863, and founder J.R. Cooper seems to have retired from the firm. The day-to-day factory role is also suggested as brother Charles assumes all responsibilities for future *manufacture* of all J.R. Cooper's patents beginning in 1863. [7] Cooper and Goodman continued as a gun making firm until it dissolved in 1886. John Goodman of course remained Chairman of Birmingham Small Arms Co at Small Heath, and he was actively involved in many other business and philanthropic concerns until his death in 1900.

An interesting announcement appeared tucked away in the back of the same issue of the magazine that published the obituary of John D. Goodman; it reads as follows:

> We understand that the George Y. Cooper Small Arms and Bicycle Co, Ltd. are now in a position to supply guns…of every description from a common flintlock to the finest hammerless breech-loaders. Mr. Cooper is the grandson of the late Mr. Charles H. Cooper of the old established firm of government contractors Messrs. Cooper & Goodman. He is occupying part of the old works which were built in the early part of this century by that firm, where he acquired his knowledge of the gun trade." [8] Formed with a capital investment of £1,000 in 1899, George may well have learned about bicycle making—The John Goodman-led BSA Co entered the field in the 1880s—from his years at Cooper & Goodman. By 1900, Birmingham had the largest number of both bicycles and bicycle part manufacturers in England. By 1915, George Y. Cooper Small Arms and Bicycle Company is no longer listed in the Birmingham Trade directory, while the company Goodman founded (BSA Co) continued in various forms well into the late 20th century. [9]

W and C Scott & Sons
W. Scott & Son(s)

The 1860s were very prosperous times for the Birmingham gun trade, due mainly to the U.S. Civil War, but some firms also had success selling their sporting guns, particularly shot guns and other high quality hunting guns in the USA, Europe, and elsewhere. The relationships in the gun trade often criss-crossed, with different gun makers sharing similar names; such was the case with several men named William Scott that both did business in Birmingham beginning in the 1840s. A gun marked "W. & C. Scott and Son" and one marked "W. Scott & Son" would be from two different firms run by two different families. The confusion is understandable, given the similarities in first and last names, but the gun making firm of "W. & C. Scott" (William & Charles) was based in Birmingham, while the W. Scott & Son firm originally came from London. They do not appear to be related. Also, trading ceased in 1875 for W. Scott & Son(s), while W. & C. Scott continued much longer in the gun trade until purchased in their entirety by P. Webley & Sons in 1897. [1] W. & C. Scott also seem to have concentrated on sporting guns rather than the military trade, though they were known to make barrels for Civil War-era P-53s.

Side by side shotgun barrel marked W & C Scott & Son, Makers. (Courtesy www.shotgunworld.com)

Beginning with the firm that had the greatest longevity, founder William Charles Scott was born in 1806. He was the eldest son of William and Dorothy Martin Scott, who had a farm in Bury St. Edmunds in Suffolk. Charles Scott, his brother, was born a year later in 1807. William Charles Scott worked on the farm with his parents until he was 21 years old, but then obtained an apprenticeship as a gun finisher with Benjamin Parker in Bury St. Edmunds. The Benjamin Parker firm specialized in flintlock and box pistols. Most young men in the gun trade started their apprenticeships at 14, so this was quite a bit late for William to make this move, but perhaps his father needed his help on the farm? [2] Younger brother Charles seems to have followed William into the gun trade several years later.

In 1834, when his apprenticeship finished, he established himself first as an outworker (gun finisher) at 11 Lench Street. Charles joined him in the business probably four or five years later, and the firm of William & Charles Scott was formed as "Gun and Pistol Makers."[3] In 1835 William Charles Scott had a son, William Middleditch Scott. In the 1851 census William Charles Scott and his family were living in Walsall Road, Aston. William Middleditch Scott (aged 15) was working in the firm as a gun finisher, and James Charles (aged 14) was employed as an engraver. There were two further sons, Frederick M. Scott (b.1839) and Edward John Scott (b.1849). There was a daughter, Amelia, who was born in 1842. At this time brother Charles Scott (aged 43) was living with William and his growing family in what must have been a crowded house. [4]

In 1855, the W. & C. Scott firm moved into larger and more prestigious premises at 94-95 Bath Street. In the 1861 census, William Scott was recorded employing 18 men and two boys. By this time Frederick M. Scott was employed as a gun stocker. [5] In 1861, William Charles Scott was appointed a guardian of the Birmingham Gun Barrel Proof House, a position he held until 1865. It appears that William Middleditch Scott became a partner in 1858, and that the firm was renamed "W. & C. Scott and Son" in that year. The new name "W. & C. Scott and Son" implies that William Middleditch Scott was made a partner, and thus selected as the future head of the firm. From 1864 on the firm also occupied premises on Bagot Street. [6] In 1864 and 1865, Westley Richards joined Moore & Harris in a partnership established to save the smaller but well regarded gun maker from closure. The new venture with Westley Richards failed, and in an interesting twist the Moore & Harris business was bought at auction by W. & C. Scott & Son.

In 1866, William Middleditch Scott was appointed a guardian of the Birmingham Gun Barrel Proof House, a position he retained until 1894. In 1869, William Charles Scott retired and William Middleditch Scott took over the running of W. & C. Scott and Son. Many of the records concerning their contributions to military rifles were lost to a fire in 1945.

W. Scott and Sons (later Son) started in business in 1841, also as a shotgun maker. The firm was originally known only as William Scott, later became W. Scott and Sons in

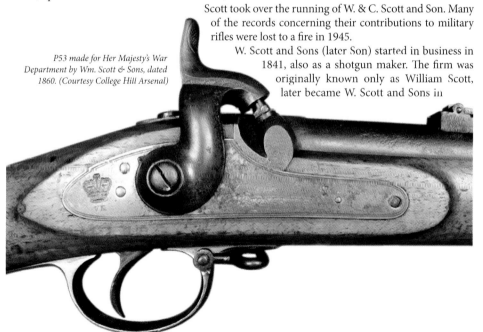

P53 made for Her Majesty's War Department by Wm. Scott & Sons, dated 1860. (Courtesy College Hill Arsenal)

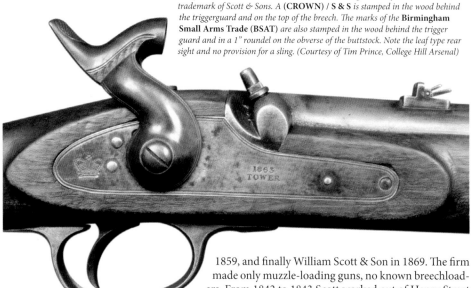

*The gun is marked with the name **W SCOTT** along the toe of the stock and the trademark of Scott & Sons. A **(CROWN) / S & S** is stamped in the wood behind the triggerguard and on the top of the breech. The marks of the **Birmingham Small Arms Trade (BSAT)** are also stamped in the wood behind the trigger guard and in a 1" roundel on the obverse of the buttstock. Note the leaf type rear sight and no provision for a sling. (Courtesy of Tim Prince, College Hill Arsenal)*

1859, and finally William Scott & Son in 1869. The firm made only muzzle-loading guns, no known breechloaders. From 1842 to 1843 Scott worked out of Henry Street in London, then moved to Leman Street from 1843-49; the firm relocated to Birmingham in 1855 to Whittall Street. In 1859, the firm of W. Scott & Sons moved to their final location on 47 Princip Street, where they stayed until 1875. The firm partially dissolved in December 1869 and "W. Scott & Son" (singular) was used on post-1869 guns. Any U.S. Civil War Enfield made by W. Scott should be marked "Scott & Sons" (plural) or S & S stamped over a crown and have commercial Birmingham barrel proofs. W. Scott & Sons was also a founding member of Birmingham Small Arms Trade, &c.

The Birmingham Directory lists the firm as follows:

Scott, William and Sons: Princip-street, and at Turin, gun and pistol manufacturers. William Scott, Frederick William Scott, Walter Scott. As regards Walter Scott, all debts received and paid by the remaining partners, who will in future carry on the business on their own account under the style of William Scott and Son. 17th and 24th December 1869. [7]

Another interesting fact about W. Scott & Son(s) is their involvement in the large scale gun stock saw mill operation located in Turin, Italy, lasting through 1877. The following appears in the Accounts and papers of the House of Commons:

Saw Mills.—Since the closing of Messrs. W. Scott and Sons gunstock factory, the principal works at Turin are those of Mr. Ferrato who employs more than 100 skilled workmen, and is in a position to supply gunstocks to foreign governments on a large scale. [8]

As referenced elsewhere in the monograph, the gun stock factory is discussed by John D. Goodman (Cooper & Goodman). He (oddly) does not mention William Scott & Sons by name, but in writing in general about the Birmingham system of manufacture states:

The stocks are of two kinds, beech-wood and walnut. The former is employed for African markets, and for the lower description of sporting guns; its liability to expand and shrink with changes of the atmosphere unfits it for any but guns of the cheapest description. The stocks are brought to Birmingham, cut from the plank into the form of the gun. Beech-stocks are grown in this country, chiefly in Gloucestershire and Herefordshire. Walnut-

*The gun marked with the name **W SCOTT** (detail on page 80) shown here full length.*

wood is free from the objection to which beech is liable; ash and maple are occasionally used, but they are very difficult to work. Walnut stocks are, with few exceptions, imported from Italy and Germany. One Birmingham contractor, to meet the demand occasioned by the Crimean war, established sawing mills in Turin and since that period has converted into gun stocks nearly one hundred thousand walnut trees. He has left few trees standing… An average-sized tree yields about thirty gun stocks; those cut from the heart of the tree are the most valued, and are used for first-class military arms and the best sporting guns; about one stock in five or six can be obtained "all heart," the remainder are "sap and heart," and "sap." [9]

As Chairman of Birmingham Small Arms Trade, Goodman would seem to be a reliable source for this information. And if so, W. Scott & Son(s) were responsible for bringing in the overwhelming majority of military gun stocks used by the BSAT, made up into Enfield Short and Long rifles, and exported by the hundreds of thousands to America during the U.S. Civil War.

William Lucas Sargant

The Birmingham gun making firm of W.L. Sargant began in the late 1700s with founder William Sargant. He came from a long line of farmers, the last of which sold the property in the 1770s and established eldest son William as an apprentice to a gun manufacturer in Birmingham. William later became a partner in Woolley, Sargant & Fairfax. They produced sporting guns as well as "trade muskets" for the North American and African market. A number of familiar names from the Civil War-era began in that lower echelon of the gun trade, including the fraternal ancestors of Barnett, Hollis, Bond, Parker, Field & Co., and Wilson.

Sargant stock stamp

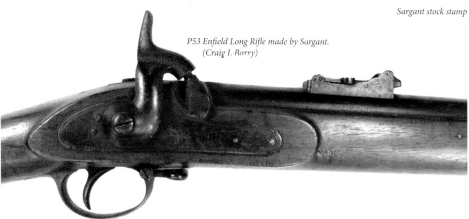

P53 Enfield Long Rifle made by Sargant.
(Craig L. Barry)

Lock marked "Woolley Sargant & Fairfax c. 1826-1830.
(Courtesy Tortuga Trading Company)

mother's side. In 1821 the father William Sargant passed away, leaving the firm to his wife and brother (Henry), as son William Lucas Sargant was at the time 11 years old. William Lucas Sargant left school at 15 and worked in a counting house for a year before entering the family business "...which my father had left and which was carried on under the management of a partner." After five years at the firm Sargant had a disagreement with the managing partner (apparently Charles Fairfax) "...who made me an offer to leave on the condition that I attend Cambridge and prepare for the bar." [1] William attended Trinity College at Cambridge for two years before "the managing partner" passed away, and he returned again to the family gun manufacturing business.

In the 1830s, the Sargant firm did business at 74 Edmund Street in Birmingham. In 1835 they leased additional premises at Charlotte Street and George Street from some timber merchants under some odd contractual terms. [2] In 1838 they were listed as W.L. & H. Sargant, and then simply Sargant Bros. Elizabeth transferred all of her rights in the firm to her son William Lucas Sargant and partner Henry Sargant in 1839. It appears that the co-partner Henry was employed primarily as a barrister at Lincoln's Inn, London. [3] Lincoln's Inn is one of four Inns of Court to which all barristers must belong. Henry's son (also Henry) and grandson Charles Henry Sargant did not enter the gun trade, but also became barristers of Lincoln's Inn and practiced law in London. In 1851 W.L. Sargant assigned the lease of the land and premises of all of the previous properties, and relocated the business to 35 Whitall Street, though directories conflict on the exact date. [4] From that point forward the firm did business as W.L. Sargant.

Of their workmanship in producing trade muskets from the early 19th century, Ramsey Crooks of the American Fur Company wrote to C.M. Lampson, his London agent, about purchasing additional guns from the Sargant firm as follows:

> The gun you sent us from Messrs Sargent (sic) of Birmingham is a better article than our usual supply and cheaper than those from London...if we could be certain that Sargent would give us guns every way equal to the one we have we would be tempted to give them

next season's order. If the reputation of Messrs. Sargent does not afford a positive guarantee for their work you need not take any further trouble in the matter. [5]

It appears they could indeed duplicate the desired level of quality, and Sargant received the promised contracts from American Fur Company. In period correspondence such as this, as well as some other surviving records, the firm name is incorrectly identified as "Sargent." The business continued to grow and innovate beyond sporting and trade guns. In 1844, William Lucas Sargant applied for a patent for improvements to gun barrel rolling, a very specialized part of the gun trade. Even in an era of predominantly hand-made guns, barrel making was the first branch of gun making to be widely mechanized.

A commission of congressmen from America visited the Sargant Bros firm in the 1840s and noted:

> The manufacturers of small arms at Birmingham having succeeded in making barrels by rolling, instead of hammering them, arrangements were making at Enfield for introducing machinery for the same purpose.
> At the gun manufactory of the Messrs. Sargent & Brothers,(sic) of Birmingham, much of their iron for barrels is formed from scraps from the button-makers, and other workers in sheet-iron. These scraps are put into a furnace faggoted together, heated, and drawn under a trip-hammer into a short thick bar, then rolled into bars of the proper thickness and width for barrels…This method of making gun-barrels is supposed to effect a considerable reduction in their cost; and the experience of the English manufacturers seems to have produced a conviction of its utility. It is not practised in any other country, nor is it proposed to introduce it into any of the manufactories that have been visited on the continent. [6]

Despite the congressional report, the rolling method as described above became the standard process for military barrel making in Birmingham and elsewhere for years to come. Gun barrel rolling was a hazardous occupation, especially for children. In a report on gun barrel rolling to the English Parliamentary Commission on Child Labour in 1864, a young man recalled his part of the job as follows:

> *Samuel Robertson, age* 11.— Catch barrels as they come red hot through the rollers. Have been at this two years…have sometimes dropped a hot barrel on my feet…but no serious burns." Ironically there were fewer and less serious injuries among barrel makers than other branches such as polishers and grinders An 11 year old boy at another well-known Birmingham firm, whose job it was to polish small pieces of gun parts at a grinding wheel states "sometimes sparks fly into my eyes…one piece stuck in the middle of it for a week and at last the grinder got it out with his pen knife. Sometime something comes over that eye still. [7]

In business, W.L. Sargant was an early member of Birmingham Small Arms Trade from the mid-1850s through the U.S. Civil War era, as the city expanded their commercial gun making enterprises. However, W.L. Sargant was not listed among the major shareholders or in any Director role in the newly formed BSA Co at Small Heath. The extent of his involvement in the venture is not known. He seems to have directed considerable attention to other pursuits. Perhaps incidents similar to those described, especially involving young children in his factory, took him down a different road.

William Lucas Sargant was active in the Birmingham community and became a Justice of the Peace in 1849. He also took an interest in schools for children and published controversial social criticism beginning in the mid-1850s with the book *Science of Social Opulence* (1856), followed by *Economy of the Labouring Classes* (1857) and *Essays of a Birmingham Manufacturer* (1869-72) in four volumes. He was a great proponent of mandatory public education for children, as well as seeing to it that they were fed.

In his writings, Sargant also has something to say about the business of commercial gun making and the offering of "perquisites" (bribes) to officials and small arms inspectors at the Tower. He confesses that "I have had a good deal to do with official persons in the way of contracts, and I hope it may please heaven to spare me from any further dealings with them. I have no complaint to make of corruption however, what I dislike is the formality and tedium incident to all their dealings." [6] Sargant suggests knowledge (at least anecdotally) that a well-known Birmingham manufacturer offered a bribe of £5,000 to an officer sent from London to superintend the fulfillment of a contract, an amount he does not find shocking. Sargant acknowledged that this was the *customary* perquisite. Of the financial chicanery involved in the gun trade, Sargant also recalled, "Some years ago an Italian called on me, and after discussing private business, told me that he was going on to the Tower to offer some timber (walnut for gun stocks). Might he ask a question? After some hesitation he inquired whether he might offer a perquisite to the inspector of small arms. I said he certainly might…and what it would give him might be the shortest route possible. He thanked me and explained that in every continental state such things were done." The point Sargant was making was that bribery was widespread, not only in the English gun trade with the War Department, but in all walks of life, "I only contend that pecuniary immorality is widespread, and is improperly attributed to the commercial classes, as though it were peculiar to them." [8]

After retiring from business in 1879 he founded the Birmingham and Edgbaston Proprietary School, and served as the first chairman of the Birmingham School Board. A particular area of interest for Sargant was the poor diet of children. His younger son, George Herbert Sargant, an accountant, continued his family's commitment to providing for poor children. He published "an interesting and practical paper" called Farthing Dinners (1887). The so-called "farthing dinner" consisted of "…a half pint of soup with a round of bread and quarter ounce of jam." [9]

Little to no mention is made of the eldest son born in 1837, also named William, who matriculated at Trinity College at Cambridge in 1858 and took his Bachelor of Arts degree in 1862, but is not heard from again. The eldest son traditionally inherited the business while younger siblings were pretty much on their own. Reading between the lines of *Essays of a Birmingham Manufacturer*, a certain picture emerges of what his eldest son may have been like. Sargant notes that the chief characteristic of the younger generation (of eldest sons) graduated from the "great universities" (like Cambridge) are "…spoiled by the luxury of home and early habits of self-indulgence, the young aristocrat has lost the power of commanding the attention, and is not only indisposed for, but incapable of, work. Profound idleness and luxuriousness have corrupted his nature. He is the foppish exquisite of the drawing-room… and beyond these spheres all life is to him a blank." [10] It is also possible William may have died shortly after graduation, but there is no record of him in the gun trade or any of the business directories during the period of time in question.

Upon his death in 1889, the obituary of William Lucas Sargant only makes passing reference to his business life and no mention at all of the gun trade. The Birmingham newspaper recalls W.L. Sargant as an "educational reformer and political economist." It lists his literary and philanthropic accomplishment and his devotion to the improvement of public life in Birmingham as his notable achievements. [11] In 1915, the Birmingham University Library received from George Herbert Sargant and Emily M Sargant (Foster), "…in memory of their father, the late Mr. William Lucas Sargant, the gift of a valuable collection of their father's books on economics. The books cover the period from the time of Adam Smith down to Mr. Sargant's death in 1889." [12]

Bentley & Playfair

Charles Playfair, gun maker and dealer at 18 Union Terrace, Aberdeen, Scotland, founded the original firm of his name in 1821. In 1845 his son, also named Charles, moved to Birmingham, England, and entered into a partnership with Thomas Bentley, "Manufacturer of Every Description of Arms" already in business at 37 Lench Street. [1] Charles Playfair was awarded the honor of 'Gun maker to Prince Albert.' The firm did business on 56 Summer Lane before moving to the factory pictured above at 315-316 Summer Lane around 1860. The earliest mention of the new factory in the Birmingham business directory is 1861. [2] The elder Charles, partner of Thomas Bentley, passed away in 1876. His son, also named Charles, took over his interest in the firm.

They remained at that location until at least 1885, when they moved to 20 High Holborn. Bentley & Playfair were doing business at 60 Queen Victoria Street (London) when Charles III (Lt-Col Playfair) supervised a merger with Isaac Hollis & Sons. Apparently business was slow, as the following was published in "Arms & Explosives," a trade periodical:

Messrs. Bentley & Playfair write to inform us, in reference to our Note in the last issue, that they are not going to give up their London premises at 60, Queen Victoria Street, E.C., and that they will continue at the same address under new management. Our Note was based on the fact that the showrooms have for some time been untenanted, most of the furniture having been removed, two gun cabinets which remain having been sold or offered for sale by Messrs. Bentley & Playfair themselves. [3]

Bentley & Playfair factory on 315-316 Summer Lane, c. 1860. (Courtesy Birmingham Gun Museum)

Like most large Birmingham gun makers, Bentley and Playfair were well-off and lived on Sherbourne Road; a neighbor of theirs was John Field Swinburn. "Sherbourne was at one time one of the most exclusive roads in Acocks Green, home, among others to three of the leading gun makers of Birmingham...These were the gun makers' houses: John Field Swinburn, Charles Playfair, and Thomas Bentley, respectively. Charles Playfair was actually listed in Acocks Green in the 1861 census on Malt House Lane. A child, Thomas Bentley, was listed as living with the Playfairs in 1861. The two men ran Bentley and Playfair." [4] The Elder Thomas Bentley passed away in 1901 at the age of 86.

On September 30, 1863, management of the BSA Co was changed at a meeting from being run by a committee to that of an elected Board of Directors (Joseph Wilson, Samuel Buckley, Isaac Hollis, Charles Playfair, Charles Pryse, Sir John Ratcliffe, Edward Gem, and J.F. Swinburn) were elected under the chairmanship of John Dent Goodman. There is no mention of Thomas Bentley as a director, but he was almost certainly involved as an investor. [5] Thomas Bentley later partnered with some of these same gentlemen in Abingdon Works, 1872-75.

Some confusion seems to exist about which Bentley (there were several) was involved with Charles Playfair in producing military Enfield rifles for the Birmingham Small Arms Trade. Some sources state the firm was owned by Joseph Bentley and Charles Playfair. This is not correct. Thomas Bentley was the business partner of Charles Playfair in BSAT, and Joseph Bentley was founder of the firm Joseph Bentley & Son at 12 S. Castle Street, Liverpool, known primarily as a maker of handguns. The J. Bentley & Son firm shared some revolver patents with Webley. [6] As far as any U.S. Civil War connection to Bentley & Playfair or BSAT, unfortunately both Joseph Bentley the elder and Joseph Bentley the younger went bankrupt on January 13, 1860. [7] Thomas Bentley and Charles Playfair continued in the gun trade well into the twentieth century. Post-bellum they continued to manufacture and sell side by side shotguns for the "fowl hunting" market and had offices in both Birmingham and London.

Joseph Bourne

Joseph Bourne was a large gun maker in Birmingham Small Arms Trade and later BSA Co. The gun making firm was established in 1840, operated under the name Joseph Bourne until 1866, and later from 1867 to 1900 as Joseph Bourne & Son. They were located at 5 Whittall Street from 1849, but by 1862 had also taken over premises at # 3 and # 4 Whittall Street, where they stayed through 1878. They relocated to 9 St. Mary's Row from 1879 and were still listed there when they acquired long time gun maker Robert Hughes in 1908. [1] The remnants of the firm remained in business until 1960, if their published catalogs are to be trusted.

Joseph Bourne was a descendant of William Bourne, among the first gun makers in Birmingham to contract with the crown to supply muskets. The 1692 contract read as follows:

The said William Bourne, Tho. Moore, John West, Rieh'l Weston and Jacob Austin do hereby severally Covenant and agree to and with the said principal Officers of their Majesty's Ordnance on their behalfe of themselves and the rest of the Gun-makers of

Joseph Bourne & Son Factory. (Birmingham)

Birmingham that they shall and will make and provide for their Majesty's Service two hundred Snaphance Musquets every Month for the space of one Yeare from the Expiration of their last Contract Bearing Date the six and twentieth day of March 1692. To be three foot ten inches long, with Wallnutt-tree and Ash Stocks. And that one half of the said Musquets shall have flat locks engraved, and the other half Round Locks and that all of them shall have brass pipes cast and brass heel plates and all the stocks varnished, and to have six Good threads in the Breech screws, and that all the said Gun

Maker's mark for Bourne.

Stocks shall be made well and Substantiall and none of them glewed. And also that the said Musquet Barrells shall be Compleatly filed before they are proved and that they shall be proved at Birmingham according to the Tower proofe and a fit person (who shall be impowered by this Office) shall inspect the same and marke them with the Office Marke, and (when finished) to survey them. [2]

In the early days of the Birmingham gun trade, when this contract was entered, Birmingham had virtually no trade unions or guilds, and the system of apprenticeships was in its very early stages. Men came and went into various branches of gun making as their mood suited them; however, there were the beginnings of specialization (such as barrel making). In the next century, as the trade grew this evolved into distinct branches of specialized craftsmen, each producing a specific part or assembly, with the "gun-maker" responsible for final assembly.

An early listing of Birmingham gun makers are recorded as follows:

Jacob Austin, Birmingham, 1689. William Bourne, Birmingham, 1689.,T. Ketland, Birmingham, before 1750 to 1791. Thos. and Wm. Ketland, Birmingham, 1803. Ketland & Walker, Birmingham, 1805. Ketland, Walker, Adams, Birmingham, 1818. Wm. Ketland & Co, Birmingham, 1823-29. Tho. Moore, Birmingham, 1689.R. Wilson & Co, Birmingham 1767. [3]

As discussed previously, the Birmingham Small Arms Trade was formed to regulate various aspects of the gun trade, as well as meet the needs of the War Department during the Crimean War. Prior to 1854 there was no formal association to resolve disputes. The following appeared in 1852, when Bourne and Westley Richards were called upon to arbitrate a labor/management dispute. The meaning of Joseph Bourne and Westley Richards being agreed upon by both sides as arbiters speaks for itself concerning the influence of these men within the Birmingham Gun Quarter.

The following advertisement, common to the more prosperous firms, appeared in 1859:

Joseph Bourne,
Contractor To Her Majesty's War Department
Manufacturer of Guns, Muskets, Revolvers, Pistols, Rifles, and Small Arms suitable for the various markets and Governments of the world.
No. 5, Whittall Street, Birmingham. [5]

One of the ten added members of Birmingham Small Arms Trade in 1854, Joseph Bourne also took 60 shares of the initial stock offering of BSA Co in 1861, but retained his factory for the manufacture (by hand) of commercial military arms during the U.S. Civil War, and later civilian sporting guns. Bourne marked Enfield rifles are quite commonly encountered, suggesting large numbers were produced. Of the few specimens examined an odd dichotomy emerges. Joseph Bourne sometimes marked the inside of the lock, the barrel, the barrel channel, and the stock behind the trigger guard with the name of their firm, rather than the actual maker. On some other Bourne marked (either "Joseph Bourne" or "J Bourne") Enfield long rifles, the barrel maker's mark appears as "Henry Clive" or "Ezra Millward", well-known barrel makers in the Birmingham gun trade which you may expect. Barrel making is a very specialized part of the trade, and Bourne is not listed in the Birmingham commercial directories in that category, only as a "Gun and Pistol Maker." The purpose of the maker's mark was so the manufacturer setting up the rifle had some recourse if the barrel provided failed proof. [6]

Bourne was also an investor in other enterprises. In 1865, when Lloyd's Bank converted to a public stock company, Joseph Bourne was one of two members of BSA Co to become an initial investor in the new Lloyd's Corporation.

Joseph's son, William Bourne of Acocks Green, was also involved in the Abingdon Works rifle making venture with most of the members of BSA Co, except Tranter, who sued. BSA Co probably settled with Tranter, because the outcome of the trial beyond the discovery stage (request for documents) is not recorded. If they did settle, Tranter may have been the only one who made money on the venture. [7] By the mid-1870s, the major shareholders in Abingdon Works were Swinburn and W.C. Scott. Abingdon Works by 1880 primarily manufactured only the "Swinburn rifle" (a rifle/carbine used in the Zulu Wars) and bicycle parts.

William Greener

The long tradition of English gun makers would not be complete without some mention of the W. Greener firm. The founder of the "W. Greener" firm was William Greener (b. 1806). He apprenticed with the famous London shotgun maker Joseph Manton until he opened his own shop in Newcastle on Tyne in 1829. Greener moved the business to Birmingham in 1844 for competitive reasons, as obviously Birmingham was then the center of the British gun trade. [1]

William Greener was completely committed to perfecting the design of muzzle-loading weapons. Muzzle-loading rifles required a bullet smaller than the bore so it could easily be rammed into the muzzle and then, paradoxically, able to become as large as the bore so that, upon firing, it would snugly fill the grooves and fully use the force applied by the ignition of the black powder charge. A number of inventors had already devised self-expanding bullets when, in 1836, William Greener developed such a bullet consisting of a flat-ended oval ball with a cavity in which a metal plug was inserted. When the gun fired, the plug drove forward and caused the bullet to expand and engage the rifle grooves. Greener submitted his invention to the British government, but it was rejected later when a French captain, Claude Minié, received £20,000 from the British government for a similar bullet; Greener sued for infringement and was ultimately awarded £1,000. It is not certain how he prevailed in the lawsuit for damages given the apparent differences in design, but Greener was not one to be shoved around by anyone, including the Ordnance Department. [2] Whatever the outcome of the case, the famous rifle-musket round that produced so much carnage and shattered limbs during the U.S. Civil War was forever after called the "Minié ball" and not the "Greener bullet."

The first success for the W. Greener firm was actually an improved whaling gun, of which he writes:

> I was then applied to by Captains Warham and Taylor of the Lord Gambier and Granville Bay Whalers, also of this port (most likely Newcastle on Tyne), to give the subject some attention. I did so by lengthening the barrel, adding a little more weight and reducing the bore to 1 ½ inches…throwing the harpoon with considerable accuracy to any distance less than 84 yards. [3]

The Scottish whaling industry held the Greener bow mounted swivel guns in high repute, even though the claim of accuracy up to 84 yards was more likely around half that distance. The Greener swivel guns were also used in America (West Coast) for whaling well into the 1870s. Harpoons were often called "Greener irons" in period references from the whalers themselves, regardless of who actually made them or where they were produced.

However, while Greener was best known for his books, which were sometimes self serving, as well as civilian fowling pieces and side by side double barrel shotguns [4], the firm also produced P53 (and P58) military arms, and a few fine specimens at that. One unusual thing about the Greener produced "Enfield pattern of 1853", or P53, is the markings on the weapon. The most common Birmingham, and to a lesser extent London commercial P53, was marked **TOWER** under or over the year of manufacture (not the pattern date of 1853, an incorrect feature found on most reproductions). The **TOWER** marking on the lock plate was intended to suggest that the weapon had been inspected with gauges at a British government facility by their employees to ensure parts interchangeability. This was a requirement stipulated in Ordnance Department contracts with private gun makers. The government obviously did not pay their employees to "inspect with gauges" commercially made military arms for sale to other countries. Greener eschewed this form of legalized misrepresentation and his lock is more simply marked with the maker's name in slanted capital letters, *GREENER*. The lock does have the usual crown behind the hammer, as well as regular Birmingham gauge and proof house marks on the barrel. The barrel often has a proprietary mark from the firm which sometimes appears as *W GREENER INVENTOR of the EXPANSIVE BULLET*.

The furniture and hardware is the standard commercial sort, bell shaped rear sling swivel, square-eared lock escutcheons, and so on. The fit and finish is good, as might be expected. The stock is stamped with only the Greener firm maker's mark on the flat. In other words, not the familiar **BIRMINGHAM SMALL ARMS TRADE** roundel on the stock flat of a great many Civil War-era P53s. This is because W. Greener was a competitor (not a member) of the consortium of gun makers who formed the Birmingham Small Arms

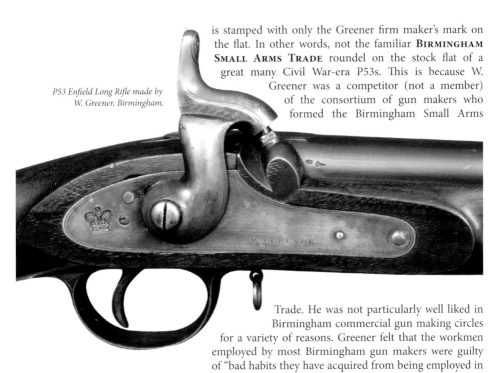

P53 Enfield Long Rifle made by W. Greener, Birmingham.

Trade. He was not particularly well liked in Birmingham commercial gun making circles for a variety of reasons. Greener felt that the workmen employed by most Birmingham gun makers were guilty of "bad habits they have acquired from being employed in the manufacture of so large a quantity of goods of an inferior quality." [5] It is worth noting that the Greener firm remains in the gun making business, with a fifth generation family member still on the current Board of Directors. At the very least, we must concede that the Greener gun making firm has stood the test of time, while most of his competitors in the Birmingham Small Arms Trade did not. Whatever history has shown, at the time his competitors no doubt found his criticism grating, as they were mostly living well while making and selling all the military arms they could produce, at least during the early years of the U.S. Civil War. And they were selling them in large quantities to both U.S. and CS governments, as well as many other foreign governments at war during the early 1860s. However, the halcyon days of seemingly endless commercial contract work at premium prices was not to last much longer. There is something Darwinian in all of this.

Greener was more than just opinionated and independent even in the "dog-eat-dog" world of the commercial gun trade. In addition to belittling his cohorts in the Birmingham Small Arms Trade, Greener, being a man of principle, held both the Birmingham and London proof houses in contempt over what he saw as their low internal standards and monopolistic practices, stating:

Many complaints are made by barrel makers that there is not the same degree of partiality shown by all the proof-masters, as though a gratuity is expected of either money or beer…a few pots of John Barleycorn will infuse more strength into (gun) barrels than you could purchase for ten times the amount in money…In fact, some barrels are sent back when there is nothing the matter with them, while those that are bulged are sent back to their maker who beats down the swellings, sends back the barrels and they are proofed again. They generally stand the second proof, though I know of one barrel that went through four proofs before it was (proof) marked. I also object to the standard of allowing best barrels to rebound into a body of sand…this is a standard calculated to destroy the efficiency of the test by 50%…the consequence is the prevalence of barrels bursting…(and) inferior guns. How can it be that such a state of things is allowed to exist? [6]

William Greener also felt that the fees for barrel proof were too high, and so on. We will leave the question to the philosophers about what it is about English gun makers (and gun collectors) that makes them stubborn and grumpy. The elder Greener appears to be quite the iconoclast, perhaps because he was an outsider coming from Newcastle on Tyne instead of Birmingham proper? We can never really know, but any casual study of human nature suggests that publishing critical remarks (as above) about those in the same trade, as well as the same city, is not conducive to any level of camaraderie. Greener may have learned these personality traits while apprenticing for Joseph Manton, who was well known in his day for being stubborn to the point of his own financial demise, or it may just have been that it was his nature to be critical.

Whatever the case, it was more than mere talk, as he backed it up with generally high standards for the firearms produced by the firm bearing his name. Of his father, the even more famous eldest son W.W. Greener (1834-1921) wrote (in retrospect):

> He was instrumental in improving the reputation of Birmingham as a gun making center, though his denunciations of "trash" made him many enemies, and his whole-hearted attacks upon the wardens of the Proof House were deeply resented…they led to better administration, improved methods and the passing of the Gun-Barrel Proof Act (1868) which has done much to protect the public and greatly advanced the interests of English gun-makers. [7]

In addition, other less legal practices were in evidence at the time. One more blatantly fraudulent practice was to engrave or stamp the name of an English gun maker on the lock plate of a commercial P53 made entirely in Belgium. This was easily done, because the lock plate forward of the hammer was blank except for the date (year) in italics. In one case where charges were filed it was documented that, "An importer obtained a number of low cost Belgian guns so proof marked, and was detected in placing the name of some English gun-makers of highest repute. Both Mr. W. Greener and Messrs. I. Hollis & Sons (of Birmingham) brought actions against this dealer and obtained judgment and damages." [8] In this instance, it seems Mr. Greener was able to cooperate against a common foe with a competing gun maker. Hollis & Sons was one of the "original four" firms from the very early days of Birmingham Small Arms Trade. [9]

W. Greener was completely committed to the concept of the muzzle loader and never entertained the advantages inherent in other designs. He was proved wrong, at least in this one matter. And when his son W.W. Greener intended to patent a newer design, he had to set up another business of his own called the W.W. Greener Company in order to do so. The younger Greener produced his first patent breech loading rifle in 1864. The days of the muzzle loader were quickly coming to an end by the mid-1860s, a trend which W.W. Greener correctly predicted. "The argument between the muzzleloader versus the breech-loader is not worth writing about, for the latter has every advantage in its favor. It is a closer distributor of shot, a stronger shooter, more readily loaded, and above all safer." [10] When his father, W. Greener, died in 1869, the two companies were joined together and managed by William W. Greener. The muzzle-loaders were naturally phased out in favor of more modern designs. W. W. Greener was responsible for popularizing several sporting gun innovations (like choke boring), and it was on the strength of these improved designs that the company was to become famous outside of Birmingham. Under W.W. Greener, the company established branch offices in London, Kingston upon Hull, and overseas in Montreal and New York.

Joseph Wilson

> **JOSEPH WILSON, 67 ½ to 70 Great Charles St. Birmingham**
> **Present Contractor to Her Majesty's War Department**
> **& Manufacturer of RIFLE MUSKETS, Guns & Pistols of Every Description,**
> **Suitable for the African, American and all other MARKETS** [1]

Joseph Wilson (b. 1817) became a member of Birmingham Small Arms Trade after the so-called "original four" gun makers to the War Department failed to deliver on the initial order of Enfield long rifles. Wilson was one of the ten or so firms added in 1854 to the "original four" to help complete the contracts. Joseph Wilson was also an initial stockholder in BSA Co at Small Heath beginning in 1861, and elected to the Board of Directors in 1863. He later served as Treasurer of BSA Co.

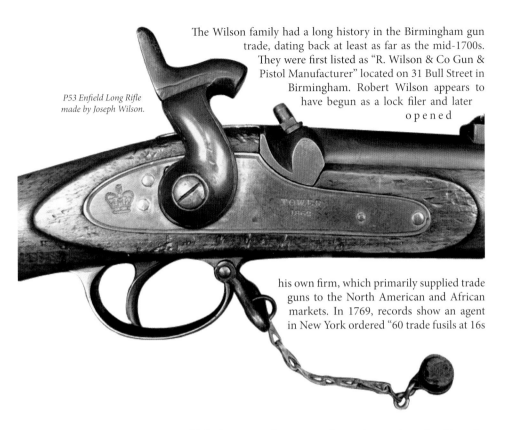

The Wilson family had a long history in the Birmingham gun trade, dating back at least as far as the mid-1700s. They were first listed as "R. Wilson & Co Gun & Pistol Manufacturer" located on 31 Bull Street in Birmingham. Robert Wilson appears to have begun as a lock filer and later opened

P53 Enfield Long Rifle made by Joseph Wilson.

his own firm, which primarily supplied trade guns to the North American and African markets. In 1769, records show an agent in New York ordered "60 trade fusils at 16s

made by Wilson & Co, Birmingham." [2] The Birmingham gun maker Robert Wilson should not be confused with the firm of Wilson & Son of London owned by Richard Wilson, with whom Robert Barnett apprenticed. There appears to be no relation between the two firms. After three generations Wilson & Son was sold to another London gun maker, William Parker (Parker, Field & Sons), in 1832, and was no longer recorded doing business in the gun trade.

However, Wilson & Co of Birmingham was far from finished. Another Robert Wilson, perhaps a son or grandson, is listed as a "Gun & Pistol maker" on New John Street in Birmingham in 1818, and under the same name at the same address in 1837. Then the next Birmingham commercial directory of 1840 shows no listing for Robert Wilson or Wilson & Co, but we find Joseph Wilson, Gun and Pistol maker, at 67 ½ Great Charles Street. [3] Joseph Wilson is most likely the son of Robert Wilson, gun maker with the multi-generational firm of Wilson & Co. The two men are listed at the same residential address in Acocks Green.

The gun manufacturing firm known as Joseph Wilson was in business from 1840 until 1886 in Birmingham. Joseph Wilson was a supplier to both the War Department and Birmingham Small Arms Trade, and at their peak employed around 150, including children, though employment numbers varied considerably with the fluctuation of demand. The factory on Great Charles Street was large and took up the block from 67½ to 70 beginning in 1845. [4] Wilson being a common name, there were several others in the Birmingham gun trade with no relation to Joseph. There was a J. Wilson & Company located on Steelhouse Lane in the Gun Quarter that was believed to be James Wilson, who went bankrupt in 1873. The firm of Thomas Wilson, 45 Church Street, was involved in the design of breech-loading weapons, but the Snider system of conversion was selected for the P53 by Ordnance and the venture dissolved in 1873. [5] These two gun makers appear to be much smaller firms. The gun makers involved in BSAT and BSA Co were large firms that were well capitalized. In other words, these men were far removed from the file, hammer, and forge many associate with the Birmingham gun makers of the U.S. Civil War-era.

The large 67 ½ to 70 Great Charles Street factory of Joseph Wilson, while still in the so-called Gun Quarter, was close to the area known as the Jewelry Quarter. Joseph Wilson had a close acquaintance with a large and wealthy jeweller named William Dudley. Dudley was known as a man who demonstrated great discrimination of character in the choice of men he trusted. When Dudley died in 1876, one of the trustees of his estate was "Joseph Wilson, a Birmingham gun manufacturer." [6]

Joseph Wilson had an eldest son, William, who did not follow him in the gun trade, but went into medicine and became the chief medical examiner for the Birmingham district. A younger son, Bernard George Wilson, studied law and became a solicitor, coincidentally listed in 1878 at 31 Bull Street, the location of the first Wilson & Co gun making firm 100 years earlier. [7] Since neither son followed Joseph Wilson in the gun trade, one assumes he saw the writing on the wall and directed their careers elsewhere, which he had the means to do. By the 1870s the English gun trade was in decline, both from the transition from hand work to mechanization and an overall reduction in demand. This trend continued until a new period of hostilities began in the early 20th century. [8]

The gun making Wilson family lived at Cottesbrook house in the Acocks Green/Sherbourne Road area, holding deeds

Inspection stamps & maker's mark

of trust on the property beginning in the mid-1700s. During the time Joseph Wilson lived there he was neighbors with other gun makers in the Birmingham Small Arms Trade, such as John Swinburn, John D. Goodman, Thomas Bentley, Charles Playfair. [9] After Joseph Wilson passed away in 1893 his son, William Wright Wilson, and wife Emily moved in and are recorded afterwards as residing at Cottesbrook house.

R. & W. Aston

R. & W. Aston was a specialist subcontractor for the Birmingham Small Arms Trade. For the first Ordnance contracts in 1854 they supplied the "original (old) four" with rammers, barrel bands, gun lock assemblies, bayonets, muzzle stoppers, triggers, nails, and screws. What follows is a report to Parliament from the Commission on Children's Labour on their inspection of the premises. It lends excellent insight into working conditions in the Gun Quarter during the U.S. Civil War-era.

Messrs. R. & W. Aston's, Gun And Gun Implement Makers, &c, Edmund Street, Birmingham

J.E. White [Commissioner]—-These are said to be about the largest works for miscellaneous gun implements. One room, where two young boys worked, was so dark that there were gas-burners alight in a bright summer afternoon. Several young boys are engaged in dark sunken shops, in constantly blowing fires for men stamping, and for this purpose stand close by the fire, or, as I noticed one, close between two. This work was remarked on to me in the works as unfit for young boys, as indeed it appeared to be and "the most unhealthy job in the place." Forming corks for muzzle stoppers is part of the work, and seems to be injurious to health from the dust.

Mr. R. Aston—We make guns, not, however, the barrels, military and sporting, and gun furniture and implements of all kinds, swords, bayonets, lances, &c. The sword trade has become very limited in England. Solingen in Prussia is now one of its principal seats. In Germany there is so much water power, and labour is cheap. With the exception of the Government factories Birmingham is the only seat in the kingdom of the gun, sword, and military weapon manufacture. A large factory is being established here for making military guns by the same machinery as that used by Government at Enfield. [1] If this succeeds it will probably bring all military gun-making into a few large factories, but the facility with which the Government can now make for their own ordinary use will throw a difficulty in the way of maintaining such costly machinery elsewhere. There are but few gun barrel rolling factories in the town, perhaps about eight.

The number of large gun manufactories here of any kind is small, but some gun makers who do but little on their own premises have very large businesses from the amount of work which they have done out, as we do also, in shops where men work, either with a few men and boys or quite alone.

There are a great many distinct branches of the trade, *e.g.,* some persons confine themselves to making the nipple only. Some gun-locks are made in Birmingham, but a great quantity of them are made in Darlaston and Wednesbury, and some in Wolverhampton by men working in their own shops, which they prefer. A factory which we built for lock-making in Darlaston is consequently not used by them.

We employ very few children, and scarcely any females. Most of the boys are paid by men for whom they work. They assist smiths, file, turn, and attend machines. The hours are from 7 am to 7 pm, with two hours for meals. Longer hours are needed sometimes, but chiefly by the men, though there may be parts of the work in which boys are wanted later also. A few hours extra will sometimes enable us to complete an order in time for a ship or some such purpose, but the occasions when this is necessary are exceptional. A limitation to a day of 12 hours only would not cause substantial inconvenience. I should prefer from 6 am to 6 pm for the work itself, and it would leave the workpeople more time to themselves at the end of the day. Mechanics are generally better off when forced to be regular. In gun work they are very irregular, as they work so much for themselves at home, and even when they work in factories the men work chiefly by the piece, and come when they please. We have scarcely any control over them in this respect. It would be better for the mechanics if they were more under control as to hours. [2]

There are occasional accidents from machinery, but not of importance. The only fatal accident that we ever had was in the grinding mill, from a stone flying and hitting a man who was walking across. A stone seldom flies, not one in three years on the average. We are very careful in having them examined when first put up, and never allow a man to go on working at one that is thought dangerous, even if he were inclined to do so himself. Grinding is men's work; a youth may get to it at 16, but generally rather later. It is not considered healthy work; but if they are steady and use precautions they may keep well enough. Leveling the stone is the worst part. Each man levels his own stone, and on the average once a day for about 20 minutes, but this varies according to the kind of work and the quality of the stone. If the work is of a rough kind the condition of the stone is not so particular. The regular grinding is done wet, which keeps down the dust. Many use a wet sponge over their mouths, but often do not begin it till too late, *i.e.,* till their lungs have begun to fail.

I think that a good many can write, and all do some reading at odd times, which helps to keep them from mischief. The cheap newspapers have done a good deal to encourage reading. [3]

Harry Feeny, age 13.—Blow bellows at a forge. Stop eight or nine times a day when the men do. It's very hot, but I don't sweat much; am "hoast" (hoarse), and have been for a week; am more so in winter. Can't speak with it at times. Wash every night at home; could at the tap here. Breakfast and tea here, dinner at home. The iron when being struck flies and burns my clothes, arms, and face, but not to hurt. This finger was cut in striking, which I do sometimes.

Don't know "A." Was at day-school when little a long while ago, and go once on Sunday, and don't miss often; but can't learn nothing, try as well as one can. Go to the Catholic chapel every Sunday almost, but can't understand what is said. They read out of a big book. Thinks it's the Bible. Don't know anyone that the Bible is about. Have only heard the lads talking about the Queen (Victoria), and heard mother say that she's a Protestant, I think. Don't know whether she is good or kind to the people, but think she does take care of us. [4]

William Morris, age 11.—Blow and strike. Have done so for three years here. Did the same for 18 months before at another place where they made railway pins, and such things (works in Edgbaston Street). My regular hours then were from 6 a.m. till 7 p.m., sometimes worked till 8 and 9; 9 pm was the latest. The work here is very hot and wets my shirt. Get *4s. 6d.* a week; pay it to my mother. Have two hours for my meals. Have not been away from work poorly. Can spell some words (can). Go to school on Sundays.

Commissioner's note: [Wretchedly pale and weak looking.]

Benjamin Mason.—Last boy works for me. He is often poorly, and is very bad in the chest, and very often complains of his chest and head when at work. A fortnight ago he was crying all day. He has had nothing given him to eat but dry bread, no tea nor coffee, not a bit of butter, nor nothing. He was so weak from it that he was no good to me, and I told him he must either leave his father or not work for me any longer; and he now lives with his brother.

Samuel Palmer, age 11.—Blow bellows all day from 7 to 7, except two hours for meals. The man pays me 3s. 6d. a week. Don't know all the letters. Was two years at the day school, and left when I got 7 (years old). Left off going to Sunday school six months ago, because I had not got no clothes. Father has been out of work two or three months; lost his work for drinking.

Frederick Cough, age 13 File; also turncorks for muzzle stoppers, on a lathe turned by the engine. Get 5s. a week for day work. Am pretty well for the corks : have worked it two years. Was badly at first,—the dust got down my throat and was always heaving me, but I shut my mouth now. It don't hurt you, only like as if there was something in your throat and you couldn't heave it up. It made me spit a good deal, and sick,—quite sick, but does not now. Don't get out of breath. Swill my mouth out with water before I eat or drink. Sometimes have a ha'p'o'th of milk, new milk as we call it. [5] It don't hurt you then. The master (man) told me to keep my mouth shut, swill it out, and take the milk. Sometimes do corks all day, from 7 to 7, and for a week together; can do 10 gross a day. My voice is always rough like it is now. Have cut my hand against the cutting wheel. (I) know a few letters. Go to school on Sundays sometimes, but not very often. Have got such ragged Birmingham clothes I don't like to go, and don't go out very often. Father was an iron caster but he lost an eye at it; apiece of iron fled into it, and now he labours at a foundry, &c.

Commissioner notes: [Pale and hoarse.].

Ephraim Randall, age 10.—Cut cork ends; b. here a year. Have cut three fingers and my arm at it.*(Shows marks.)*Feel sick sometimes. Have dinner in the shop here, and the other boys does too. Get meat on Sunday, and other days bread and cheese.

CD... age 14.—Work a press for plates, triggers, and small things; the only other girl in this shop does the same. My hands are black with the oil from the tools, which are all oiled. Wash me at home, not here. There is a tap, and we could bring soap and towel, but there is no bucket in this shop. Have to live away from home, because my father is dead, and the young man that lives with mother, who is not married, don't like us to be with him, so I pay 3*. 6d. out of my 4*.6d. a week to live with a woman. Was quite a little one when at school. Can tell my letters, but not spell them.

Julia Kerr, age 14.—Press girl. Know the letters; cannot spell. "Say" is "was." Was never at a day school. Go Sunday sometimes.

Frederick John Hughes, age 14.—Slit screws at a steam lathe.Was at day school from 9 years old till 11. Can read and write. (Reads "delight," &c, imperfectly.) Cannot tell what the word means, why the Saviour is called so, or what is the Queen's name.

Richard Shipley, age13.—Go on errands for the men. At school two years, but was often away at home for two or three weeks or more, to mind the young 'uns. Sisters were at pins.

James Smith, age 15.—Cannot read. Was at day school four years, but not regular,' though more there than away. They taught mine to try to read. Go to night school when there is any ; don't pay. Have left Sunday school a good while.

John Chapman, age 14.—Go on errands. Have worked at four places. Was never at a day school. "h"is"v."

William Wiseman.—Foreman. He is surprised to find how few can read; should have thought most could, but the men (mechanics) take whom they please. The boys take their meals when they please. If a case of ill-treatment were to occur it would be brought to the master's notice. It happens very seldom.

Source: House of Commons papers, Volume 22. White, J.E., "Children's Employment: Factories. Second Report of the Commissioners," By Parliament of Great Britain. House of Commons, Sesson of 1864, p 76.

Charles Reeves "Toledo Works"

Charles Reeves & Co, Gun and Sword Makers, Birmingham

Charles Reeves was first listed in Birmingham as a sword maker beginning in 1820, as partner in the firm of Reeves & Greaves at 6 Fazeley Street. In 1842, the eldest son of Charles Reeves joined the firm, which was then titled Reeves, Greaves & Reeves. They had moved to Bartholomew Street and were well established as the principle maker of swords by the time of the Great Exhibition of 1851. Their display (booth # 244) consisted of dress swords and military sabers, along with a massive two-handed Scottish Claymore. Their booth won a prize of honorable mention, which was quite an accomplishment given the hundreds of displays.

The Reeves, Greaves & Reeves partnership dissolved in 1852 and became Chas Reeves & Co. See the following from the London Gazette:

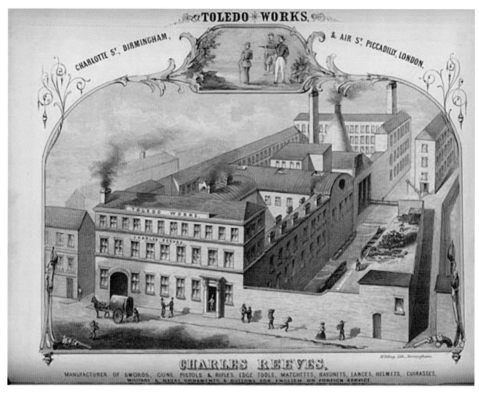

Chas Reeves, Toledo Works.

NOTICE is hereby given, that the Partnership hereto
fore subsisting between us the undersigned, Charles
Greaves and Charles Reeves the younger, both of Birmingham,
in the county of Warwick, Sword Cutlers, carrying
on business under the style or firm of Reeves, Greaves, and
Reeves, was dissolved by mutual consent, as and from the
1st day of January 1852. All debts due and owing to and
from the said firm, will be received and paid by the said
Charles Reeves the younger, by whom the trade will in
future be carried on.—As witness our hands this 11th day
of May 1852. *Charles Greaves. Charles Reeves, Jr.* [1]

By 1854, Chas Reeves & Co had opened a factory at 28 Charlotte Street and was already a large manufacturer of socket bayonets for the War Department. They were one of the main suppliers for the "old four" gun makers who set up the early War Department contract for the first Pattern 1853 long rifles. Reeves' factory was named "Toledo Works." However, there was no connection to Toledo steel or Spain. [2] The Charlotte Street location was actually outside the so-called Birmingham Gun Quarter, nearer the center of town and the Jewelry Quarter. The transition from swords to gun making seems to be a natural one. The following report on a visit to Chas Reeves & Co in 1861 provides an excellent insight into the small arms manufactory of the mid-19th century.

THE MANUFACTURE OF SWORDS, GUNS, AND IMPLEMENTS OF WAR.—THE TOLEDO
WORKS OF MR. CHARLES REEVES, CHARLOTTE-STREET. [3]

In reference to the introduction of the manufacture of Guns, there is some ground for discussion… be this as it may, it is certain that, previous to the commencement of the American (Civil) War, the gun-trade did not assume the importance it then did, and has since done. The most significant and comprehensive idea of the extent to which the trade has now reached, may be gathered from the fact, that in the period which elapsed from the 1st of December, 1854, to the 31st of March, 1857, the number of guns supplied to the War Department amounted to no less than 231,800…The period in which these guns were made was certainly an extraordinary one: from peace we were suddenly called to do battle, and the shores of the Crimea, of the Chinese seas, and the rivers of India, gave back the echoes of Birmingham-made guns or Minie rifles. Our admiration of this power of production is increased, when we consider the amount of real workmanship expended upon the "setting up" of a single gun, "Minie," or "Enfield" it is only by the intelligent process of the subdivision of labour that such numbers of guns could have been produced in the time;—thus we have gun-barrel and gunlock forgers, filers and fitters, stockers, ramrod-makers, browners, engravers: these are again subdivided by the artisans who finish the separate parts which form stock, lock, or barrel.

Our limits preclude the possibility of our entering into anything like a description of the making of guns, or of the various materials out of which the barrels are made, and which pass muster under the denominations of Damascus, stub-Damascus (formed by the union of old horse-shoe nails with Damascus iron), or of charcoal iron, three-penny, and Wednesbury skelp, two-penny and "sham-damn." In the early periods of the manufacture of fire-arms, the barrels were probably formed by drilling out a mass of solid iron; they are now produced by welding on a mandrill. To reduce into the form of ribbons what had previously been a multiplicity of small fragments of iron; to unite these together; to twist, weld, re-weld, and then wind the ribbon, or thin bar, round a mandrill in a spiral form, thereafter to incorporate the whole by welding and hammering into a tube, may be taken as the routine of the manufacture of a gun-barrel. The boring out is accomplished by "bits," either propelled by machinery or worked by the hand; the external surface is turned, filed, or ground; the fibres and their windings are revealed by the operation of acid, which attacks the softer and leaves the harder particles of the material of which the barrel is composed comparatively untouched, and covers the whole surface of the barrel with a rich deep-brown hue.

The manufacture of Swords may be briefly glanced at. These are made from pieces of steel called "sword moulds; in each mould there is sufficient steel to make two blades, the flutes or greaves being produced by "swages," which correspond to the indentations to be made on the blade they are then, if curved, bent and fitted to a gauge, the process of "hardening" follows, then "tempering; the final test as to temper is arrived at by striking the blade on the back and edge of a wood block, and bending it into a curve, in its entire length, or half a circle. After due trials have been satisfactorily gone through the blade is delivered to the grinders, who, seated below enormous grinding-stones, propelled by steam power, speedily obliterate the marks of the hammer man. To clear out the grooves, stones with raised beads are used: glazing follows, by means of revolving discs of wood, on the surface of which emery powder is attached by glue; and the blade is finely polished on a similar revolving disc, or "bob," with fine emery and oil,—powder of frottstone, or crocus, give the brilliant polish. The deep rich blue colour observable in swords of all ornamental kind is produced by means the gilding of the ornaments by amalgam of gold. Damascening is effected by incising into the blade various lines, and fixing into these by pressure threads of gold or silver, etching, by covering the blade with an etching ground, cutting through it the various lines which make up the design, a solution of acetic and nitric acid is applied, which attacks the steel exposed; after remaining a sufficient time, the acid is removed, and the ground cleansed off, when the ornamentation will be found bitten in on the surface of the blade.

Steel sheaths are made by bending thin plates of steel round suitably-formed templates or mandrills: they are soldered with hard solder at the junctures, then ground and polished, as already described in the operation of sword-grinding and polishing.

In the production of Swords, Guns, and Implements of War, THE CHARLOTTE-STREET WORKS OF MR. CHARLES REEVES is a leading one; it has been in existence for many years, and

Pattern 1821 light artillery saber from R, G&R. (public domain)

is justly celebrated for the excellence of the various articles therein made. These consist of Swords, Muskets, Rifles, Bayonets, Sword Bayonets, Revolvers, Lances, Helmets, Cuirasses, Military and Naval Ornaments; Cutlasses and Boarding Pikes, various kinds of Edge Tools, as Machetes and Sugarcane Knives. The Works cover a large extent of ground. The machinery is of the most ingenious and costly kind, and is set in motion by steam-engines equal in power to that of 100 horses, which is distributed over the Works, giving motion to enormous tilt-hammers, grinding-stones, polishing-wheels, lathes, &c. Upwards of 300 pairs of hands are constantly employed. The proprietor of the Works is the Inventor and Patentee of the improved Cavalry Sword, and the originator of the present Pattern Sword Bayonet, which may be used in the hand as a sword, or, when attached to the gun, may be employed by our foot-soldiers with that terrible effect which has ever distinguished a bayonet charge made by the infantry of our land. Mr. Reeves also materially facilitated the production of the ordinary bayonet, by the invention of improved machinery for its manufacture; by these means he supplied the Government with immense, almost incredible numbers during the late Russian (Crimean) War: by hand-labour or the ordinary methods of production this would have been impossible.

The Swords of all kinds which have been sent from these Works, in number are immense, and in quality have been considered as unexceptionable; while to those of an ornamental kind, for Presentation or for Dress, the highest praise has ever been awarded; their elaborate and carefully-worked handles, basket-hilts, and sheaths of steel, saw-pierced and perforated, or of metal, chased and gilt, emulate the doings of the artists of all times. Many of these have been selected as worthy of illustration in the various works devoted to the progress made by our manufacturers. We introduce, as an example of these, a sword exhibited by Mr. Reeves in the Exhibition of 1851. The example alluded to was, however, surpassed in beauty and excellence by a sword presented by Mr. Reeves to His Royal Highness the Duke of Cambridge, on the occasion of a visit paid by him to the Toledo Works in 1857. It was made entirely

JUNE 28, 1862. **ILLUSTRATED TIMES.** 145

THE WORKSHOPS OF ENGLAND.— No. VIII. MR. CHARLES REEVES'S IMPLEMENTS OF WAR MANUFACTORY, TOLEDO WORKS, BIRMINGHAM.

SWORD-BLADE, BAYONET, SWORD-BAYONET, AND MACHETE GRINDING MILL.

The grindstones inside of Charles Reeves' "Toledo Works" factory in June 1862. (Courtesy Craig L. Barry)

of the finest steel; the hilt being richly chiseled and worked out of the solid metal, with gold introduced in the manner described by Benvenuto Cellini, in his interesting biography where he says, "Soon after there fell into my hands some little Turkish daggers, the handles of which were of iron as well as the blade, and even the scabbard was of that metal; on these were engraved several fine foliages in the Turkish taste, most beautifully filled with gold. I found I had a strong inclination to cultivate this branch likewise. My performances were much finer and more durable than the Turkish, as I made a much deeper incision in the steel than is practised in the Turkish works, and I varied my ornamentation from that of chicory leaves to the grotesque, *i. e.*, introducing festoons of leaves, flowers, masks, and figures of animals. In such taste I made foliages filled up in the manner above mentioned, which were far more elegant and pleasing to the eye than the Turkish works." In order to show the excellence of temper in connection with good finish, we may allude to a sword produced by Mr. Reeves, which readily finds its way into a coiled, serpent-like scabbard, and which, on being withdrawn, becomes a perfectly straight blade.

This manufactory has been visited by many distinguished personages belonging to this and other countries; among others may be mentioned the Princes of Oude, the Siamese and Spanish Ambassadors, military officers in the service of France, Russia, and recently by the Prince of Orange. The Jury of Class 8, in the Exhibition of 1851, awarded to Mr. Reeves a Prize Medal for his "beautiful collection of Swords and other field arms, admirably embellished. In concluding our notice of this establishment we may add that the ingenious proprietor has recently added to his previous remarkable achievements the production of a newly-constructed gun, which loads from the muzzle or the breech. Mr. Reeves's London (Retail) Establishment is in Air-street, Piccadilly. [4]

Birmingham gun and sword makers in the mid-19th century employed over 7,000 workers during peak times. As John Goodman stated, because of the up and down nature of commercial contracts for military arms, exact employment numbers are very difficult to determine. [5] However, it is more easily accomplished for individual firms. For example, Ward & Son employed between 100 and 120 workers during the peak for the Birmingham gun trade during the U.S. Civil War-era. If the article above is correct, Charles Reeves & Co employed 300 hands as early as 1861. By 1864, the firm grew to about 400 workers manufacturing rifles and swords. [6] There was not always better tor small arms makers, in fact in terms of longevity Ward & Son of 26 and 27 Bath Street was still in business in the middle of the 20th century. Even though Charles Reeves was much larger than Ward & Son, more famous, and had been around much longer, by 1869 Chas Reeves & Co accrued about £26,000 in liabilities and was essentially insolvent. [7] The Bankers Journal stated after the announcement, "...the economic condition of affairs in the financial and commercial world continues discouraging, and at the present moment there seems little or no prospect of recovery. The advice from all the manufacturing districts is very unsatisfactory."

Wilkinson & Son, which had done business with Chas Reeves & Co since 1853, bought a majority interest in the Toledo Works factory. Wilkinson was an 18th century gun maker of longstanding that came to sword making rather than the other way around. They acquired Chas Reeves & Co for the production capacity to compete for government contract work with R. Mole & Sons, another sword and bayonet maker from the early War Department contracts of the Crimean War era. [8]

CHAPTER FIVE:
History of Larger London Gun Makers

London Armoury Co.

Background

Due to scant surviving company records on London Armoury, historians have depended on English, U.S., and CS documents as the main sources for information on the firm. That and the weapons themselves are all we have to study. London Armoury Company was started in Bermondsey, part of Southwark, which was across the river from the city of London. It was a poorer district from at least the Elizabethan era. Charles Dickens immortalized the infamous slums in "Oliver Twist." Bermondsey was an area where most residents expressed considerable enthusiasm for moving out. Two major commuter railways serving the city of London produced a huge complex of east/west railway arches, effectively severing the area in two. [1] London Armoury was constructed there on the site of the old Southeastern Railway Company. The enterprise was started in 1856 by Robert Adams as principal shareholder, along with F. Edward, Beaumont, Harding, and J. Kerr for purposes of manufacturing the Adams hammerless double-action revolver. His cousin and fellow investor, James Kerr (pronounced CARR), was employed at the firm as well. The Adams revolver would fire its five chambers as quickly as you could pull the trigger, and for that quality it caught on with the British Army during the Sepoy Rebellion of 1857. London Armoury Company did so well with the Adams revolver that Colt folded their London revolver manufactory and left England. The LA Co directors were offered a large contract by Ordnance for Enfield rifles if they would purchase a duplicate set of machinery identical to what was used at Royal Small Arms Manufactory. Adams disagreed with the new direction, sold his stock in 1859, and left the company. He moved into the premises of his former partners, the Deane Bros on King William Street, and continued manufacture of the revolver in Birmingham. The Board of

PREMISES OF THE LONDON ARMOURY COMPANY.

The London Armoury Company, Henry Street (Bermondsey S.E.), circa 1861. Frederic William Bond, Manager, Archibald Hamilton, Superintendent. (Courtesy Southeast Railway Co)

Adams self cocking revolver. (Courtesy of Tim Prince)

Directors named Frederic Bond as manager, and James Kerr took over as the factory Superintendent. Kerr had his own revolver design in both .36 and .44 caliber with an external hammer and a back action lock. Production of the Kerr's patent revolver began in April 1859, but sales got off to a slow start. The British government did not make an immediate order for the new weapon, retaining the Adams revolver as its official sidearm (until 1880). At some point before Caleb Huse came along in May 1861, Archibald Hamilton (of Sinclair, Hamilton & Co) was hired as Superintendent, and James Kerr assumed other managerial duties for LA Co. [2]

Confederate Contracts

Confederate arms buyer Caleb Huse was prepared to offer a contract for all the Enfield rifles and Kerr revolvers that London Armoury Company could produce, except he exceeded his authority, even with his initial order of 10,000. Huse had only $50,000 in hand for Enfields he agreed to purchase at $19.50 each. Confederate records, as well as Huse's account in his memoirs, support that he quickly found additional funding, and an arrangement was reached in May 1861 for a large order, including Kerr revolvers. Huse felt he was "not only justified but required to go beyond his orders." Cavalier spending "beyond his orders" would lead to a major financial scandal for Huse in a few years. Caleb Huse reported the details of his first visit to London Armoury in May 1861 to Gorgas as follows:

> London, England, May 21, 1861.
> Sir: In compliance with instructions from the War Department I left Montgomery on the ___ of April, on my way to Europe, via New York. It was my intention to have left New York by the steamer Persia on the 24th of April. I became satisfied, however, after arriving in that city, that it would be very imprudent for me to attempt to sail from that port; and acting under the advice of the gentlemen through whom my financial arrangements were made, I left New York for Canada on the evening of the same day that I arrived. From Canada I came to England, and there took passage in the steamer of the 27th. I arrived in Liverpool on the 10th of May, and at once put myself in communication with the house of Fraser, Trenholm & Co., on whom I had letters of credit. I found these gentlemen, and especially Mr Prioleau, member of the firm, ready to do everything in their power to assist me in carrying on successfully the object of my mission. On presenting my letters it appeared that I had actually but £10,000 with with it to purchase arms, &c.
> The letter of the Secretary of the Treasury to Messrs. Fraser, Trenholm & Co., informing them that my drafts on the U. S. Treasury would be honored to the amount of $200,000, would, I was assured by Messrs. Fraser, Trenholm & Co., be of no value in a commercial transaction. They expressed themselves disposed, however, to do everything for me in their power. I left Liverpool the same day for London, and called on Mr. Yancey, of the commission from the Confederate Government. I then lost no time in possessing myself of information concerning the possibility of obtaining arms and artillery in England. A very short time sufficed to satisfy me that of small arms there were none in market of the character and quality required by the Department. There were muskets to be purchased in

any quantity, called by different names. I heard of not a few Enfield rifles. These, when I came to examine them, I found to be for the most part altogether worthless. I could have purchased a few, perhaps 500, short Enfields of good quality. To ship so small a quantity as that, however, after the proclamation of the British Government it would have been an impossibility.

After fully satisfying myself that small-arms that I was willing to send to the Confederacy were not to be had either in England or Belgium, I made inquiries at the London Armoury Company for Enfield rifles to be manufactured by them. This establishment is in some respects superior to every other musket manufactory in the world, and in every respect is equal to the Government works at Enfield. *Since it was first put in operation it has been constantly employed by the British Government, and they have work on hand for this Government which will require eighteen months to complete.* The rifles made at this establishment interchange in every part and with perfect accuracy. The importance of the principle of interchange of parts I need not dwell upon. It is fully recognized by the war departments of every civilized nation. The London Armoury Company is the only establishment in Europe, excepting the Government armories, that works upon this principle. It seems to me highly important to obtain rifles from this company, if possible. I found that they were willing to entertain a proposition for 10,000, but not for anything less than that number. After conferring freely with the commissioners and receiving from them an entire approval of my action, I proposed to take from the London Armory Company 10,000 Enfield rifles of the latest government pattern, with bayonet, scabbard, extra nipple, snap-cap, and stopper complete for £3 16s. 6d. This price is somewhat above the limit given in my instructions from Major Gorgas, and I engaged to take 10,000 instead of 8,000. Under all the circumstances, I believed myself not only justified, but required, to go beyond my orders.

The necessity of the Confederacy arming at once is so great, judging from the accounts that appear in the papers, that if I could in any way obtain arms that I thought would be serviceable I should purchase without delay, and I have little doubt that I would be able to send or bring them to some port of the Confederacy. The arms are not to be had, however. Everything has been taken by the agents from the Northern States, and the quantity which they have secured is very small, and many of them of indifferent quality. They have paid enormous prices, and worthless muskets are now held at fabulous prices. One man had orders to purchase 60,000. They were not to be had. He would have contracted with the London Armory Company for all that they could furnish for a year to come, but his instructions were to obtain the whole number within two months. The next steamer will without doubt, as I learn from a reliable source, bring orders for him to close with that company. The greatest number this company can supply is about 1,300 per month. They are under a contract to supply the North with 100 per week for three months, the contract to cease with one week's notice. If the company accepts my proposition this notice will be given, and at least 1,200 Enfield rifles that would go North will be secured for the Confederate Government. The company will accept my proposition if they can obtain a release from their contract with the Government. This they have no doubt they will be able to obtain. Application has been made, and an answer will be obtained in a day or two. If I could have offered to take 20,000 they would have broken with the Government. This, however, was so far beyond my instructions that I could not make the offer…

The agent sent by the United States Government to purchase arms is the best man for the duty that could have been selected, namely, Mr. McFarland, who was the superintending engineer of the London Armoury during its erection and until it was in complete working order. [4] His instructions to make a similar contract with that company for the United States Government will come too late. In my contract I specify that I shall be the preferred purchaser for from 6,000 to 10,000 in addition to the number now ordered. If I could contract for the entire 20,000 I think I could secure them at 70 shillings, and if the Confederate Government intends to purchase a further supply, I would respectfully suggest that the great importance of interchange of parts, in a country where repairs of arms will be for many years a great expense, should be fully considered. Even in England, a nation of workers in metals, this principle is considered invaluable. In the present condition of affairs I do not think it possible to send a sample to Montgomery. I shall avail myself of the first opportunity to do so…

I am very respectfully your obedient servant,

C. Huse,
Captain CS Army [5]

Whatever the case, the London Armoury Company eventually became a leading arms supplier to the Confederacy, providing parts interchangeable Enfield rifles and also selling as many as nine thousand or so Kerr's patent revolvers.

To Whom Did L.A. Co. Sell Enfield Rifles?

We will discuss some of the highlighted passages in greater detail, starting with the notion Huse propagated about L.A. Co. being some kind of proprietary Confederate weapons factory from some point early in the war until the last shipments ran the Union blockade in early 1865. Historians have been quick to latch on to the concept, stating as a matter of fact that "…the London Armoury was an exclusive manufacturer of guns for the Confederacy", or that the "Southern contracts tied up their full production capacity," etc. It was true that the full production of Kerr revolvers went to the Confederacy, but not their entire output of Enfield rifles. [6]

For example, L.A. Co. also supplied British Volunteer units. In fact, they advertised their weapons to Volunteer units as soon as the units started to form in the late 1850s and continued to advertise them for sale through the mid-1860s. One historian stated, "By late 1861, London Armoury guns were being shipped to the Confederacy. It is often reported that all L.A. Co. (rifle)-muskets produced after the Huse contract were sent to the Confederacy. This isn't true. The company continued to supply the Crown, but shipped all their excess production to the southern states. Most of their 1863 output was destined to run the blockade. Almost all of the 1864 production went to the South, and even a portion of 1865." [7] Actually that isn't entirely true either, though it is correct that L.A. Co. had "excess production" available beyond what was sold to the British Army. L.A. Co., like any other commercial gun maker, offered military arms to whoever it was legal to do business with and could afford them, including the enemies of their principal client, the Confederacy. See the following letter from Federal agent Marcellus Hartley on his purchases from London Armoury for the Union in late 1862:

To Hon. E. M. Stanton.

4/ HAMPTON ST., BIRMINGHAM, December 20, 1862

Dear Sir,
My last was from here under date of the 17th inst, No. 21, containing an offer from the London Armoury Company. I now have the pleasure of inclosing invoices of our last shipment, being the largest and best yet made. By the steamer Hammonia, which was to have sailed the 17th inst. from Southampton, but was delayed owing to some disarrangement of her machinery (inclosed you have newspaper account) and sailed to-day, have been shipped

1,700 interchangeable Enfield rifles
28,060 hand-made ditto
10,978 Austrian 54/100 and 58/100 calibers.

The balance of Enfields to make the amount of inclosed invoices will be shipped by steamer New York, to sail the 24th inst. from Southampton with the 69/100 calibers, viz:

500 interchangeable Enfields
7,300 hand-made ditto
13,860 French rifled muskets — 69/100.

The above, no doubt, is the largest shipment ever made by one party, or ever obtained in the same time of first-class Enfields, 37,560. I have made every effort here, in London and Liege to obtain all the Enfields in hand. In London and Liege I cleaned the market out, but here could have obtained 5000 more if they could have been viewed. We have worked day and night for the last sixteen days. It has required care and caution to push the manufacturers to this unusual quantity, without materially advancing the price. In London and Liege, though I advanced the price for a short time, I gave them larger orders than they could complete, and bought them at the low price, and in Liege from 2 francs to 5 francs less. Here in Birmingham I started at 42/ on the 29th of November, but had to advance to 50/, or should have lost many of the guns.

I shall not be able to obtain the freight bills of the Hammonia and the New York until the beginning of the week, which will delay my accounts, but they shall be forwarded with the vouchers next week.

I have not insured any of the arms; they all have arrived in safety, as far as heard from. The shipment by the Hammonia is very large and valuable, amounting to, say, £110,000. As this advice will reach you before her arrival, if you think it proper they can be insured in New York.

I have used about £110,000 of the last credit. Amount of Enfields shipped to date, 110,140; total amount of arms shipped, 204,848.

Yours respectfully,
MARCELLUS HARTLEY [7]

It is clear that in late 1862 the Confederacy was not L.A. Co.'s only customer (besides the British Government), nor even their only American customer. Further, it suggests the Union was quite aggressive about procuring available foreign arms. Marcellus Hartley was the founding member of Schuyler, Hartley & Graham (New York) and he knew the English Gun Trade. The broader point here is that London Armoury was also doing business with the Union for "interchangeable Enfield rifles" when many (including Huse) thought that the entire output of London Armoury Company was going to the Confederacy.

How Many Enfields Were Produced by L.A. Co.?

One reason that the production capacity of L.A. Co. Enfield rifles was believed to be relatively low is that surviving examples are scarce today. That doesn't mean L.A. Co. Enfield rifles were rare during the U.S. Civil War. Instead, being grade one/interchangeable weapons, the vast majority were sold back into the Gun Trade after the Civil War and converted post-bellum to Snider breechloaders. Various misunderstandings about L.A. Co.'s business practices seem to have become the basis for presumptions about what their actual production capacity might have been. Huse states of L.A. Co.'s capacity, "The greatest number this company can supply is about 1,300 per month," and then (separately) that L.A. Co. has an "Ordnance contract that will take 18 months to complete." Huse is not working from firsthand knowledge here, but rather reporting what he has been told by L.A. Co.. From these figures, at least one historian has derived a production capacity for L.A. Co., which appears to be well understated. [9] What does Huse actually mean to say here? Huse does not say that L.A. Co. is supplying Ordnance with their entire production capacity of 1,300 per month; rather, he is saying that 1,300 per month was the most L.A. Co. could supply until their contract with Ordnance was concluded in 18 months. These similar sounding statements mean two very different numbers.

To get an accurate feel for the production capabilities of L.A. Co., it would be helpful to know about how many arms were subject to the British Army contract that still had 18 months to go in May 1861. The following appeared in a period journal on the subject, "...Up to the present time the Government has had no contract for interchangeable arms, *excepting one for 30,000 with the London Armoury Company.*" [8] This contract with the government was made in 1858, with the stipulation that L.A. Co. obtain the same machinery from Ames Mfg that Royal Small Arms Manufactory was using for their Enfield rifle. Deliveries of parts interchangeable L.A. Co. Enfield rifles began in 1860, meaning L.A. Co. was about a year into their Ordnance contract when Caleb Huse arrived in May 1861. "He (Huse) was much impressed with the Enfield rifle made by the London Armory Company, which had been making arms for the British Army, and wanted to contract with them for 10,000 arms. The British Government, though, would not release the firm from their contract." [10] This jibes with what Huse reported to Gorgas initially (in May 1861) as well.

If London Armoury had no excess production capacity to sell when Huse arrived and wouldn't for 18 months, then how were L.A. Co. Enfield rifles among the first weapons to run the blockade aboard the steamship *Bermuda* in September 1861? How could L.A. Co. have entered into that small Union contract with McFarland, who had arrived just ahead of Caleb Huse? How did L.A. Co. just fill an earlier rifle contract with the state of Massachusetts? What about all the weapons L.A. Co. was advertising for sale to British Volunteer units? We also know L.A. Co. told Caleb Huse that future contracts had to be made for "not less than ten thousand Enfield long rifles," which suggests they had the ability to produce that number in a timely manner. If 1,300 per month was not their full production capacity, what other figure is more likely to be correct?

There is one simple statistic that will help establish a sensible number for the Civil War-era production capacity of L.A. Co., since they employed the same machinery as Royal Small Arms Manufactory. Thomas Greenwood of Greenwood & Batley (Leeds) reports in 1861, "There were not any of the machines at work yet in Birmingham" while at Enfield (Royal Small Arms Manufactory) "…there were *two sets of the machines* and also **a nearly similar set** at London Armoury's works in London." [11]

As of 1861, Royal Small Arms Manufactory had *two* full sets of machinery from Ames Mfg, while London Armoury had purchased *one* full set. The output of Enfield rifles from Royal Small Arms Manufactory was (on average) 6,000 per month. [12] With the identical set of manufacturing equipment, shouldn't L.A. Co. produce a proportional ratio, all things being equal? 1,300 rifles per month represented too small a fraction (20%) of the Royal Small Arms Manufactory output to be correct. To wit, could a commercial enterprise dependent on profits for survival be that much less productive than a Government-run facility? Well, of course not. The English Gun Trade was not a nursery for weaklings. Huse recalls of his contract dealings with L.A. Co. Superintendent Archibald Hamilton that "…in trade he haggles over the half-penny." If L.A. Co.'s total output was in proportion to Royal Small Arms Manufactory, than it would have been much nearer to 3,000 long arms per month when Huse visited in May 1861. With L.A. Co.'s various other contract work and sales to the Volunteers and the British Army contract, that left 1,300 per month available for the Confederate to purchase. If so, this should clarify Huse's comments on availability from L.A. Co. and puts a different perspective on just how many Enfields they may have produced for the Confederacy. It is also important to understand that in 18 months (after the British Army contracts were finished), the number of L.A. Co. Enfield rifles available for sale to the Confederacy would have increased substantially.

Evidence of excess production capacity can also be found in early-to-mid-1800s British shooting publications. L.A. Co. purchased an advertisement in a book for riflemen offering Enfield long rifles for sale. See the following advertisement from *Notes on Rifle Shooting:*

LONDON ARMOURY COMPANY (LIMITED), 36 KING WILLIAM STREET, LONDON BRIDGE
SOLE MANUFACTURERS OF THE
Regulation Interchangeable Long Enfield Rifle, and the Interchangeable Kerr Small bore Rifle.
PATENTEES OF THE
Kerr Revolver Pistol, Deane & Adams' Revolving Pistol Gunners' Brass Sheathed Ramrods
WORKS:-VICTORIA PARK MILLS,
OLD FORD, E. [13]

Additionally, you will note in the text of the ad that there are new premises for L.A. Co. in Victoria Mills Park. This move took place in 1863. What possible business strategy was there for relocation of the factory from Bermondsey to Victoria Mills Park? It was most likely done to increase their production capacity and with it, their profits. Whatever the case, L.A. Co. was offering Enfield rifles for sale during the last half of the U.S. Civil War, and obviously had guns to sell beyond what they were producing for the Confederacy. In 1863, when L.A. Co. moved their premises to the new location in Victoria Park Mills, the factory was first offered to the Confederate government, and Gorgas favored the purchase, either running it in England or shipping the machinery overseas (to Macon, Georgia). Rather than risk losing it all to the Union blockade, the Confederacy instead decided to put their resources into purchasing finished arms. In another ironic twist, Robert Adams, the original founder and major stockholder of L.A. Co., purchased the factory in Bermondsey to produce the same revolvers for which the facility was first built in 1856.

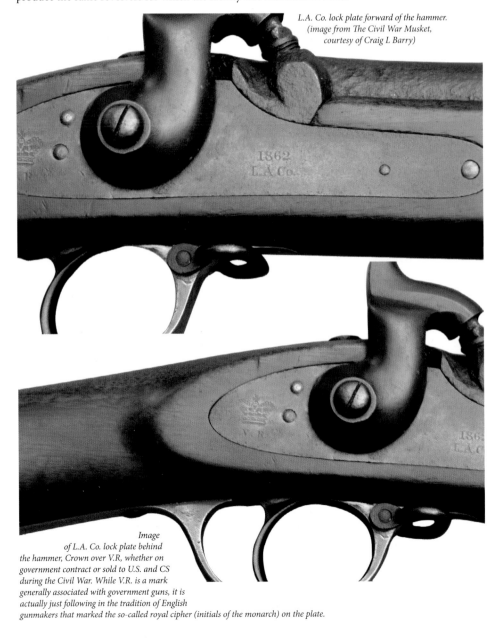

L.A. Co. lock plate forward of the hammer.
(image from The Civil War Musket,
courtesy of Craig L Barry)

Image
of L.A. Co. lock plate behind
the hammer, Crown over V.R, whether on
government contract or sold to U.S. and CS
during the Civil War. While V.R. is a mark
generally associated with government guns, it is
actually just following in the tradition of English
gunmakers that marked the so-called royal cipher (initials of the monarch) on the plate.

The Kerr Small Bore Rifle

Besides the availability of Enfield rifles, the advertisement also mentions the LA Co Kerr small-bore rifle (in .451). According to cfspress.com, "The most widely used match rifle in England was the Kerr, made by the London Armoury Company. This finely crafted rifle outwardly resembled the Enfield— just about all the parts were interchangeable—but fired a .446 caliber bullet through a 37-inch barrel that featured a patented, six-groove progressive rifling system. While extremely accurate its shorter, somewhat lighter bullet lacked the carrying power of the Whitworth at very long ranges. The ten-pound Kerr used a rear sight similar to the standard Enfield ladder sight and an adjustable globe sight on the front." [14] This specialty rifle was also interchangeable with other LAC products. What were the Kerr rifles like?

The 'London Armoury Or Kerr Rifle,' with which most excellent practice is made, is thus described by Mr. Kerr, the Superintendent of the London Armoury Company :—

Diameter of Bore.—*451 of an inch, shape circular.

Grooving.— Six grooves, Ratchett form, without angles; and as the deep part of the groove is on the side of which the bullet turns.

Spiral.—At the breech end the grooves are nearly straight, increasing in twist until, at the middle of the barrel, they attain the full spiral of one turn in 20 inches, which is thenceforward maintained at the same pitch to the muzzle. *Weight of Barrel.*—About 5 lbs. 4 oz. *Weight and Shape of Projectile.*—The ordinary cylindro-conoidal bullet, weight 530 grains, diameter *442 of an inch.

Charge.—2f or 3 drahms of No. 6 Smallbore rifle powder.

Lubrication.—Solid grease or lubricated wad, as made by Eley Brothers.

Price at which the Rifle is supplied.—From £5 16s. 6d.; but Mr. Kerr strongly recommends the rifle at £6 10s., which is complete, with steel furniture, small grip, light detanted lock and chequered hand and fore end.

Mr. Kerr claims the following as the peculiar excellences of his rifle:

"The straight part of the grooving allows of perfect expansion of the bullet, thus avoiding windage and consequent fouling; stripping, of course, is also prevented. A great advantage connected with this rifle arises from the system of manufacture, as the lock and all other parts and limbs are interchangeable with the Long Enfield rifle, thus rendering the repair of any accident a mere matter of writing for a duplicate part; and whenever a purchaser, whether at home or abroad, is within reach of a garrison town, the armourer is always competent to supply any defect." [15]

The Confederacy imported a small number of those costly target rifles made by L A Co. The Kerr rifles (like the Whitworths) were highly prized by those fortunate soldiers that got them. In the autumn of 1863, Patrick Cleburne organized a sharpshooter or "marksmen" company made up of men armed with thirty Whitworths and sixteen LAC Kerr rifles. The Kentucky Brigade received eleven from "an English admirer, and Cleburne's division at one time deployed a forty six man sharpshooter corps that boasted thirty Whitworth and sixteen Kerr rifles. During the battle at Dalton, Georgia, in 1864, Cleburne's 46 sharpshooters silenced the Union artillery at 800 yards and stopped cold an advancing skirmish line. A Federal officer reported, "...so galling was the fire that every man who attempted to rise was shot dead." [16]

The Kerr target rifles were not set up to accept a bayonet, but they came with two barrels: one in standard .577 caliber (for drill) and another .451 caliber "small-bore" barrel for match shooting. When Whitehall mandated the use of the regulation P'53 Enfield in 1962, many British volunteers sold their old target rifles to Confederate buyers.

The Kerr Patent Revolver

The Kerr Revolver featured a side-mounted hammer with an actual lock plate, marked either London Armoury Or London Armoury Co. It began production in 1859. Unlike other revolvers of the day, the lock mechanism of the Kerr revolver was of a back-action rifle design. The back action was designed to be easily repairable in the field without requiring model-specific spare parts. The problem with that approach is very few back action lock rifles were in use during the U.S. Civil War. The Kerr had a top strap over the cylinder, which is held in place by a pin that runs into the back of the frame below the hammer. The pistol is 12.25 inches overall, with a barrel length of about 5.3 inches. Most were "54 bore" or .44 caliber with fewer in the smaller .36 caliber.

The Kerr is often described as a five shot double action revolver. That is true as to only the earliest Kerrs produced, but all the later production appear to be the single action mechanism. The barrels were cast integral with the top strap, lug, and lower section of the frame. The grips were checkered walnut reinforced by the lock plate, a butt cap, and an upper and lower tang. These were rugged revolvers in terms of the main components and framework. The first shipment of Kerr patent revolvers were delivered to the Confederacy aboard the steamship *Bermuda* in September 1861.

In terms of total produced for the CS, Kerr patent revolvers have the advantage of consecutive serial numbers. The lowest serial number known with Confederate inspection stamps (JS/anchor) is #1050, and the highest known is #10,164. [17] The squad rolls of the 18th Virginia Cavalry issued Kerr revolvers show serial numbers as high as #9974. Other than being of interest to collectors, the higher serial number does not mean that same number of revolvers were in CS hands. Obviously, not all the Kerr patent revolvers shipped from L.A. Co. made it through the blockade.

Kerr Patent Revolver. (Courtesy Tim Prince, College Hill Arsenal)

How Were L.A. Co. Enfield Rifles Different?
We have established some background on London Armoury during the U.S. Civil War-era and their products, as well as cleared up some possible misconceptions about production capacity. What characteristics differentiated the L.A. Co. Enfield rifle from the more common London and Birmingham handmade commercial variety? Previously in this monograph we explored the time and labor intensive processes used by the Gun Trade to produce a "handmade" commercial Enfield rifle. Here is an explanation of the time required to "set up" a rifle from parts made by machinery:

> Mr. Greenwood replied that the time required for putting together a gun was now only six minutes, including the ramrod, bayonet, &c. The lock was finished and put together beforehand ready for the workman, and the screw holes being ready drilled in the stock all he had to do was to put it into the recess in the stock and screw it in. All the other parts of the gun furniture were taken up promiscuously from a lot of each sort, and put into the stock, and the only tool used by the workman was a hand brace with a screwdriver in it. [18]

And how good were these machine made rifles compared to those produced by the handiwork system of the English Gun Trade?

> Whatever may be said by the defenders of the old system of fitting the various pieces of a rifled musket by hand, it is unquestionable that the muskets now made at Enfield are

turned out in a manner with which no human hand, under any amount of skill or practice, could possibly compete. The work is so accurate and so sound that there can be no hesitation in pronouncing the Enfield rifle to be the best weapon that ever was placed in the hand of the infantry soldier. As regards the musket, there can scarcely be a difference of opinion. It is marvelously good…Excellent guns for service may be, and are, made by hand—that I do not deny—but when the quality of the work is impartially surveyed by the educated eye, there is a sharpness and precision, and an almost invisible fitting of part to part which render comparison out of the question. And this advantage of strict accuracy, although it may be of little moment to the individual soldier using the musket, becomes a great national consideration when a whole army has to be supplied, and when the manufacture can be conducted on the principle of interchangeability—namely, that any part of any musket will fit the parts of another musket equally well; so that in the manufacture it is not requisite to make muskets and to store muskets, but only to make a complete supply of parts, for any lock will fit any stock, and vice versa. [19]

Aside from the quality and accuracy of the work, the machine made Enfield rifles from L.A. Co. had some differences in detail by which they can be easily recognized. The lock internals are stamped "LAC" on all moving parts except the springs. The inside of the lock plate is also stamped "LAC." The outside of the plate is plain (not line engraved), as is the hammer. There is a crown behind the hammer with the initials V-R underneath. The "V-R" stands for Victoria Regina, and it was simply

London Armoury Bermondsey stock roundel. The last digit [2] in 1862 is slightly off center, leading to speculation that the stock stamps made use of interchangeable digits which could be changed when the year changed. (Collection of Craig L Barry)

a way the English sometimes identified their military service weapons, whether they did military service or not. For example, all L.A. Co. Enfield rifles made after 1860 have a V-R under the crown whether they were sold to the Volunteer units, the British Army, the Union and Confederacy, or any other commercial customer. If there is a reason that the commercial output of L.A. Co. is marked this way, it is lost to history. To the front of the hammer the lock is marked simply "L A Co" with the date. You will need also to recall that all London Armoury Enfields were marked L A Co with the date and name were marked London Armoury Company with no date. This is false. There is a picture of an original London Armoury Enfield rifle circa 1858 (with no date on the lock plate) marked with the full name London Armoury Co in the same script original style as the W R Revolver. It appears in *The Civil War Musket, a Handbook for Historical Accuracy* (by the author) [20]. After 1860 when L A Co. began production by machinery, the engraving on the lock plate changed to the initials "LA Co" date and crown over V-R markings.

The hardware is also distinct in several ways. The British Army contract called for weapons which were interchangeable with the production at Royal Small Arms Company. When the British updated their barrel band and swivel designs to what we term the "fourth model" (these distinctions were not in use at the time), L.A. Co. had to follow suit for their Ordnance contract work. The barrel bands in use on the vast majority of commercially made Enfield rifles were called Palmer bands. These are a straightforward split iron design that fastened by way of an exposed screw at the bottom. In 1861 Major Baddeley, Superintendent at Royal Small Arms, submitted an improved barrel band design that recessed the exposed screw and eliminated the potential for snagging on the accoutrements as with the Palmer type. The War Department approved the new design on June 3, 1861, and it went into production later that year for the bottom two barrel bands, but for some reason the top barrel band was left as is. The fourth model lower sling swivel was changed to an oval design in contrast to the Palmer triangular type common in shape since the early colonial-era Brown Bess muskets. This oval

London Armoury lock plate lettering pre-1860. (Collection of William O Adams, courtesy of The Civil War Musket by the author)

Triangular Enfield lower sling swivel. (Courtesy Peter Dyson Ltd with permission)

Oval rear swivel (fourth model). (Courtesy Peter Dyson Ltd with permission)

rear swivel has been found on examples of L.A. Co. commercial Enfield long rifles with type III Palmer bands. [21]

The majority of L.A. Co. Enfield rifles with identified U.S. Civil War provenance are the type III with Palmer bands. The "Palmer" bands are found on the overwhelming majority of commercial London (and Birmingham) P53s other than the later type IVs produced by LAC, Kerrs (also LAC), and Whitworths. The fourth model LACs are rarely found in America, regardless of the year on the lock plate. Baddeley bands have been found in "dug" condition on at least one Civil War battlefield in Georgia. The fourth model LACs were comparatively much rarer than the type III, but were in existence. [22] One peculiarity of the hardware on the machine made L.A. Co. Enfields is that the lock plate screw escutcheons are of the rounded ear variety, not the squared-off version used on the majority of hand-made type IIIs from the Gun Trade. This is because of the stocking machinery. The Robbins & Lawrence "WINDSOR" marked Enfield rifles from the mid-1850s share this same characteristic for the same reason. [23]

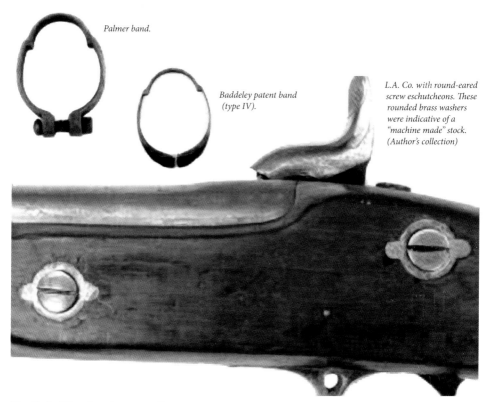

Palmer band.

Baddeley patent band (type IV).

L.A. Co. with round-eared screw eschutcheons. These rounded brass washers were indicative of a "machine made" stock. (Author's collection)

The End of London Armoury Company

The loss or destruction of records from both the Confederacy and London Armoury Company make it difficult to determine the exact financial state of affairs post-bellum for L.A. Co.. Could London Armoury have survived the fall of the Confederate government, even if they had paid their bills? It is difficult to say, because it appears that L.A. Co. was reeling from a one-two punch that included the loss of their biggest customer (CS) and a worldwide glut of small arms. At least 100,000 Enfield rifles were sold back into the gun trade after the Civil War to reduce the Union war debt. What appears to have finally done L.A. Co. in was the so-called "Financial Crisis of 1866." The export-led boom broke that year. Economists regarded the crisis of 1866 as having been generated in the credit system, rather than within industry or manufacturing. These panics were associated with excessive capitalist speculation and the growing vulnerability of the British economy to downturn in the business cycle. The crisis of 1866, which weighed so heavily on all the money markets of Europe, caused shareholders who had met with losses to get rid of their liabilities. [24] Banks called in their loans and L.A. Co. liquidated, rather than selling the factory outright to investors.

Well, at least the enterprise in Victory Mills Park called "London Armoury Company, Ltd" shuttered its doors. In July 1866, most of L.A. Co.'s gun makers and staff started "London Small Arms Co" in Tower Hamlets (London), which continued in the manufacture of military arms until 1935. Their first contract with Ordnance in 1866 was for the conversion of Enfield long rifles to the Snider breechloading system, of which they completed 85,200. [25] It is fairly common to find Martini Henry, Martini-Enfield, and Lee Enfield rifles made for Ordnance stamped LSA Co. As with the L.A. Co. Enfields, the quality of these arms is generally a cut above the rest. James Kerr continued to market his revolvers, which were produced out of existing stock for years running, and the Bank of England made them the official sidearm of their security guards. Messrs. Sinclair, Hamilton & Co were involved in post-bellum litigation over Federal capture of their steamship *Agrippina* under the British flag during the Civil War. The bark was loaded with war material and the effort was unsuccessful. Apparently little the worse for wear, the firm continued, as merchants "engaged in the South African trade." [26]

A letter from August 20, 1868, is of particular interest, if London Armoury had indeed shuttered its doors in 1866. It is addressed to "The Manager, London Armoury Company" and reads as follows:

Sir,

Be so good as to supply my son, Mr. Edward Dickens who is going out to Australia, with a rifle in accordance with his choice. Will forward a checque for the amount on knowing what it is.

Faithfully Yours
Charles Dickens [27]

J.E. Barnett & Sons
Robert Barnett (Founder)
The Worshipful Company of Gun-makers took their charter in 1637, and a member of the Barnett family became the first President of the Gun-makers guild. The term "Worshipful Company" means Livery companies or trade guilds made up of skilled craftsmen that operate in London. *The Worshipful Company of Gun-makers* ranks 73rd on the order of precedence, just ahead of the *Worshipful Company of Fan-makers* (76th) and *Playing Card-makers* (75th), but far behind the obviously much more essential *Worshipful Company of Brewers* (14th).

In June 1737, the famous gunsmith Richard Wilson took his third apprentice, Robert Barnett, and in so doing founded the beginnings of the dynasty of Barnett gun makers who would play a significant role in the gun trade during the nineteenth and first half of the twentieth centuries. The family history can be confusing, as several descendants share identical names. Hence, a little background is in order. Robert Barnett came from Kirkby-Stephen in Westmorland, the same town as Richard Wilson (now modern day Cumbria). Robert Barnett began with the manufacture of trade fusils and rifles while working as apprentice for Richard Wilson, and then for 15 years as a journeyman gun maker. He became a master gun maker in his own right in 1761 and set up at 157 Minories, London, in 1777. Minories was a street between Aldgate and the Tower of London and mostly occupied by armorers and gunsmiths. Barnett continued to make components and complete arms for the Wilson firm, and was almost undoubtedly a member of "Wilson & Co." which functioned from 1755, when William Wilson was taken into partnership. Richard Wilson employed a total of eight

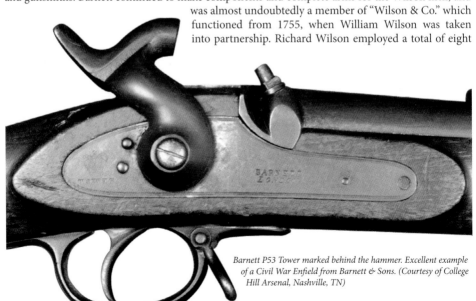

Barnett P53 Tower marked behind the hammer. Excellent example of a Civil War Enfield from Barnett & Sons. (Courtesy of College Hill Arsenal, Nashville, TN)

apprentices: Robert Barnett (1737), Benjamin Hartwell (1741), Robert Loy (1744), William Wilson, John Rookin/Rukin and Robert Yeatts (1747), and Thomas Rukin and Anthony Barnes (1755). All but two of these (Loy and Hartwell) were later recorded as gun makers, although none of them except William Wilson and Robert Barnett achieved any special longevity or notoriety in the gun trade. [1] Robert Barnett retired due to ill health in 1781 and went back to live in his place of birth, Kirkby-Stephen in Westmorland (Cumbria).

Robert Barnett (Nephew of Founder)
The Barnett firm continued in the gun trade with Robert Barnett's nephew, also named Robert, who was apprenticed by his uncle in 1771. He was elected assistant in 1781 and became a master gun maker in 1785, then set up the workshop at the more familiar address of 134 Minories in 1790. Robert Barnett (nephew of founder) died in 1793. The business was continued after his death by his widow Elizabeth until 1794.

Thomas Barnett
Thomas Barnett was the next Barnett to continue in the trade. He became the apprentice of Robert Barnett (the nephew mentioned above) in 1778. Thomas was then sent to William Wilson in 1780. He took livery in 1788, and

*Thomas Barnett & Sons'
"Northwest Trade" musket.
(Courtesy Craig L. Barry)*

was elected master gun maker in 1799. The firm became Thomas Barnett & Sons from 1794 to 1832 at 134 Minories, London. Barnett & Sons became contractors to the Ordnance Department in 1820 and supplied the East India Co between 1797 and 1831, as well as the Hudson Bay Company from 1821-32. Barnett muskets were also made for fur trading companies in North America during the early and mid nineteenth century, most notably by the Northwest Fur Company and after 1821 by the Hudson Bay Company. However, the American Fur Company, the Mackinaw Company, and the U.S. Indian Trade Office also traded Barnett muskets to native Americans. Trade guns, like the Barnett musket were typically referred to as "Northwest guns," "Mackinaw guns," or "Hudson Bay fukes." Less expensive than guns destined for Europeans or American buyers, these trade guns were lightweight with relatively short barrels, were usually designed to fire a shot weighing no more than an ounce, and had an oversized trigger guard large enough to allow the musket to be used with gloves or mittens during the coldest months of the year. Typically, Barnett muskets featured a side plate embossed with a dragon ornament that decorated the side of the gun opposite of the locking mechanism, offering Indians an easily recognizable mark of authenticity. [2] Contracts for trade muskets often stipulated that the weapon be "equal to the Barnett." Thomas Barnett died in 1831 and was succeeded by John Edward Barnett.

John Edward Barnett
John Edward Barnett was the son of Robert Barnett (nephew of original gun maker Robert). He was apprenticed to Thomas Barnett in 1801 and became a master in 1828. In 1832, the company was known as John Edward Barnett & Sons. They supplied the East India Co and Hudson Bay Co, as well

as continuing to be contractors to the Ordnance Department. Around 1840 the firm started to produce a double-barrel carbine of .74 calibre for the "Cape Cavalry." London gun maker Thomas H. Potts (Potts & Hunt) was an apprentice to Barnett prior to becoming a freeman in 1846 and opening his own firm. John Edward Barnett passed in 1849.

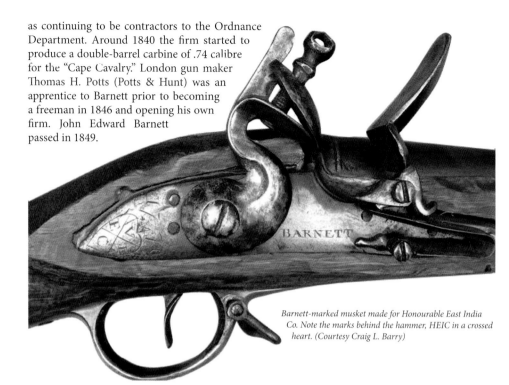

Barnett-marked musket made for Honourable East India Co. Note the marks behind the hammer, HEIC in a crossed heart. (Courtesy Craig L. Barry)

Barnett During the American Civil War

Subsequently, his two surviving sons Edward and John Barnett took over the firm. John Barnett was born in 1819 and was aged 42 in 1861. John had been apprenticed to his father in 1833 and took livery in 1840. He became a master gun maker in 1846. [3]

Edward Barnett was born in 1824 and was aged 37 in 1861, and was apprenticed to his father. He took livery in 1844 and became a master gun maker in 1849. In 1851 he was living at 2 Glebe Place, Hackney, and London. [4] Another brother, Robert Barnett, also worked for the firm as a gun maker. Robert was born in 1820 and was aged 41 in 1861. He took livery in 1841, but did not become a master gun maker until much later in 1867. As well as the workshops in the Minories, the company also opened a new site at Brewhouse Lane, Wapping (London), in 1860, which closed in 1874.

It is this firm of J.E Barnett & Sons, and the brothers Edward and John Barnett working in partnership, with whom Confederate Major Edward C. Anderson secured the first contract for arms for the Confederacy—especially the Enfield long rifle or "rifle musket"—nipping Union purchasing agent William McFarland in the process. McFarland had already made agreements with all the commercial gun makers in London for their output of Enfield rifles for four to six months. However, Colonel George Schuyler was officially the U.S. Government procuring agent in Europe. Schuyler had final say, and he failed to complete the contracts by the drop-dead date. English companies were demanding large down payments up front in case the war in America concluded suddenly and the demand for munitions from the CS and U.S. were to suddenly cease. Sensing an opportunity, Samuel Isaac (S. Isaac, Campbell & Co) alerted Major Anderson to the situation. Anderson asked Isaac to call on Barnett & Sons to see if he could secure the contract. Samuel Isaac successfully negotiated the deal for the Confederacy. Edward Anderson (the Confederate purchasing agent) wrote on July 1, 1861:

> It is only necessary to add that McFarland's remittances from the U.S. government did not come up to time and that we got the Barnet (sic) muskets and shipped them over to the Confederacy in due time… [5]

On July 3, 1861, funds finally arrived from the Confederate Government and Anderson put down a large down payment of £10,000 to secure the deal with JE Barnett & Sons, ensuring these weapons would see Confederate service only. So doleful was the situation in London for the Union buyers attempting the procurement of the sought after Enfield rifles that U.S. consul in London F.W. Morse communicated the setback, writing on October 26, 1861:

> Mr McFarland obtained the best offer he could from all the armouries here (London) for all the thoroughly inspected guns they could dispose of for a period of four to six months. When Mr Schuyler first came here we had everything ready. Mr Schuyler did not feel authorized then to take charge of the matter and close the contracts, and consequently the supply from this city has gone into Southern hands. [6]

During the summer of 1861, the initial efforts of Huse and Anderson resulted in the purchase of Enfield long rifles, of which 3,500 were the coveted P1853 Enfield long rifle, from several London firms. These were loaded on the seven hundred ton Blockade Runner *Bermuda*, which sailed on August 22, 1861, arriving in Savannah, Georgia, on September 18, 1861. The majority of these Enfield long rifles were from Barnett; surviving specimens with consecutively marked rack numbers suggest these were almost all State of Georgia marked. These were the first Enfield rifles to reach Confederate soil since the start of the war. [7] State of Georgia arms are easily distinguished by the rack numbers on the butt plate tang and a capital letter *G*, usually 5/8" high, stamped in the stock.

The story, of course, does not end there. Before very long the firm of J.E. Barnett & Sons had cancelled at least one Confederate contract in late 1861 for non-payment, and the Union stood prepared to step in and take any immediately available weapons. Such were the vagaries of the commercial Gun Trade during the U.S. Civil War. It was all about profits and which buyers had the funds ready at the time. Writing about the Barnett firm, the U.S. Consul made the recommendation to the Secretary of War as follows:

> Consulate of the United States of America,
> London, November 6,1861.
> Sir:
>
> …I have the satisfaction of informing you that one of the gun manufacturers here, who had a contract with the rebels running to March (1862), has had a difficulty with them, broken the contract, and will hereafter send his guns, Enfield rifles, to New York on his own account. His name is Barnett, and his rifles stand very well here.
>
> Your obedient servant
> F. H. Morse, Consul [8]

The main point illustrated here is that J.E. Barnett & Sons, like virtually all other London (and Birmingham) commercial gun makers, did not provide their output strictly to one side or the other. Many Barnett marked guns went to the Confederacy, but as documented here, Barnett freely and without guilt sold to the Union as well. In 1873, the firm moved to Duncan Street with additional premises in Leman Street, but the Leman Street workshop closed within the year. In 1901, the firm became a limited company, J.E. Barnett & Sons Ltd, and the company finally closed its doors in 1908. [9]

Barnett buttplate variation: block letters, no line engraving, and plain hammer.

Workmanship of J.E. Barnett & Sons

What sorts of long rifles were produced by Barnett during the U.S. Civil War and how did they differ from their competitors? To use a rough analogy, Barnett was the "Eli Whitney" of the British gun trade. Barnett was an opportunist, producing firearms that ranged in quality from nearly class one rifles to "African trade guns" assembled from surplus or rebuilt parts. Like virtually all commercial London and Birmingham gun makers (except LA Co), Barnett produced grade two/hand fitted arms that had locks, hammers, and hardware resembling those on first class (grade one) arms, but were not gauged or parts interchangeable. Additionally, the Barnett firm sometimes stamped their locks with a cipher consisting of a letter B surmounting a downward pointing arrow, which resembled the British government crowned broad arrow acceptance mark. They apparently did this for reasons that could gently be called deceitful and less kindly be termed fraudulent. The practice by Barnett of stamping over government condemnation marks on rejected parts was much like an open range cattle rustler changing the brand on a maverick steer. Eli Whitney (*Whitneyville*) in the U.S. was another gun maker widely associated with the practice.

Barnett produced mostly grade two/ non-interchangeable Enfield rifles, of which some number had "Tower" marked under the crown behind the hammer. Barnett was the only London gun maker to mark the lock plate in this way. Unlike most commercial gun makers, JE Barnett & Sons varied on the practice of how their engravers marked their lock plates. Barnett guns can be found marked "Tower" over the date, fancy hammer and double line perimeter engraved, like a Birmingham lock at first glance, however, with Barnett stamped in the wood on the other side between the lock plate screws. Other Barnett locks are more like most of the London gun makers, meaning not dated at all, no crown behind the hammer and plain hammers. Others have Barnett in block letters over London or Barnett over *London*, slanted with or without engraving or a crown behind the hammer.

Enfield rifles marked Barnett on the outside of the lock may be found to have internal markings of another maker, such as Pritchett, who supplied the lock or even the complete arm to Barnett. Conversely, some locks with standard Birmingham "Tower" markings and dates are found marked Barnett on the inside of the lock. Some Civil War-era Enfields have been found with Barnett barrels and Liege (Belgian) made locks. One illegal practice of the Gun Trade was to fob off a Belgian-made Enfield rifle as English. This combination of Belgian and Birmingham markings suggests that Barnett may have been re-branding inferior Belgian P-53s, or at least recycling dissociated Belgian parts to put together weapons marked Barnett and sold back into the gun trade. Both Isaac Hollis and W. Greener sued an individual gun maker (not Barnett) caught putting fake "Tower" marks on a Belgian Enfield and recovered damages. Such were the practices of the bottom feeders in the International gun trade during the early 1860s.

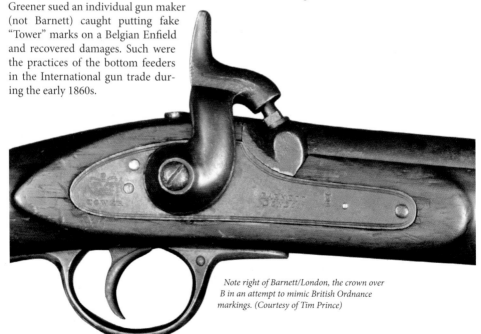

Note right of Barnett/London, the crown over B in an attempt to mimic British Ordnance markings. (Courtesy of Tim Prince)

How big of a Confederate supplier was JE Barnett & Sons? By the beginning of 1863, the Confederacy had already imported 70,980 Long (3-band) Enfield Rifles, 9715 "Short" (two-band) Enfield Rifles, and 354 Musketoons (carbines) to total 81,049 military arms, and the most common of these were Barnetts and L.A. Co. [11] The contract Enfield rifle-muskets from the Barnett firm that went to the Confederacy were a mixed lot in terms of quality. No single gun maker made "best grade" firearms all the time, but Barnett furnished quite a few inferior arms. Whatever their various deficiencies might have been, J.E. Barnett contracted and sold a volume of commercial rifle-muskets that were serviceable and shot well, and the firm stood ready to supply their weapons to the highest bidder. It is interesting to note that S. Isaac, Campbell & Co did a large volume of business with J.E. Barnett, but while these two firms were known for very questionable business practices, Barnett does not show up in litigation nearly as often as S. Isaac, Campbell & Co, but he did show up as a witness in a theft case from 1858 as follows:

Records of Central Criminal Court of London, Fifth Session, 22nd Feb 1858.

Joseph Edges (40) , Stealing 50 pieces of gun furniture and 24 lbs. weight of brass, the goods of John E. Barnett and another, his masters; and John Warren (27) , Feloniously receiving the same; to which Edges pleads GUILTY.

MR. HORRY *conducted the Prosecution.*

JOSEPH EDGES (*the prisoner*). I have been a porter in the service of Mr. Barnett, a gun maker, in the Minories, for about two years—I have pleaded guilty to stealing some brass—there was a great quantity of it loose about the factory, and it was a very great temptation to anybody—I had been told by Mr. Barnett to knock some stocks off, and this was the remainder of it—I took it to Mr. Warren and sold it—I only went there once; it was twice in one evening—the first time, I think I took about eighteen pounds; but I will not be certain—he did not ask me any questions when I took the first lot; I swear that—I took the second lot about a quarter of an hour afterwards; he did not ask me any questions then—he paid me 11s. 6d. for the two quantities—I did not tell him where I got it from.

Cross-examined by MR. ORRIDGE. *Q.* Was not that a fair price for it? *A.* I do not know—I have known Warren about three months—I do not know how long he has been in business.

COURT. *Q.* What is Warren?

A. A marine store dealer—I knew him by living close by.

WILLIAM COPPIN (*Policeman, K 379.*) On the evening of 11th Feb., I was in Charles Street. I know Warren's shop, No, 1, Princes Street, which leads into Charles Street—I saw a female, who I have since ascertained to be his wife, leave the shop. I saw Warren, at that time standing just inside the door; he was a short distance from me, perhaps fifteen yards— I followed her up to Charles Street Waterloo Road, Mile End New Town—she was carry something very heavy underneath her shawl—I asked her what she had got; I examined it; it was a quantity of brass. I sent her with the brass to the station house by a constable before doing that, I had some conversation with her. I then went back to Warren's shop; he was then closing his door. I asked him whether he had bought any brass of any man during the evening, he said, "Yes, I bought about three farthings' worth"—I asked him how long it was since his wife was there; he said, "Two hour. —I said, "Are you sure of that?" he said, "Yes"—I said, "Has she taken any brass away from here?" he said, "No". I said, "Then if she has told me she has just brought some brass away from here, she has told me an untruth?" he said, "Yes." I said, "Your wife had better come to the station, you had better come on with me." he said, "Very well" as we were going along he said, "I bought the bronze my wife has got of a man that lives in Charles Street, a gunsmith, he did not give me any name. he told me the house."

Cross-examined Q. How long have you known Warren?

A. I should say about three months— I think that is about the time he has been in business—I cannot say what he was before—I was not absent from his shop more than five minutes before I returned —I was not laying any trap for him—I did not ask these questions to see if I could catch him out in a falsehood—I never laid a trap for any man in my life.

EDWARD SHERIDAN (*Policeman, K* 433.) I was with Coppin on 11th Feb.—I stopped Warren's wife—I saw the metal, and saw it weighed—there was twenty-four pounds.

JOHN BARNETT, I have a partner; I carry on business in the Minories—Edges has been in my employment about two years, as porter—some months ago, I told him to break up some old muskets—he had access to that metal—this is the description of metal; I have every reason to believe that it is my property.

Warren's statement before the Magistrate was read as follows:—"This man came to me about 8 o'clock last night with seventeen pounds of brass, and asked me what I gave for old brass; I said 6*d.* a pound; he said he had bought a lot of old gun stocks of his master, and had knocked them off; in about a quarter of an hour afterwards he came with six pounds more, and I paid him 11*s.* 6*d.*; I should not have bought it, only he said he knocked it off the old gun stocks he bought of his master."

(*Warren received a good character.*)

WARREN— GUILTY *of Receiving—Recommended to mercy by the Jury, it being his first offence— Confined Twelve Months.*

EDGES— *Confined Twelve Months.*

Source: Proceedings of the Old Bailey, London's Central Criminal Court, reference # t18580222-296. JOSEPH EDGES, JOHN WARREN, Theft: stealing from master, Theft: receiving stolen goods, 22nd February 1858.

One purchase of Barnett arms sold directly to the Confederacy was made on July 3, 1862, for:

"413 chests", "8,250 muskets," "29 chests"580 Rifles" "129 moulds", and "1 case" worth £12,153.4s.6d were purchased directly from JE Barnett & Sons, these were to be shipped from Liverpool. [12]

Note: Here is a Barnett P53 which illustrates the amalgamation of parts used in hand-made guns. The outside of the lock plate is marked **Barnett** over **London**, but it is also marked inside by the lock maker in an arc around the mainspring boss **J Bridgewater**. J. Bridgewater was a lock maker who operated during the Civil War-era in Darlaston beginning about 1855. So, although **Barnett** was a "London" gunmaker, the lock has features that would be typical of locks found on Birmingham P53s. For example, the outside of the lock plate has the double line engraving around the perimeter, as well as "flames" engraved on the hammer. Other Barnett-produced P53s have plain unengraved locks and plain hammers. This means, in the typical English gun trade methodology, while Barnett had the contract to deliver this gun, he utilized subcontractors from various regions of England to produce parts, then assembled and delivered the finished product.

The "Tower" markings on the lock plate of most Barnett produced arms are very likely to be bogus, as most Barnett guns were not military gauged. [13] Compare a Barnett P53 to a machine made, parts interchangeable LA Co Enfield and note the differences. When Samuel Isaac (S. Isaac, Campbell & Co) went bankrupt in 1869, one of the creditors named in the bankruptcy court documents was one Edward Barnett of 134 Minories London, occupation gun maker.

Edward P. Bond (London) and Eyton Bond (Birmingham)

The English gun trade is interspersed and intertwined with multi-generational family members taking over as older generations either retire or pass on. And usually the descendants remain within the original firm like a dynasty, even though the name may change. Barnett is a well known example of this and it seems to be the norm. [1] What makes the Bonds different is not that several descendants of the founding gun maker followed their father in the English gun trade, but rather that the brothers split up into two separate firms and operated independently in two different cities.

The name Bond is prominent in the listings of London gun makers starting with the first Edward Bond, who apprenticed with Samuel Blanckley in the 1740s. Bond was granted his "Freedom from the Company of Gun-makers" of London in 1754, meaning he could do business under his own name, and set up shop at 59 Lombard Street. In 1780 he became Master of the Worshipful Company of Gunmakers. His son, Philip John Joseph Bond, took over the firm until 1810, at which time the firm passed to sons Edward and William Bond. They did business as E. & W. Bond from 1826-54, moving to 45 Cornhill until 1856 and then to 154 Leadenhall Street with a second location at Hoopers Square, Goodman Fields, until 1865. The firm was a supplier to the Honourable East India Company (HEIC), but they do not

Barnett P53 with London proof marks.
(Courtesy of Craig L. Barry)

Stock rounder used by E. Bond of Birmingham compared to the common D3AT stock stamp.

EP Bond, London. (Courtesy collection of Tim Prince, College Hill Arsenal)

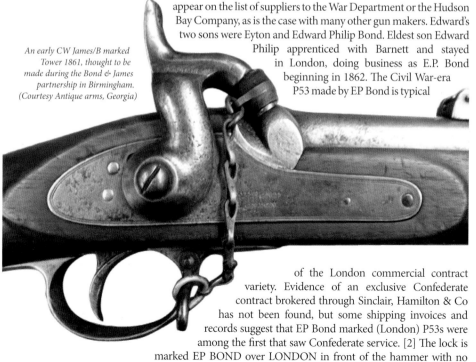

An early CW James/B marked Tower 1861, thought to be made during the Bond & James partnership in Birmingham. (Courtesy Antique arms, Georgia)

appear on the list of suppliers to the War Department or the Hudson Bay Company, as is the case with many other gun makers. Edward's two sons were Eyton and Edward Philip Bond. Eldest son Edward Philip apprenticed with Barnett and stayed in London, doing business as E.P. Bond beginning in 1862. The Civil War-era P53 made by EP Bond is typical of the London commercial contract variety. Evidence of an exclusive Confederate contract brokered through Sinclair, Hamilton & Co has not been found, but some shipping invoices and records suggest that EP Bond marked (London) P53s were among the first that saw Confederate service. [2] The lock is marked EP BOND over LONDON in front of the hammer with no date, and the lock plate/hammer is often double line engraved.

Eyton Bond entered the ship brokerage business in 1851 with Malcolm Inglis, trading under the name Inglis, Bond & Co at 54 Old Broad Street, London. They were listed as Merchant /Ship brokers/ Chapmen (merchants) and insurance agents. The firm went bankrupt in 1855. [3] Eyton Bond at some point then went back into the gun trade. It was not uncommon for members of a gun making dynasty to eschew the family business in favor of other trades, but it was somewhat unusual to return to the gun trade but not to the family firm. Eyton Bond went upcountry to Birmingham instead. The evidence suggests Bond took over the premises at 36-37 Loveday Street previously occupied by gun makers Moore & Harris [4]. E. Bond is listed at that address, doing business as Bond & James in the early 1860s. The firm advertised in the Birmingham city directory as follows:

> Military arms contractors and manufacturers of every description of breech and muzzle-loading *guns*, revolvers, &c. Patentees of improved snap-action breech-loaders. *Guns* for the African market supplied. [5]

His partner was likely Charles Wedge James, a gun and pistol manufacturer previously located at 6 Bath Street. [6] CW James used a circular stock roundel that read "CW JAMES/BIRMINGHAM/ MAKER". Neither E. Bond nor CW James were members in the Birmingham Small Arms Trade, which was driving many of the smaller gun makers out of business. Hence, they may well have partnered in the early 1860s to better compete against BSAT. Whatever the case, in 1863 Eyton is registered separately as "E. Bond" at 6 Shadwell Street in the Gun Quarter of Birmingham, right next to R&W Aston at 8 Shadwell Street. He invested in an oval stock stamp which reads exactly that way. After 1868 the firm again appears as Bond & James at 36-37 Loveday Street with no mention of the Shadwell Street premises, and finally in the 1870s as E. Bond at the 36-37 Loveday Street address and CW James at 48 Whitall Street. [7]

During the early Civil War era the 6 Shadwell Street address may have been a second factory location or a retail facility, with the main factory on 36-37 Loveday Street. It is believed that some of the Tower 1861 marked P53s from CW James, which were among the first to run the blockade aboard the *Bermuda*, were marked with a "B" when part of the on-again-off-again Bond & James partnership.

(*Courtesy of the Firearms Museum*)

Parker, Field & Sons

The firm of Parker, Field & Sons evolved from the merger of two late 18th century gun makers then doing business as "William Parker" and "Field & Clarke." Clarke passed away about 1791 and John Field entered into a partnership with William Parker. The new firm is first listed as Field and Parker in the 1794 Directory of London and Westminster. Field passed away soon afterwards, but his son, also named John, continued with the firm and later married Mary Parker, daughter of William Parker. The couple had three sons, two of whom followed their father and grandfather in the gun trade. Eldest

(Courtesy of The Firearms Museum, www.firearmsmuseum.org/au)

sons John William Parker-Field and William Shakespeare Field took over running the enterprise upon the passing of William Parker in 1840. The old firm of Field & Parker became Parker, Field & Sons in 1841. The firm is continuously recorded in business under that name until 1877. They relocated to 59 Lehman Street and 22 Tavistock Street from 1877-1883, doing business as Field & Sons. John William Parker-Field and William S. Field passed away during this period of time. The firm ceased to produce firearms, but continued in business at least through the early 20th century. The advertisement below ran in 1901, but who was running Parker, Field & Sons at 10 Crescent Belvedere Road remains a mystery. [1] The firm is not recorded afterwards.

In the mid-19th century Parker, Field & Sons was a major domestic supplier to both Ordnance and HEIC, along with the Hudson Bay Company and the London Metropolitan Police. [2] Apparently the firm did enough business overseas in India that they took out the following advertisement in 1857, addressed "To Sportsmen" living over there:

> PARKER, FIELD, & SONS'
> Newly Invented Spring Cartridge Set,
> REGISTERED ACCORDING TO ACT OF PARLIAMENT.
> PARKER, FIELD, &SONS beg to inform their Sporting Friends and the Public, that they have recently invented a SPRING BELT for the purpose of carrying Shot Cartridges, an article which, in combination with the UNIVERSAL CARTRIDGE lately introduced, will facilitate loading, and supersede the Shot Belt altogether.
>
> The REGISTERED BELT is extremely simple; protecting the Cartridge completely from injury, enabling the Sportsman to carry them with the greatest ease, and saving more than half the time in loading. They are worn round the waist of the Sportsman,

and by the simple pressure of a spring, as soon as one Cartridge is removed another supplies its place—two Cartridges always being ready to the fingers; and for battues and quick loading they are invaluable.

Officers supplied with the Regulation Houlster Pistol for every branch of the Service.

First-rate Second-hand Guns and Pistols.

PARKER, FIELD, & SONS,

Gun Makers to Her Majesty, the Honourable Board of Ordnance, the Honourable East India and Hudson's Bay Companies, Armourers to the Metropolitan Police, &c., 233, HIGH HOLBORN, LONDON. [3]

As with most of the larger English gun makers, Parker, Field & Sons produced a variety of products besides sporting guns, as evidenced by the list of display items at the Great Exhibition of 1851:

> Double-barreled fowling and rifle guns, in cases, complete.
> Inlaid and ornamental pistols.
> Air-gun in case, complete.
> New spring belt for carrying shot cartridges.
> Percussion musket and bayonet, as employed in the Hon. East India Company's service.
> Percussion fusil.
> Sapper and Miner's carbine.
> Cavalry carbine and pistol.
> Flint and steel single gun, used by the Hudson's Bay Company as a trade gun.
> Truncheons, rattles, spring handcuffs, leglocks, and spring-hilted cutlass, used by the metropolitan and city of London police.
> Brass pocket staff and pistol used by the inspectors and superintendents.
> Chain, with wrist shackles and lock, used at prisons for removing prisoners. [4]

Of the Parker, Field & Sons products displayed at the 1851 Great Exhibition, "Punch," a London magazine famous for humor and wit but never accused of understatement, ran the following commentary:

> Not the least interesting of the products of native industry, now in course of astonishing mankind at large, in Hyde Park, are certain specimens of a peculiarly national weapon, exhibited, together with a variety of fire-arms, by Messrs. Parker, Field, And Sons…The sight of these truly English contributions figuring in the World's Fair, the reflection how much more potent are such simple truncheons to maintain tranquility amongst us, than bayonets and artillery are to keep the peace in foreign lands, inspired Punch with thankfulness for the possession, by ourselves, of that "moral instinct of deference to a policeman" which Dr. Newman sneers at, in apologizing for the political state of popish countries. As Punch gazed on these symbols of law and order, a glow of patriotic enthusiasm flushed his cheeks with such a colour, that they looked like red apples; and a paroxysm of the same sentiment, dilating his bosom, occasioned one of his waistcoat buttons to fly with a loud pop. [5]

Besides military and sporting arms, perhaps the most unusual other products that Parker, Field & Sons sold were manacles and handcuffs. These came from Birmingham, but it is not known if they were manufactured by Parker, Field & Sons or if they merely sold the output made by someone else (probably Hiatt). Whatever the case, the Parker Field marked manacles were not only widely used by law enforcement in England, but large numbers were also sold to the antebellum Southern states for the slave trade. However, manacles and chains were not the only connection that Parker, Field & Sons would have with the Confederacy. The firm was one of the top five or six London suppliers of commercial Enfield long (and short) rifles shipped to the Southern states during 1861-62. Many of the first Parker, Field & Sons Enfield rifles that ran the Union blockade ended up in the states of Georgia and North Carolina. [6]

The other larger London gun makers that were documented suppliers to the CS during the Civil War were Barnett, EP Bond, LA Co (London Armoury Company), Potts & Hunt, and E. Yeomans & Son. [7] While the commercial gun making firms in both London and Birmingham were famously indifferent about selling to both the Union and the Confederacy, many of the larger London firms had their entire production totally committed with Confederate contracts early in the war. Caleb Huse landed in England just days ahead of Union buyers, and according to correspondence from F. H. Morse, the U.S. consul in London:

> Mr. Schuyler did not feel authorized then to take charge of the matter and close the contracts, and consequently the entire supply from this city (London) have gone into Southern hands...The Confederates are getting the same guns at Birmingham, but not enough to disturb the market. [8]

According to Confederate buyer Caleb Huse, there were seven Enfield long rifles for each short rifle purchased. As stated elsewhere in this monograph, the long rifles were actually about 20% less costly to produce as a "stand of arms." [9]

John William Parker-Field registered a patent for "improvements to breech loading firearms" in late 1862 as recorded by the *London Gazette*. Other than that, the firm does not appear to have been as innovative in terms of the evolution of gun design as some of their competitors. William Greener of Birmingham, for example, immediately comes to mind. A review of 19th century London court cases did not reveal any legal activity either brought by the Parker, Field & Sons firm or against them. The closest Parker, Field & Sons seems to have gotten to the courtroom during their history was when a set of their manacles were worn by a prisoner appearing there.

Close up of lock plate markings. PARKER FIELD & SONS of LONDON in slanted letters. (Coll. and of Craig L Barry)

Potts & Hunt

Another firm associated with Confederate Enfield purchases was Potts & Hunt of London. Like most gun makers, Potts & Hunt produced Enfield rifles on contract for whichever side had the money to afford them. The firm worked through Colt (as agent) to fill a Union contract for 4,000 Enfield rifles with 24 gauge (.58 caliber) 40" polished barrels like the U.S. Models for 65s/ each, and an additional 1,940 short rifles with saber bayonets at $25 each. [1] These particular Enfield rifles were believed to be the only Civil War-era commercial Enfield rifles that left the factory in England with polished instead of blued barrels. Colt is fairly well known to most Civil War enthusiasts, so a little background on the gun makers Potts & Hunt is in order. It begins with Martin Brander, who was apprenticed to his father in the mid-1700s. Thomas Potts (the elder) was in turn apprenticed to Martin Brander in 1792. In 1827 Martin Brander died. Thomas Henry Potts (the elder) took over the firm and kept the name Brander & Potts. Potts was a contractor to the Honourable East India Co. from 1827 to 1842. Thomas Henry Potts (b. 1824) joined as an apprentice in the firm of Brander & Potts when it moved to Haydon Square, Minories. The

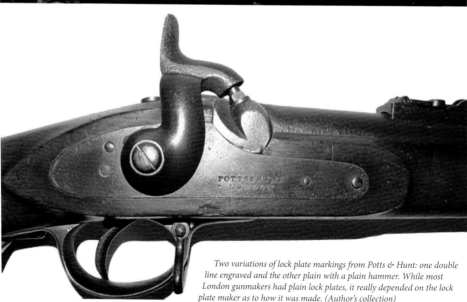

Two variations of lock plate markings from Potts & Hunt: one double line engraved and the other plain with a plain hammer. While most London gunmakers had plain lock plates, it really depended on the lock plate maker as to how it was made. (Author's collection)

elder Potts died soon thereafter in 1842, and the firm was managed by his mother Mary Ann Potts, who completed the remaining contracts. Thomas H Potts the younger was then turned over to the London gun maker J E Barnett & Sons at age 18 to finish his apprenticeship. In 1846 Thomas H Potts was made a freeman. He went into business and changed the name of the firm in 1848 from Brander & Potts to T.H. Potts. [2]

The T H Potts firm was unusual, as it listed an address in the Minories (London), but also listed premises on Shadwell Street in Birmingham beginning in 1848. It was not unusual for Birmingham firms to have a London retail operation, but it was not the norm for a well known London gun maker to have factories in both Birmingham and London gun quarters simultaneously. Potts was in the process of moving day-to-day operations of the firm to the Birmingham gun quarter. Private correspondence states that he made trips back to London only to conduct business there. In 1849, Thomas Potts was elected assistant in the Gun-makers Company of the London Trade Guild, so clearly the firm did business from their premises in London as well. [3] However Potts was, at the time, living full time in the Midlands and socializing with the gentry of the city. This is where he met his betrothed, Emma Phillips. Potts married Emma at Bourton on Dunsmore, Warwickshire, on April 2, 1850. Warwickshire is approximately twenty miles from Birmingham. Within a few months Emma's parents and brothers left for Canterbury, New Zealand.

In 1851, Thomas Potts had a display at the Great Exhibition in London. According to the Official Catalogue:

Exhibition # 207. POTTS, THOMAS HENRY,
Haydon Square, Minories - Inventor and Manufacturer.
1. A double-barrel gun (finished), with improved breeches, bolted triggers, etc.
2. Similar gun, in a bright (unfinished) state.
3. An instrument for drawing the breeches, applicable to all sorts of fire-arms. [4]

In 1852, the London firm moved to 32-33 Leman Street and had additional workshops at 27 Tenter Ground. However, the day-to-day business became increasingly centered in Birmingham, where Potts was residing. [5] During late 1853, Potts apparently turned over most of the operations to Thomas Hunt, left for New Zealand, and the firm traded as Potts & Hunt from 1853 to 1874. There is evidence in Potts' surviving personal correspondence that he was involved in the formation of Birmingham Small Arms Company, perhaps from its origins as Birmingham Small Arms Trade before he departed. Whatever the case Potts returned to England only once in 1862 "to sort out troubled business matters" involving BSA, according to his correspondence. BSA was run by committee up until September 1863, when they settled on a Chairman (John Goodman) and Board of Directors. [6] However, Potts was not listed among the new Board of Directors or major shareholders after the reorganization of BSA in 1863 and he never returned to England again. This suggests the "troubled business matters" were resolved by Potts liquidating his shares.

Thomas Potts and his family left England for New Zealand in late 1853. They sailed on

Thomas Potts posed with a stuffed Kiwi, circa 1875. (Courtesy NZ Birds Hall of Fame)

the *Balnaguith*, arriving at Lyttelton four months later on April 24, 1854. The couple already had three sons, and another ten children were born in New Zealand. More so than gun making, Potts enjoyed the pursuit of natural history and conservation. He spent virtually all of the rest of his life in New Zealand studying botany, ornithology and horticulture. He wrote for the *New Zealand Journal* and discovered two new species of bird. [7] During his time in New Zealand Potts also explored the interior. Mount Potts and the Potts River in New Zealand are named for Thomas Henry Potts. He was described as an "alert, congenial, vivacious, peppery, little man." [8] The economic depression of the 1880s impoverished him, as he had tied his fortunes up in properties which were suddenly worthless. Estranged from his wife, Potts lived with his daughter and son-in-law during his last years. Never sick a day in his life, Thomas Potts collapsed with a heart attack while making purchases in a stationery store and died July 22, 1888. His estate at the time was worth £70.

Back in England, it appears Thomas Hunt was involved with the firm T.H. Potts as early as 1852. Even before the firm was renamed "Potts & Hunt" Thomas Hunt applied for two patents in 1852, and he listed premises at 32/33 Leman Street, the London address of T.H. Potts. The patents were as follows:

> THOMAS HUNT, of Leman-street, Goodman's-fields, gun-maker: For improvements in firearms. Patent dated August 19, 1852. The first part of this invention consists of improvements in the breech-loading firearm, commonly known as the Prussian needle-gun. The construction of the piece does not differ materially from that in general use, the improvements being principally confined to matters of minor detail. The lock, instead of being secured to the sliding bolt by a screw is held by means of the sear spring; the needle is projected, as in the ordinary form of this gun, by a coiled spring, but is secured in place in the lock by a stud taking into a groove on its head, there being a longitudinal groove in the needle to allow of its being brought at first into a correct position ; the sliding bolt, instead of having its handle a fixture has it contrived so as to fold down against the side of the gun, and is held up against the permanent case in which it is situated, by a spring-catch instead of a screw ; the trigger lever is placed at the back of the trigger, instead of occupying its usual position; and the permanent case of the sliding bolt is enclosed by a moveable cover, which can be turned round when required so as to protect the working parts from the access of rain, &c.

TH Potts estate "Ohinetihi" in New Zealand. He, his wife Emma, and 13 children lived there from 1854 to the 1880s.

The second part of the invention has relation to double-barrelled guns, and consists,—1, in forming the breeches of such guns with a single "hut" intermediate of the breeches, instead of with two "huts," which is the common practice;—2, in an arrangement of apparatus for removing and fixing the breeches, in which the barrel is cramped between two surfaces faced with wood and screwed together, while the removal or screwing in of the breeches is effected by means of a screw acting against a lever, which embraces the " hut" on the end of the breech; and 3, in a safety-bolt for preventing the accidental discharge of double-barrelled guns. This bolt is attached to the rear end of the sliding loop or trigger-guard, the ends of which work through slots in the guard-plate, and hold the triggers fast by taking into a notch formed on each of them, either at half or full cock. The bolt is released by applying a slight pressure to the front end of the loop, which withdraws the bolt from the notches in the triggers, and leaves them free to act on the lock-spring.

Claims.—1. The improvements in breech-loading fire-arms. 2. The method of making the breeches of double-barrelled fire-arms, and the apparatus for removing and fixing the breeches, 3. The means of forming a safety bolt. [9]

Thomas Hunt also applied for patents for the improvement of sights in March 1853, and then another breech-loading design still using the same London address (32-33 Leman Street) in 1866.

According to the London *Daily News*, on October 23, 1854 there was a gas explosion at the Leman Street address of Potts & Hunt "the minie rifle maker" and a 65 year old night watchman named Robert Blake was killed in the tragic accident.

Londoner Thomas Hunt was not found listed in the Birmingham directories as a gun maker. He does not appear to have had any direct connection to the Birmingham Small Arms Trade or BSA Co. T.H. Potts, on the other hand, was listed on Shadwell Street in Birmingham from 1848 right up until he left for New Zealand in 1854. It appears from historical records and what can be pieced together that in the late 1840s Thomas Hunt began as an employee or gun maker for the T.H. Potts firm in London, perhaps so Potts could spend more time in Birmingham. Thomas Hunt may have already been as well off as Potts, since he most likely bought the firm from him after Potts left in 1853. Hunt continued to run the London and Birmingham operations, but appears to have lived in London. Rather than remove the former proprietor's name, Thomas Hunt may have merely added his own name to the masthead. At first glance the title "Potts & Hunt" suggests a partnership. This was not the case in the sense of the men sharing office space or even correspondence with each other. So why would Thomas Hunt not remove Potts' name from the title of the firm? The Potts firm was considered one of the eminent gun makers in London, dating back to the Brander & Potts-era. Thomas Hunt no doubt wished to continue to be associated with the gun making legacy of Potts, who was half a world away.

The working relationships in the gun trade can be confusing. When Potts returned to Birmingham in 1862, there is no evidence that he travelled down to London to visit the firm still bearing his name, but he found the time to head off into the heath for some bird watching. [10] This strongly suggests his lack of any further financial interest in Potts & Hunt. Whatever remaining financial interest Potts may have had in the English Gun Trade seems to have been limited to his involvement with investments in Birmingham Small Arms Co. BSA Co is the only firm which he directly mentions in his personal correspondence. And after returning to New Zealand later in 1862, Potts never mentions BSA Co or returns to England again. We should conclude that after 1862, Thomas Henry Potts is no longer involved directly or indirectly in the English Gun Trade. He spends the rest of his days indulging his interest in ornithology and conservation in New Zealand.

The majority of surviving Civil War-era Enfield rifles from Potts & Hunt are stamped "London" on the lock plate. There were at least some Enfield rifles made in Birmingham, as there are cavalry carbines stamped "Potts & Hunt Birmingham" It seems likely that the Birmingham factory supplied parts and components to the London factory to be "set up," or perhaps even provided finished guns. The Enfield rifles marked "Potts & Hunt London" may have commanded higher prices, if the Colt contracts are representative. Post bellum, Potts & Hunt (Birmingham) produced 77,000 bolt action Chassepot rifles under contract from the French government. The contract was not affiliated with Birmingham Small Arms, supporting the lack of involvement by Potts & Hunt in that enterprise. The firm of Potts & Hunt is not recorded after 1874.

E. Yeomans & Son: Gun and Sword Maker

Yeomans was a contractor to the War Department and Supplier to the Honourable East India Co (HEIC) during the 19th century. The firm had premises located at several addresses convenient to the Tower (of London). The etymology of the name "yeoman" dates from the Middle Ages and evolved in meaning and usage. Under feudalism, it was a rank of servant in a royal or noble estate. "Yeomen" were the first class of peasants and served their manor in feudal wars, often as archers. The medieval fighting men were classified as follows: knights, squires, yeomen and (lastly) pages. [1] By the 17th century "yeoman" meant a freeman with his own land or farm. In England, there was an aristocracy even in the peasant class.

None of this has much to do with the London gun making firm of Yeomans, but it is a good English sounding name with a history to it which could suggest the ancestry of the family. The firm is first listed in the London Post Office Directory in 1814 as *James Yeomans, gun maker, 46 Chamber Street, Goodman's Fields*. [2] However, there are surviving examples of flintlock muskets made on contract for HEIC marked *Yeomans* and dated as early as 1807. The founder passed away in 1839, and in his will left the business to his eldest son, also named James (#2). [3] Yeomans maintained premises on Chamber Street, an area of tenements which are located near the Tower. After 1843, Yeomans is listed in trade as follows:

> *Yeomans, James (1844-1849)* Gun Maker. Premises at 1 Magdalen Passage, Great Prescot Street and 67 Chamber Street, London. The address known as Magdalen Passage was very narrow (almost an alley)—on that street was housed a combination rescue mission and hospital for repentant prostitutes dating from the mid-18th century. Presumably James Yeomans did not share premises with the inmates.
>
> *Yeomans, James & Son (1850-1852)* Premises at 67 Chamber St, Goodman's Fields, London Supplier to Her Majesty's Ordnance Department and Honourable East India Company. During that time period, by permission of the Royal Commission for the Great Exhibition of 1851 (Crystal Palace), Yeomans & Son attended with a modest booth featuring "an assortment of muskets." The "Son" in the title of the business is James (#2) who passed away in 1851. [4]
>
> *Yeomans, Mrs Elizabeth (1853-1854)* Premises at Tenter St West, Goodman's Fields, and Chamber Street, London. James Yeomans' (#2) will, dated 9 Oct 1851 left the business to his wife Elizabeth, which was unusual since they had an eldest son, also named James (#3). It is most likely that James (#3) was either underage, still an apprentice in the gun trade or both.
>
> *Yeomans, E. & Son (1855-1864)* Gun and Sword Maker, with premises at 7 St Mildred's Court in the Poultry, Tenter Street West, Goodman's Fields, 3 Union Row Tower Hill, Chamber Street, 42 Great Tower Street, 35 Upper Street Smithfield, London. "E" refers to Elizabeth and "Son" refers to James (#3), now officially a partner in the business. There were two more sons in the family: Horace Yeomans, who specialized in sword and cutlery making; and William Arthur Yeomans, a minor child. [5]
>
> *Horace Yeomans & Co (1865-1870)* Sword maker and Cutler, 42 Great Tower Street, London and 35 Upper Smithfield London. The Yeomans firm is not recorded in the English gun trade again after 1870.

On April 8, 1861, James Yeomans testified in court with regards to two barrels stolen from the factory by an employee. The court transcript is as follows:

> Charged: JOSEPH MOCOCK [19] *First Count*, with stealing 2 gun-barrels, value 12/s, property of James Yeomans. *Second Count*, feloniously receiving the same.
>
> MR. GIFFARD *conducted the Prosecution.*
>
> JAMES YEOMANS: I am a gun manufacturer, and have a factory at 3 Union-row, Tower-hill—the prisoner was an under worker for us, in the employment of a man of the name of Clode—on Wednesday, 28th January last, I missed twelve musket barrels and a quantity of other brass that had been stripped from different finished guns—at that time the

prisoner was at work in my factory—in consequence of some information I received from Messrs. Devey and Vale, brass-founders, in Shoe-lane, I went to their premises—I there saw two barrels and identified them as part of the number I had missed on the 28th—in consequence of something I heard from them I went to a person named Shea, and Shea and myself went to one of my factories, where the prisoner, together with other men, were waiting to receive their work, and he identified the prisoner as the lad that had sold him the barrel—I called the prisoner into the counting-house and taxed him with it—he at first denied it, but afterwards admitted it—he said he had been led into it by another man of the name of Harvey—the value of the two barrels is about 12/s.

Cross-examined by MR. COOPER. Q. I believe he said that Harvey had given them to him to sell. A. Yes; and he had been led to do it, believing it was right—there was such a man in our employ; he is gone now—he is now in the workhouse—he is not here; he was at the Mansion-house, but was discharged—the prisoner at first denied it, but afterwards admitted that he did steal them, or rather, that he was led into it by Harvey, to sell the barrels—he did not say, "thinking it was all right"—I suppose he meant that.

MR. GIFFARD. Q. Tell us what he said. A. In the first place, Shea asked him if he was not the lad who had brought him the barrels—he said, "I did not; I did not sell the barrels"—Shea then said, "You certainly are the lad that sold them to me," and called his foreman to identify him too—the foreman also identified him—and on hearing that, the prisoner said, "I did sell the barrels, but I was led into it by a person of the name of Harvey"—that was all that passed as far as I recollect.

COURT. Q. Who is Harvey? A. He was a man in the same employ—an under worker, the same as the prisoner—I think Harvey is about twenty-three or twenty-four years of age—the prisoner is about nineteen.

JOSEPH SHEA. I am a marine store dealer, at 51, Great Ailie-street, Goodman's-fields—I bought these two brass musketoons from the prisoner, one on 18th January, and the other on the 24th—the first one was purchased by my foreman—I paid him ten shillings for the one I purchased—I asked him where he brought it from—he said, he was sent with it by his master, and brought a note; this is it (*read*)"January 23d, 1861—Sir,—The bearer has with him the barrel of a blunderbuss which does belong to me, but as it is perfectly useless I give him my sanction to sell it, as he has many times before, for old metal You may trust him, as he has been employed by me three years.—S. J. Harrison, 29, Chamber's-street"—on reading that note I purchased it, and paid him the money.

Cross-examined. Q. Are you quite sure he is the man? A. Yes, quite positive—I think he came somewhere about six or seven o'clock in the evening—he brought it openly.

The Prisoner's statement before the Magistrate was here read, as follows:—About the beginning of last month I went upstairs to go to work, I saw Daniel Harvey outside the door with one of the barrels in his hand, I asked him what he was going to do with it, he told me to mind my own business, and told me not to say anything about it as he had bought it at half price. I met him again in the evening and he brought the barrel with him; he said he would give me two or three shillings to sell it. I asked him if it was his own he said "Yes," and if I said anything about it he would put a knife into me. Mr. Shea bought the first, and the last one I took he refused, and I brought it him again in the evening and told me to take it home with me. I would not and left it in his care he came two or three days afterwards and brought a note with him and told me to take that in, and that would do, and if they asked me where I brought it from, to say it was my master's

The prisoner received a good character.

GUILTY of receiving — *Confined Twelve Months.* [6]

The London Confederate States Commercial League was formed in September 1863 with the mission of fostering business relations. Meetings were held every Wednesday at 7 St. Mildred's Court, Poultry; coincidentally, the offices of James Yeomans. [7] The London Confederate States Commercial League was advertised for several months but never gained enough traction to succeed, and the effort was discontinued. The attempt at "fostering business relations" smacks of desperation. It appears that business was off significantly in the gun trade (at least for Yeomans), no doubt due to the disappearing War Department contracts for military arms and a minor economic recession. By 1863, the War Department was getting close to 2,000 grade one, interchangeable P53 long rifles from Enfield Lock each week. As a result, domestic commercial military contracts with the London and Birmingham gun makers had dried up. However, the U.S. Civil War was such a boon to the English gun trade during mid-1861 to 1863 that it more than made up for it. Then, in September 1863, the U.S. Government cancelled all their existing orders, as they were able to meet their own needs domestically. The effect of the sudden cancellation created a temporary glut of military arms in the trade. Birmingham bore the brunt of the impact, as they had most of the U.S. contracts. E. Yeomans & Son must have been on shaky ground already, because by March 1864 they were in the process of liquidating their holdings to their creditors. See the following:

> London Gazette, March 8, 1864: Assignments for the benefit of creditors, E. Yeomans & Son, Gun Manufacturer and Sword Cutlers, 7 St Mildred's Court NOTICE is hereby given that the following is a copy of an entry made in the book kept by the Chief Registrar of the Court of Bankruptcy for the Registration of Trust Deeds…Date of execution by Debtors— 8th March, 1864, and 5th July, 1864. Names and descriptions of the Debtors, as in the Deed- Elizabeth Yeomans and James Yeomans, both of No. 7, Saint Mildred's-court, Poultry, in the city of London, and Tenter-street West, Goodman's Fields, and Chamber-street, Goodman's Fields, and No. 35, Upper East Smithfield, all in the county of Middlesex, Merchants and Gun and Rifle Manufacturers, and Sword Cutlers, trading under the style or firm of E. Yeomans and Son (debtors). [8]

In the matter of leases and sales of settled estates, the holdings listed for Yeomans included quite a bit of real estate:

> Lot 1. Four houses, numbered 60 to 63, inclusive, in Chamber-street, Goodman's-Fields. –

> Lot 2. A very substantial newly-erected warehouse, of three floors situated in the rear of Nos. 68 and 69 Chamber street; with the seven houses numbered 68 to 73, inclusive on Chamber-street, and No. 1, Magdalen-passage, Goodman's Fields. At the same time will be sold by the owners

> Lot 3. Comprising two houses, numbered 63 and 67 and Lot 4. Comprising two houses,-numbered 14 and 65, both in Chamber-street... [9]

Horace Yeomans continued in the small arms trade after the bankruptcy of E. Yeomans & Son. Oddly, although listed as a sword maker and cutler, he also produced muskets and revolvers. The National Maritime Museum (London) has five examples of the "old pattern" .75 caliber smoothbore muskets made by H. Yeomans/London and dated 1865. This is the same pattern musket based on the Brown Bess, which they were selling to the HEIC in the early 1850s. [10] It is unclear why the obsolete "old pattern" smoothbore muskets were ordered or by whom, but there are five of them in the NMM collection, all marked exactly the same way. The curator of the NMM states they may have been used aboard merchant ships, but why the old pattern at a time when more modern rifled muzzleloaders were being converted to breech-loaders by the hundreds of thousands? Keep in mind, Yeomans did not make the arms; they just had the parts "set up" at their premises.

By January 1866, Elizabeth Yeomans had left London and was living in Saxony. In legal records she is listed as mother and guardian of William Arthur Yeomans, an infant (under 18) and on behalf of James Yeomans, her eldest son. It appears she was finishing up the final sale of estate properties and then dividing the assets among herself and her children. [11] E. Yeomans & Son was a multi-generational firm considered one of the major "setters-up" of commercial military arms in London during the 19th century. Few Englishmen left both their profession and country for Saxony in those days. The sense of latent provincialism in Great Britain is too great for that drastic move to have resulted from merely the

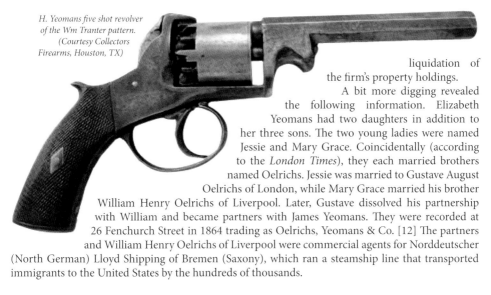

*H. Yeomans five shot revolver
of the Wm Tranter pattern.
(Courtesy Collectors
Firearms, Houston, TX)*

liquidation of the firm's property holdings.

A bit more digging revealed the following information. Elizabeth Yeomans had two daughters in addition to her three sons. The two young ladies were named Jessie and Mary Grace. Coincidentally (according to the *London Times*), they each married brothers named Oelrichs. Jessie was married to Gustave August Oelrichs of London, while Mary Grace married his brother William Henry Oelrichs of Liverpool. Later, Gustave dissolved his partnership with William and became partners with James Yeomans. They were recorded at 26 Fenchurch Street in 1864 trading as Oelrichs, Yeomans & Co. [12] The partners and William Henry Oelrichs of Liverpool were commercial agents for Norddeutscher (North German) Lloyd Shipping of Bremen (Saxony), which ran a steamship line that transported immigrants to the United States by the hundreds of thousands.

CHAPTER SIX:
Enfield Rifle Implement Appurtenances Issued with the P53 Enfield Rifle Musket

On May 21, 1861 Captain Caleb Huse wrote to Josiah Gorgas, the Confederate Chief of Ordnance, "I propose to take from the London Armoury Company 10,000 Enfield rifles of the latest government pattern, with bayonet, scabbard, snap-cap and stopper complete for £3 16s 6d." What exactly were these *appurtenances* – as the British military termed them – that were issued with the P53 rifle musket?

The P53 Enfield Socket Bayonet

Large numbers of bayonets issued with the London and Birmingham commercial made P53 Enfield rifle muskets issued to Confederate troops during the American Civil War were made by the firm Geo. Salter & Co of West Bromwich, England. The company is today still best remembered for the manufacture of weighing machines and scales, and is still making these items today. But in the 19th century the company was noted for making quality bayonets for the Birmingham and London gun trade.

Original Salter P53 Confederate-used bayonet. (David Burt collection)

The company was formed in 1760 by two brothers, Richard and William Salter. The brothers established a business manufacturing springs and pocket steelyards (spring balances) in a cottage in Bilston, near Wolverhampton, in the English West Midlands. In 1770 the company moved to West Bromwich, where it became the leading employer. After Richard's death in the 1790s, the business was taken over by William's sons, John and George Salter; it was the sons who, as well as making springs, also began to make bayonets to the gun makers' specifications. The company's bayonet manufacture came about because the steel used in spring manufacture was ideal for the making of bayonets.

Blade of an original Salter & Co Confederate imported bayonet. (David Burt collection)

In 1824, after John Salter's death, George took over the running of the company and the company was re-named George Salter & Co, a name by which it became best known. In 1849 George Salter died, but the firm remained in family hands, and continued to make a wide variety of spring balances used in weighing equipment, steam pressure gauges, irons, and musket bayonets. [1]

After the adoption of the P53 Enfield musket in 1853, the bayonet for this new gun was manufactured by the company. It was these commercially made bayonets that made their way over the Atlantic during the American Civil War to arm the Confederate Armies. The P53 Enfield musket was sold complete with a bayonet, scabbard, snap cap (nipple protector), and muzzle stopper.

G. SALTER,

WEST BROMWICH,

MANUFACTURER OF THE IMPROVED AND

PATENT SPRING BALANCE,

A PORTABLE AND CONVENIENT

DOMESTIC WEIGHING APPARATUS;

AND AN

Indicator of the Pressure of Steam,

WHEN ADAPTED TO

LOCOMOTIVE & other ENGINES.

Vertical Spring Roasting Jacks, &c. &c.

An 1839 Company advertisement.

The Salter P53 Enfield Bayonet

The P-1853 Socket Bayonet was adopted by the British Board of Ordnance in 1853, and was the first British socket bayonet to utilize a locking ring to secure the bayonet to the musket. It was also the first pattern of British bayonet to incorporate a steel blade and *elbow* (or shank) with an iron socket. An original *SALTER & CO* bayonet in the author's collection is typical of the commercial bayonets made for the Confederate P53s during the American Civil War. The blade is 17 inches long and the socket is three inches long. This socket was made of iron, and was blued right down the shoulder of the bayonet to the beginning of the blade. This bluing matched that of the gun barrel. The blade on the original is made from steel, which is triangular in shape. The *Fuller* or *blood grooves* are located on all three sides of the blade. This bayonet is devoid of any British military marks, and therefore must have been provided with a P53 for export to the South during the American Civil War. Stamped onto the blade is the name *SALTER & Co*; there is also a Birmingham inspector's stamp of a *Crown over B.S.A.T.* (*Birmingham Small Arms Trade*). There are also the letters *S.H.* stamped on the blade, and this could be an inspector's initial.

On the rear of the socket itself there is stamped an *X*, this is likely to be a bending mark for proof of blade. This mark proved that when the blade had been tested against easily bending

This newspaper article from 1859 shows how the bayonet was made:

> The bayonet first arrests attention, and we observe a stout little cylindrical chunk of iron, about four inches in length, which we are told is the first state of the bayonet. This is merely the iron, which is supplied from Sheffield, and which is to be educated into the deadly weapon, for the use of which the English soldier has ever been famous. Hammering and hammering are the earliest ordeals to which the bayonet is subjected. Heavy hammers, swung in circles by strong arms, descend with unerring precision on the required spot.

The Salter & Co C.S used bayonet with original "Salter" and "Birmingham" inspection stamps. (David Burt collection)

One man, with a pair of iron fingers, holds and turns the metal, while the other knocks it about. To a nervous bystander; this process is very trying; for he who holds will certainly receive the blow of the hammer on the center of his forehead, if he does not move his head just one inch and three-fourths. The hammer approaches; the man bends back only just in time, and only just the required distance. Again he is in danger - again he escapes; and thus he has gone on, blow after blow, day after day, month after month. Talk about confidence in princes, let us see on earth more confidence than this holder places in his hammerer. We are, however, convinced that sooner or later the final catastrophe must come, and the blacksmith will be killed by his partner. It was here that we saw the water-gauge, by which the amount of iron requisite to form a bayonet is accurately tested - a tube containing a given quantity of water; into which the iron is thrust. When the water reaches the top of the gauge, the correct quantity of iron has been inserted. However irregular the iron may be in form, the right amount is sure to be thus obtained.

Our attention is now called to a curious machine behind us. This looks like some nervous infuriated monster mouth, which is armed with a row of grinders. The creature is evidently in a rabid state, for the grinders are being gnashed together with fearful rapidity, while the water runs over them. A smith boldly approaches this, holding in his hand a red-hot bar of iron, which he places between the grinders. Delight at once seizes them, for they move more rapidly than before; and instantly the bar of iron is chawed out a couple of inches longer.

The bar is then inserted in a fresh place, is again lengthened, and so on until we are shown a stick of iron not at all unlike a bayonet. A most formidable individual then measures and inspects, gauges and tests, this piece of iron; length, breadth, weight, and colour are examined. Should the bit be below or above gauge, below or above par, 'mulct so much' is the fate of the last workman. Each man thus has his responsibility, from which there is no escape, and for which there is the simple remedy, "a fine." [1]

Unmarked Confederate used Pattern 53 Enfield bayonets are often found in private collections and museums in America. It was common practice during busy times for the London and Birmingham gun makers to contract work to foreign suppliers, as was the case during the American Civil War. These bayonets were made in places like Liege in Belgium and Solingen in Germany (Solingen was known as the *City of Blades*). Other British commercial bayonet suppliers that supplied the P53 bayonet to the London and Birmingham manufacturers included: R &W Aston, Wilkinson, S. Hill & Sons, Heighton & Lawrence, G.W. & E. Roe, J. Roe & Son, and Charles Reeves and William Deakin & Sons. [2]

THE P53 ENFIELD BAYONET AND SCABBARD DIAGRAM

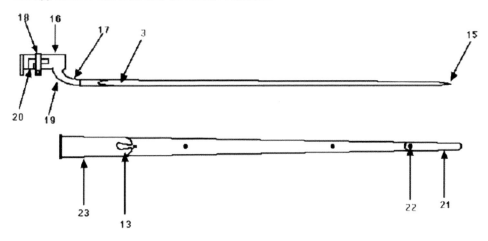

3. Fuller or blood groove. 13. Frog Stud. 15. Tip 16. Socket. 17 Shoulder. 18. Locking ring. 19. Elbow. 20. Zig Zag slot .21. Chape. 22. Rivet. 23. Locket.

The Pattern 1860 Scabbard

The first pattern scabbard for the P53 bayonet was based upon the earlier P1842 design, with the brass frog hook mounted directly through the scabbard body. The scabbard tip was made of sheet brass and secured by three brass pins. This way of attaching the frog hook directly to the scabbard body did not hold up well in the combat conditions of the Crimean War, and following the conflict a new scabbard was introduced. The new second pattern P1860 scabbard called for a heavier throat, with the frog stud attached to it for greater strength and durability in the field. It also now had the seam of the scabbard at the back instead of the side as in the first pattern.

The List of Changes for the British Army noted.

The new style throat for the second pattern bayonet scabbard. Note how the frog hook is now attached directly to the throat, or "Locket." This throat was excavated at Petersburg, VA.

123. 28th April 1860, Scabbard for Bayonet Pattern 1853
The brass chapes and locket secured by rivets, the hook fixed to the locket, and the seam at the back instead of at the side.
Proposed by Superintendent Royal Small Arms Factory [1]

The new scabbards provided for the P53 bayonets were made from black leather (with smooth side out and of waxed (rough side out) leather. The fittings on the scabbard, locket, chape, and frog stud were made from brass. There was no internal sheet metal or wooden liner as would be seen in later versions.

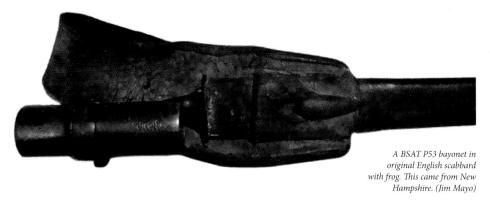

A BSAT P53 bayonet in original English scabbard with frog. This came from New Hampshire. (Jim Mayo)

The scabbard was not part of the *accoutrement* set as issued by the British Army, nor that imported to the Confederacy by S. Isaac Campbell & Co. It was instead issued along with the P53 rifle musket and bayonet. When the soldier received the *frog* with his set of accoutrements, the scabbard was simply attached to it by sliding the scabbard through it and fastened by using the frog stud on the scabbard, which passed through the opening on the front of the frog.

The Sword Bayonet and Scabbard

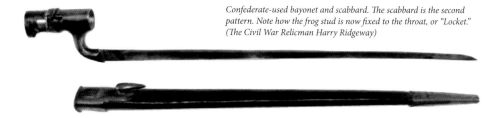

Confederate-used bayonet and scabbard. The scabbard is the second pattern. Note how the frog stud is now fixed to the throat, or "Locket." (The Civil War Relicman Harry Ridgeway)

THE SWORD BAYONET DIAGRAM FOR THE P1856-60 TWO BAND ENFIELD RIFLE

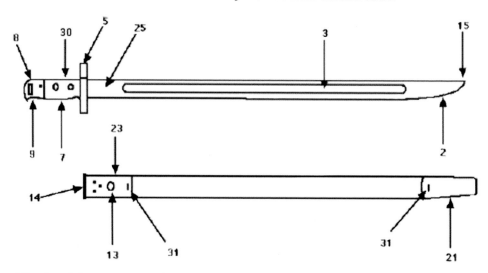

2. True edge. 3. Fuller groove. 5. Crossguard. 7. Grip. 8. Pommel. 9. Locking grip. 13. Frog Stud. 14. Mouthpiece. 15. Tip. 21. Chape. 23. Locket. 25. Ricasso. 30. Hilt. 31. Wire lace.

The sword bayonet was intended for use with the P56 and P60 two band *short* Enfield rifle, and it is featured in lots of original photographs of Confederate soldiers, along with the two band Enfield rifle. In 1859, the scabbard for this bayonet underwent changes; the LOCs noted:

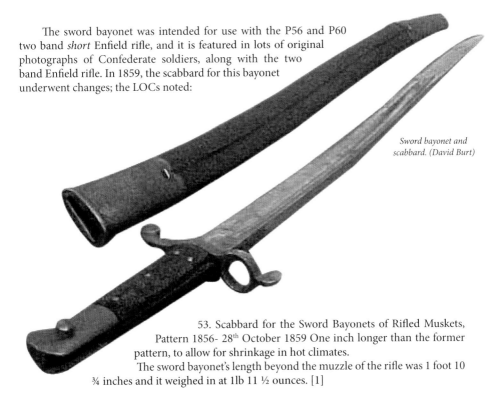

Sword bayonet and scabbard. (David Burt)

> 53. Scabbard for the Sword Bayonets of Rifled Muskets, Pattern 1856- 28th October 1859 One inch longer than the former pattern, to allow for shrinkage in hot climates.

The sword bayonet's length beyond the muzzle of the rifle was 1 foot 10 ¾ inches and it weighed in at 1lb 11 ½ ounces. [1]

Other Parts (Appurtenances) Issued with the P53 Enfield Rifle Musket

The Pattern 1853 Rifle musket was issued a bayonet, muzzle stopper, and snap cap.

The Muzzle Stopper

The muzzle stopper is self-explanatory; it was inserted into the muzzle to keep any inclement weather out.

An article entitled *Instructions in Musketry* for the P53 Enfield written in 1857 stated:

> At all times when not shooting, stoppers should be in the muzzles to keep dust as well as moisture from entering. [1]

British Regulations called for the muzzle stopper were as follows.

> The Muzzle Stopper consists of 3 parts
> 1st Head or Cap
> 2nd Pin or Shank.
> 3rd The Cork.
> The Head or Cap is made of iron or brass according to the mountings of the arm for which they are intended it having been decided by order of 26 August 1865 81/B/156 No 7, New Series, paragraph 1134, that brass headed stoppers are to be issued with brass mounted arms and iron headed stopper with iron mounted arms irrespective of service.

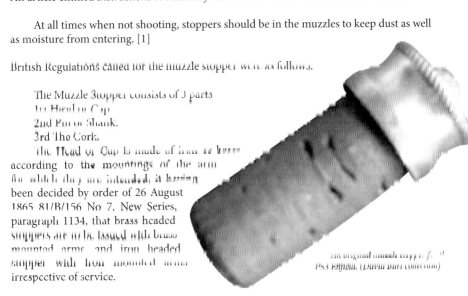

The original muzzle stopper for the P53 Enfield. (David Burt Collection)

The brass cap on the muzzle stopper for the P53 Enfield.

The "cupped" iron shank. (David Burt)

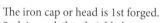

The iron cap or head is 1st forged.
2nd Annealed and pickled
3rd Recess for Cork bored
4th Turned on the outside.
5th Screw hole for the shank drilled & tapped.
6th Case hardened.
The shank is made out of square iron.
1st Wire clipped to length.
2nd Washer punched out of sheet iron
3rd Washer riveted on wire and cupped.
4th Washer brazed on wire.
5th Shank milled & threaded.
6th Head polished.
7th Blued.

The Cork is sawn into strips, then milled to diameter & afterwards a hole is drilled through the center from end to end, for the Shank.
Assembling
This consists in passing the Shank up the cork, screwing on the head & riveting it.
Marking
The Muzzle Stopper is marked on the head with the usual view mark.
NOTE - The Cork for a Muzzle Stopper should last 2 years after which they may be condemned for "wear & tear." [2]

The P1857 Snapcap

The snap cap was issued with all exported P53 Enfield muskets supplied to the Confederacy, including all the commercial gun makers that supplied arms. The purpose of it was for training in the British Army; it allowed the soldier to *dry fire* the weapon during training so as not to damage the nipple of the rifle. It is widely seen on original Confederate P53s in museums and at antique fairs still attached to the original weapon.

The snap cap was first introduced into the British Army in 1857, as a letter written by GA Wetherall Adjutant General explained:

Snap Caps For Rifles 1857

The snap cap. (David Burt collection)

The following circular has been forwarded from the Horse Guards to the commanding officers of those regiments and depots which are now undergoing a course of rifle instruction. In consequence of it having been found that the practice of snapping which was ordered by the circular memorandum of September 25 1853 to be discontinued on account of the injury caused thereby to the firelock is of the utmost importance to the effectual carrying out of the position drill as prescribed by the Instruction of Musketry the late Field Marshal Commanding in Chief. In concurrence with the Secretary of State for War decided upon the adoption of snap caps of a pattern which has been for some time under trial at the School of Musketry without any breakage of either cock swivel or any other parts of the rifles with which they have been issued. A number of these new snap caps being now ready his Royal Highness the Duke of Cambridge has entered into an arrangement with the War Department for their being issued to every regiment and depot at home and abroad according to their establishment and without the necessity of separate requisitions from commanding officers. The snap caps will be attached to the musket by a small chain or elastic band and with every fresh issue extra leathers in the proportion of 20 per company will be supplied for the purpose of being fitted into the metal frame in lieu of others as they become worn out an operation attended with no difficulty and one which it is stated can be effected by any handy man in a company. In the event of a soldier losing his snap cap either wilfully or through neglect the cost thereof as fixed by the War Department viz 3d each will have to be made good by him at his own expense.

By Command GA Wetherall Adjutant General [1]

British Army regulations called for the snap cap to be made as follows:

The snap cap for all arms with guard swivels consists of 4 parts. For those not having guard swivels 5 parts.

The 4 parts are -

1st Snap Cap head of iron, 2nd Chain of brass, 3rd Split ring of steel wire and 4th Pad of leather

The Head is manufactured on the same principle as the other parts of iron furniture, and when finished polished or blued

The Chain is made of thick brass parts being punched out sufficient to form each link.

The Steel Split Ring is supplied by contract.

The Pad consists of two bits of leather fastened together by fish glue. The under piece of leather has a hole in it for the supply at the bottom of which there is a small thin disc of brass punched out of sheet brass & pressed into the bottom of the hole to protect the leather which is expected to last 1 year. The leather is pressed into the hole by a pin at such an angle as to receive the hammer fair on the surface of the leather.

Assembling
When all the parts are manufactured the Snap Cap is assembled by fastening the chain on to the head & putting in the leather pad & attaching the ring.

Mode of Attaching
The Snap Cap is secured to the Rifle by passing the split ring over the guard swivel. Those pieces which have no guard swivel have an eyelet screwed into the swivel plate of the trigger guard to which the split ring is attached. This is the 5th part previously. [2]

The Enfield Gun Sling

The use of a musket sling is a continuously controversial subject that elicits strong opinions on both sides of the debate. On one side is the great horde of Enfield toting Civil War (re)enactors all equipped with 72" long leather brass hook style slings, all flopping around loose. On the opposite side is the contrarian arguing that musket slings were a thing practically unknown during the Civil War-era. There exists a general lack of understanding of the role the sling played for the common soldier of the U.S. Civil War and how it was issued. The four U.S. and C.S. manuals of arms

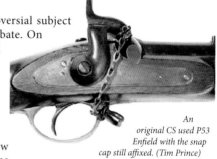

An original CS used P53 Enfield with the snap cap still affixed. (Tim Prince)

from the Civil War-era do not make specific mention of carrying the musket by any sort of sling at all. When the command of "at the route step" is given, it is only stipulated that the musket be carried with the muzzle upright. [1] It is not specific as to the use of a sling to carry the musket or otherwise. Civil War-era photographs fail to depict slings in evidence about as often as they are shown, and surviving Civil War-era slings in good condition are rare. The most common question asked is how prevalent sling usage was in the Civil War, when a better question might be "Is a musket sling appropriate for *my impression*," and if so, "which sling is most correct and how should it be used?"

Slings were an item ordered through the Ordnance Department and not the Quartermaster, as they were considered part of the accoutrements set. Research using existing documents also suggests that large numbers of accoutrement sets (including slings) were issued to the Confederate armies, not only from Richmond, but also Atlanta, New Orleans, and Baton Rouge before these cities fell into Federal hands. Did they ever get to the troops that were on campaign, or otherwise deployed in the field? We may never know definitively. However, prior to the war, various southern states entered into contracts for full sets of accoutrements, which they had on hand in 1861. In correspondence dated January 1863 the CS Ordnance Bureau reported over 282,000 complete sets of accoutrements (which would have included slings) had been issued, with another 25,000 in reserve. In addition, numerous crates of slings and other accoutrements ran the blockade such that in February 1863, an additional 40,240 gun slings were reported as having arrived in southern ports. [2] If soldiers initially received all the equipment that the government intended them to have, what might have happened to it in the field? An insightful period account by a boy who enlisted in the 2nd Mississippi in 1861 at age 16 is suggestive of what he did with at least some of the equipment originally issued:

The first year of the war (1861) was a picnic compared to the three remaining years. We had good tents in which to quarter, plenty of clothing, with little marching and fighting to do; also we had plenty of rations… It was not until April, 1862, that the war began in earnest… At that period of the war every soldier had either a trunk or valise in connection with his knapsack, and every company had its tents, cooking utensils, and baggage wagons. In order to lighten my load I took from my knapsack and placed in my trunk everything except one change of underwear, one towel, a cake of soap, a comb, and a little book on how to cook fancy dishes—a thing that the Lord knows I had no need for. I also had two heavy blankets, a rug, a knapsack, three days' rations, a heavy musket, and a cartridge box containing forty rounds of ammunition—a good load for a broncho (sic)…After some three miles' march (in the rain) my rug weighed about fifty pounds, so I decided to drop it. A few hundred yards farther on I abandoned one of my blankets and a little later my knapsack… We were so completely worn out that after partaking of a few bites of hard-tack and boiled beef we searched for places to sleep. I slept under my wet blanket with my cartridge box for a pillow. [3]

In the southern armies of the U.S. Civil War it seems reasonably clear that slings were initially issued by the government as part of the accoutrements. The period accounts of camp life early in the war suggest the armies had plenty of everything. Then, as the armies went out on campaign, items either wore out or were discarded. What kind(s) of slings were issued? There were U.S. type, CS linen and also British P-53, P-56 Enfield slings (and accoutrements), which while rare in the Federal army were common to the Confederacy. The correct Civil War-era British slings are a subject of some debate and several different slings are made for the P-53 Enfield. There are British leather slings that are the "loose leather thong, tied at the bottom" type with one fixed and one sliding or "friction" keeper. A thong tied sling is found documented as in use *before* the U.S. Civil War period on the 1808-39 Brown Bess muskets, and *after* the U.S. Civil War, on the Martini-Henry, but was it in use *during* the U.S. Civil War? Let's consider the facts as much as they are known. At the time of the U.S. Civil War, and just prior to it (Crimean War and in British colonial India) the British Army issued buckle type leather slings to their infantry units along with the P-53 and P-56 Enfield rifles. There are period photographs of British soldiers in the field where these waxed black and white buff leather buckle slings are clearly visible. Having established that, the question we have left unanswered is not (specifically) what the British Army used, but rather what did the commercial London and Birmingham Enfield gun-makers ship to the U.S. and CS during the U.S. Civil War?

The slings included with crates of P-53 Enfields shipped here during the 1860s were (unfortunately) not specific as to any particular type or style. If the London and Birmingham commercial gun-makers ever kept records of what specific style of sling were in their Enfield shipments they are now lost to history. There were a few rare instances where Federal units received British accoutrements along with their P-53 Enfield rifle-muskets. These are well documented as to the type of sling. One known shipment was from the Massachusetts state contract on which delivery was received in mid-1861. The slings included were consistent with what the British Army used at that time. They were leather with a fixed leather loop at the bottom, *a buckle closure* and a sliding leather keeper to take up the slack at the top. It was known as the Pattern of 1854 rifle sling, for use with the new Pattern of 1853 long rifle (also known as Enfield). [4] Actually, the era of the British buckle sling seems to have been rather short lived, perhaps from the Crimean War through the end of the 1860s. This would be understandable to anyone attempting to adjust a sling with a buckle closure while on the march. It seems to take a minimum of three hands. The fixed leather loop/sliding keeper sling is very easy to adjust on the march, and it is therefore reasonably clear why the British went back to that design again in the early 1870s.

The argument often brought up in favor of Civil War provenance for the post-bellum loose leather thong/sliding keeper sling goes something like this: "If these British slings were known to be in wide use pre-U.S. Civil War (they were), wouldn't the British gun-makers have fobbed off their current inventory of obsolete loose leather thong-tied slings before shipping the newer buckle fastened variety?" We can't really know for certain, but what we do know is at least some British gun makers were already shipping the buckle type slings very early in the war as part of the accoutrement sets ordered along with rifle-muskets in mid 1861. The Massachusetts state contract(s) P 53s counted among the first Enfield shipments received by either side. We don't know conclusively what other commercial gun-making firms were shipping to the Confederacy along with their Enfields in use, or what type slings they may have had leftover in inventory. It is pure conjecture. As students of history and of the Civil War P 53 Enfield we attempt to reach conclusions based on the available records of the time and what can be observed in period "field" photographs. Hence, we are somewhat at a loss

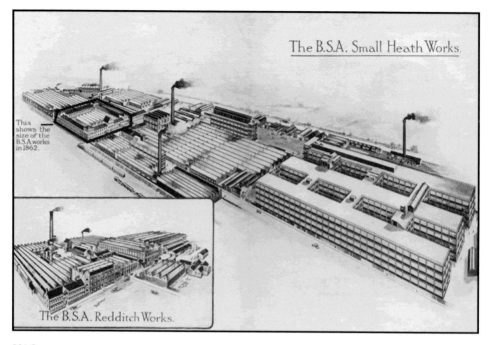

BSA Co

A correct buff white leather P53 rifle musket sling. (Courtesy of Craig L Barry)

here. British military records reveal that the "loose leather thong/sliding keeper" sling were used pre-U.S. Civil War on their Brown Bess musket and post-Civil War on their Martini-Henry and SMLE Mk I military rifles. The UK companies which make reproductions for British Military (re)enactors seem to be of one accord on this point as well. In terms of what was in use there during the U.S. Civil War period, as cited in the book *Arms and Equipment of the British Army 1866*, known alternately as "Petrie" (as he was the illustrator), plates XV and XVI show two slings in use by the British infantry, one in black for rifle regiments, and the other in "buff leather" made for rifle-muskets. The rifle musket sling is described as having one fixed leather keeper at the base (not a loose leather thong), a sliding keeper at the top and being fastened with a brass buckle. This all seems clear enough. Five years later the sling has apparently been changed back to old type, and the new description reads "20 November 1871 Musquet Slings. Having lower end when passed through guard swivel fastened by a white horse-hide thong instead of a brass buckle." See *Arms and Equipment of the British Army 1866* edited by John Walker, Greenhill books, 1986, p. 49. Also Ian Skennerton, *List of Changes of British War Material in Relation to Edged Weapons, Firearms and Associated Ammunition and Accoutrements 1860-1886* (1980), p. 67.

Incidentally, the change in British sling design back to leather thong tied with sliding keepers would happen just in time for the 1871 Martini-Henry rifles, and those rifles are widely found in period (Zulu war-era) photographs with this type of sling. There are no known images from 1861 to 1865 where a loose-leather thong tied at the bottom sling can be identified.

Conclusion
What Lessons Were Learned?

While much of this has been covered in detail elsewhere, it bears a final summation here. As the Industrial Revolution evolved it ushered in the efficiency gains of manufacturing by machine beginning with the textile trade in the 18th century. One of the last of the traditional trades to be affected was the military gun and leather trade. And the era of hand-made commercial small arms in England was quickly coming to a close as well. [1] The English system of military supply was one of the last industries to be impacted. The Birmingham Small Arms Trade (and the London gun-makers) recognized the threat of the new Ordnance Department strategy of manufacturing military arms in-house, but largely ignored it in favor of their time honored system of setting-up finished guns from hand manufactured piece work performed by independent craftsmen. [2]

The secession of the Southern states from the Union and the resulting Civil War was an immediate economic boon for the commercial military suppliers in Birmingham and London. Suddenly small arms of every description were in short supply, and it was a seller's market. The Southern buyers—representing either the Confederate government, speculators or individual states—acted quickly to tie up most of the current (and future) production capacity of the larger London gun-makers. [3] The CS buyers then moved on to Birmingham, which would also supply the Union with Enfield rifles in large quantity. Birmingham enjoyed a much greater production capacity, and manufactured more than 70% of the total number of commercial Enfield rifles produced for the U.S. Civil War. [4] The contract terms were often generous and times were good once again. Unfortunately, the U.S. Civil War contracts only prolonged the inevitable, and when the war ended so did the large scale commercial military contracts with the English gun trade. [5] It turned out that the late-war Confederate contracts were the last large orders that many in the gun trade would ever see. [6]

The needs of the fledgling Confederate government to field an army of the necessary scale to win their fight for independence did not begin and end with the gun trade, though. During the first two years of the war, up until February 1863, some 34,655 knapsacks, 34,731 sets of accoutrements, 81,406 bayonet scabbards, 40,240 gun slings and 650 sergeant's accoutrements all costing the Confederate Government £54,873 16s 3d were imported from Great Britain. With some 8,000 successful runs into Southern ports bringing in this vitally needed war materiel from England; with around 84% of over 2,000 runs into North Carolina and South Carolina ports from mid-1861 to February 1865 being a success. Entire companies and regiments received English Enfield long rifles.

British accoutrements, mess kits, and knapsacks, including:

38th Georgia
39th Georgia
45th Georgia
61st Georgia
4th Florida
10th Mississippi
8th Louisiana
2nd South Carolina
5th South Carolina
26th South Carolina
37th North Carolina
1st Florida

Those imports do not include the vast amounts of leather and fittings imported to copy the British equipment from the middle of the war onwards. These items were desperately needed by the agrarian Southern States while the Confederate government got their own arsenals and clothing factories up to speed. The amounts of British imported arms and accoutrements by Huse and Anderson that ran the Union blockade equipped tens of thousands of Confederate troops during the first two years of the war. We know that if they had not succeeded, the U.S. Civil War would have likely been a short-lived conflict.

Finally, the impact on the British economy proved far-reaching. There was a major misunderstanding among English investors concerning the assumption that the U.S. government had to make good on CS financial obligations if the Confederacy ultimately failed. After all, they were all Americans, right? Aren't the two sides now a band of brothers and reunited once again? However, the U.S. government once reunited with the former Confederate states had no such intentions towards honoring any of the Confederate debts, or releasing the cotton that was used as collateral on the Erlanger bonds. Fortunes quickly made were quickly lost. What

CS soldier.

followed in England (and Europe) was a series of recessions and in the mid-1870s, bank failures on an alarming scale. There were, of course, many economic reasons such as free trade restrictions and tariffs unrelated to the U.S. Civil War. However, in the post-reconstruction United States of America rapid economic development fueled the evolving modern industrial economy while settlement of the Western U.S. opened up new markets for goods and services. By 1890, the manufacturing output of the United States surpassed Britain for the first time. [7]

APPENDICES

APPENDIX A:
The Numbers Game

B irmingham gun maker John D. Goodman (Cooper & Goodman) provides some eye-popping figures in his report on the state of the Birmingham Gun Trade as presented to the British Association for the Advancement of Science in September 1865, and later to Parliament. Goodman states in his report on the Birmingham Gun Trade that:

> From the proof house returns I obtain the following numbers, showing the extent of the supply of arms from this country to America:
>
> Birmingham supplied...733,403
> London supplied.........344,802

Some explanation of what these figures represent is in order and is provided. Goodman offers that:

> The effect of the American war on the gun trade of Birmingham will be shown by the following monthly table, commencing with October, 1861, the earliest date at which a separate classification is given of military barrels. The attack at Charleston on Fort Sumter commenced on the 12th April, 1861, and the first orders for arms reached Birmingham on the following 9th May. We can only judge of the number made in 1861, previous to October, by the fact that the number of plain iron barrels, including all descriptions, increased from 13,445 in January to 36,275 in September, after which date the number of military barrels is separately given. [1]

MILITARY BARRELS PROVED AT THE BIRMINGHAM PROOF-HOUSE.

	1861	1862	1863	1864
JAN	13,445	16,573	40,206	2,527
FEB	N/R	23,632	38,706	2,704
MAR	N/R	17,643	11,025	3,660
APR	N/R	12,983	13,729	1,389
MAY	N/R	20,189	13,419	1,893
JUN	N/R	19,026	13,669	4,010
JUL	N/R	29,307	24,534	3,720
AUG	N/R	37,644	17,078	4,946
SEP	36,275	46,439	6,715	4,955
OCT	32,348	60,345	5,454	4,116
NOV	28,693	48,758	5,307	3,937
DEC	29,828	54,507	10,226	4,385
TOTAL	142,819	388,264	210,078	42,242

NR = not recorded

Although the chart tracks only Birmingham output, the production statistics are immediately revealing of the month-to-month "feast or famine" aspect of the commercial gun trade. Some of the variation is impacted by political events. Goodman elaborates on that as follows:

> An important falling-off in the number will be observed in January, 1862. This is explained by the occurrence of the Trent Affair, which led to the Order in Council, laying an embargo on the export of arms, issued on the 4th of December, 1861. This embargo was removed early in 1862, and we therefore find the trade again actively employed throughout 1862, until in October of that year the barrels proved in Birmingham alone, in addition to a very large number supplied to the London trade, which would be proved in the London Proof house, reached the unprecedented number of 60,345. These barrels would be made up into rifles during the following month. This number is altogether unequalled in the history of the trade…the demand for the Northern States suddenly ceased in September, 1863. Without notice the orders were withdrawn, as at that time the manufactories at Springfield and elsewhere in the United States were found sufficient to supply their wants. The smaller numbers made subsequently must have found their way to the Confederate States. We thus find that during the four years the number of military arms made in Birmingham amounted to 783,403; of these something less than 50,000 were shipped to other countries, leaving 733,403 for America. The London trade during the same period supplied 344,802 — making a total of 1,078,205. [2]

At first glance, the highlighted figure of "…less than 50,000 shipped to other countries" seems strangely understated, given the likely demand for Enfield rifles as a result of the worldwide political upheaval of the 1860s. For example, there were wars going on in South America (Triple Alliance) which were conducted on a fairly large scale, and involved British interests. There are period images of a South American soldier holding an Enfield long rifle with a white buff leather English buckle-type sling. There were also wars in Italy (Garibaldi), China (2nd Opium War), New Zealand (Maori), Austria, Prussia (territorial), and so on. The market for English commercial military arms ought to have been brisk. We should keep in mind that Belgium was producing Enfield rifle clones by the hundreds of thousands, and they cost 20% less than the same rifle from the English Gun Trade.

A closer look at Goodman's London and Birmingham totals "sent to America" (1,078,205) contradicts figures generally agreed upon by most historians that estimate U.S. and CS government Enfield rifle purchases at 800,000 (give or take), with about 400,000 going to each side. In fact, we know the U.S. purchases are 428,292 if the official records (ORs) are to be trusted. [3] *Ipso facto*, was the huge balance (649,913) made up of Confederate purchases? According to historian James Whisker, the problem is that the "paucity of surviving Confederate records makes an accurate number of CS imports from England difficult to determine." Another historian arrives at "…a figure greater than 400,000" from examining the shipping manifests of blockade runners alone. The use of shipping manifests is problematic for several reasons. First, they are seldom complete records, and additionally, the documentation varies from the different ports. According to C. Lon Webster III (*Entrepot* 2009), "Charleston invoices are particularly problematical. This is because for one reason or another the Charleston manifests were often much more generic than the Wilmington manifests, and there is no corresponding Wayne ledger to tell us anything further. Through December 1864 most of Caleb Huse's Enfield purchases came in through Charleston. [4]

Some discussion here is in order. It is agreed that an exact total number of Enfields in CS hands is not known down to the last rifle, but an idea as to some order of magnitude here is what we do have. According to the *Official Records of the War of Rebellion* (a.k.a. "ORs") as of December 1862, J. Gorgas provides a summary abstract to Secretary of War Seddon of purchases made by Caleb Huse as follows: "131,129 stands of arms consisting of 70,980 long Enfield rifles, 9,715 short Enfield rifles, 354 carbine Enfield rifles, 27,000 Austrian rifles, 21,040 British muskets, 20 small bore Enfield, 2,020 Brunswick rifles. There were also 23,000 Enfield rifles in London awaiting shipment…[.]" [5] In terms of long and short Enfield rifles, this would be 80,695 currently in Confederate hands. Later correspondence from Gorgas (again to Secretary of War James Seddon) in November 1863 states that "…the supply of small arms on hand has been steadily increasing despite the losses at Vicksburg, Port Hudson and

Gettysburg of 75,000 stands of arms." In the section of his report labeled "*IMPORTATION*," Gorgas states that from late 1862 through late September 1863, 113,504 additional small arms were imported. It is likely at least half of these were Austrian rifles, if the shipping manifests are to be trusted. Therefore the ORs show the total number of Enfield rifles (more or less) in Confederate government hands at or around 137,447 as of September 1863. [6]

September 1863 is a key date, because it is also the date given by Goodman when all Union small arms contracts with the English Gun Trade were suddenly cancelled. The remaining Birmingham production of 69,944 from the rest of 1863 and all of 1864 is what Goodman opines "must have found its way to the Southern states." Indeed, from the shipping manifests there is documented and verifiable receipt of 45,340 Enfield rifles that arrived in the port of Wilmington between July 1863 and December 1864. The number was probably larger, as not all shipments of arms were so listed. Of course, the Union blockade was also becoming more effective at intercepting shipments as the Civil War went on as well. Roughly 600 cases of Enfields came into Charleston after April 1863. Assuming the standard 20 rifles per case, there are another 12,000 documented Enfield rifles from April 1863 through the end of 1864. The Gulf ports and Trans-Mississippi received another (perhaps) 20,000. [7] To summarize, adding up the ballpark numbers from all these sources (the underlined figures), we can account for 214,747 Enfield rifles in the hands of the Confederate government through January 1865, when the port of Wilmington, NC, was closed after the fall of Fort Fisher.

Analysis and Conclusions

The ballpark figure of **214,747** Enfield rifles gleaned from the Confederate records is well short of the **649,913** that John Goodman contends were sold to the South during the U.S. Civil War. So what happened to the all the hundreds of thousands of missing Enfields? To address the question of where all these rifles went, let's take a look at the factors affecting Confederate Government military supply logistics during the U.S. Civil War. Goodman's figure on the output of the gun trade (649,913) is simply the first step in a military procurement process called "production." Goodman bases his production figures on the number of barrels passing proof, which may or may not be exact, but it would be unwise to dismiss the figure as a total fabrication. Goodman was confident enough in the number to use it in his report to Parliament. There were penalties associated with the misrepresentation of figures to that audience. The next step is "procurement" both by Confederate authorities and private parties. While Caleb Huse and Gorgas imported impressive numbers of small arms for the Confederacy, individual Southern states and private ventures (speculators) on their own contracted for and imported even larger numbers on top of that. According to *King Cotton Diplomacy* (1931), these other sources "would successfully import over 270,000 additional stands of arms…mostly Enfield rifles." [8] The significant smuggling abilities of entrepreneurs circumvented Confederate government, state, and local controls in response to the demands of the wartime black market economy. For example, of the first Enfield rifles to arrive in the Confederacy aboard the *Bermuda*, there were those for the Confederate Government and the state of Georgia, and a substantial additional number were also brought in privately. These may have been listed in the portion of the shipping manifest under "cases of hardware" or some other non-sequitur. [9] Other than working backwards from step one (production) as we have done here, we have no way of arriving at a more precise number. Of course, the black market was based entirely on the prospect of quick profits and not record keeping. Consider the fact that the Confederates shipped commercially for the most part, and a portion of the cargo space was always reserved for the speculators and the black market.

The broader point here – which is backed up rather than contradicted by John Goodman of BSAT – is that the Confederate soldiers in the Southern armies appear to have had in hand a much greater number of Enfield rifles during the U.S. Civil War than most modern historians have acknowledged. In fact, there were times throughout the war when Confederate soldiers were better armed than their Union counterparts. One such instance was recorded in a letter home by Sgt Carlos W. Colby of Company G, 97th Illinois Infantry. He wrote about the capture of Fort Hindman (Arkansas) on January 12, 1863 as follows:

It was here all our men threw away their old guns and took Enfield rifles captured from the enemy…these guns were up to date English make. When the ordnance officer found we made the change he made a terrible kick, for he had no cartridges to fit the new guns and a lot of the old ones on hand that he had no use for, but the kick came to (sic) late, for we had the newer guns and the old ones had been turned over as captured property.

Colby would later put that captured Enfield to good use in the Siege of Vicksburg, where he was awarded a medal of honor for bravery. An additional number of Confederate Enfield rifles were captured when Vicksburg fell in July 1863. General Grant instructed his men still carrying imported Belgian smoothbore muskets to exchange them for the newly captured CS Enfield rifles. [10]

APPENDIX B
The Enfield Rifle

E verybody has heard of the Enfield rifle, which is in course of adoption by the service, as fast as stores for that purpose can be made; and everybody has heard almost fabulous accounts of the immense cost at which the gigantic government establishment where they are made has been founded and is carried on. Had our limits allow us to do so, we should have wished to have fully gone into the matter, and the manufacture of the rifle throughout, and to have described the various processes which it undergoes, and the wonderful machinery by which it is accomplished. This, however, we have not space for, but will at once proceed to describe the rifle itself, by the aid of a very carefully executed engraving, showing its various parts. It will, however, be well to premise that the rifle, the stock, and every part, is made and finished by steam machinery, that there are 719 different processes in its manufacture, that the number of hands employed is 1,250, and that 1,200 rifles per week can be made with ease. Thus, at the rate of one rifle every three minutes, are our forces being supplied with these deadly arms. The cost at which the Enfield factory for the manufacture of small arms has been established is as follows. The buildings alone cost no less than £91,618, and the machinery and stores, £117,845, making, with later additions, and exclusive, of course, of salaries, wages, &c, about £250,000. This, it must be owned, is a great outlay; but it has been wisely made, and the rifles turned out are not to be equalled by those of any other country.

The Enfield rifle is composed of sixty-three different parts, including all the screws and other minute portions. As we have not before given this information, we append a list of them in their proper order. The number of pieces in other rifles is nearly the same, so that this will serve as a general guide:

1 Stock
1 Barrel
1 Breech screw
1 Front sight
1 Bayonet
1 Locking ring
1 Locking ring screw
1 Bayonet stop screw
1 Lock plate
1 Hammer
1 Tumbler
1 Sear
1 Bridle
1 Swivel
1 Main spring
1 Sear spring
1 Tumbler screw
1 Sear spring screw
1 Sight bed
1 Sight leaf
1 Sight slide
1 Sight leaf top
1 Sight spring
1 Sight spring screw
1 Sight leaf screw
1 Sight axis pin
1 Nose cap

1 Nose cap screw
1 Ramrod
1 Ramrod stop
1 Ramrod spring
1 Ramrod spring pin
1 Band upper
1 Band screw upper
1 Band middle
1 Band lower
2 Band screws, middle and lower
3 Nuts for band screws
1 Swivel for upper band
1 Swivel for guard
1 Swivel screw for guard
1 Trigger guard
1 Trigger guard pin
3 Trigger guard screws
1 Trigger plate
1 Trigger
1 Trigger screw
2 Side cups (washers)
2 Side screws
1 Tang screw
1 Butt plate
2 Butt plate screws, large 2 Bridle and sear screws
1 Cone

Total = 63 pieces. [1]

NOTES
1. Frederick Llewellyn and William Jewitt, *Rifles And Volunteer Rifle Corps: Their Constitution, Arms, Drill Laws And Uniform* (London) 1860, p. 8.

Appendix C
The Mechanics Magazine:
Saturday, June 20, 1857 p. 584-5

THE MANUFACTURE OF SMALL ARMS

"An article in the *Times* of June 2nd (1857) on the above subject has elicited from Mr. Goodman, chairman of the Birmingham Small Arms Trade, a letter containing certain allegations, which have been replied to by Lieut-Col. Dixon, Superintendent of the Enfield Small Arms Factory. Mr. Goodman's statements are to the following effect: —

GOODMAN: "*That the weapon known as the Enfield rifle is emphatically a Birmingham weapon, modified from the original Minie* rifle in the workshop of Mr. Westley Richards; that a return, made up to the 31st'of March last, shows that from Birmingham 220,000 rifles have been received by the Government, and from Enfield not one; that the Birmingham manufacturers can scarcely owe anything to examples of superior workmanship received from Enfield when an Enfield-made gun (the production of the new establishment) has never been seen in Birmingham ; that the head viewer in Birmingham never visited the establishment at Enfield to see what is being done there, and it is not probable that any one of the sixty-four viewers under him ever did; that the enormous sum already expended at Enfield, and the high wages paid to secure the services of men taken from the workshops in Birmingham, render the attempt to compete with the Birmingham makers in the price of the gun utterly hopeless ; that before Enfield can produce a standard to afford an example, Enfield must first attain the step of making as good a gun as the Birmingham makers can make; and that he (Mr. Goodman) has not the slightest hesitation in promising that, whatever the standard may be to which Enfield in future may attain, Birmingham shall attain a still higher.*"

(DIXON): "*This system is one,*" says Lieut-Col. Dixon, "*which can only be pursued and successfully carried out by a proper condition of manufacture, where all is conducted under the supervision of one head, who watches the progress of every part from the forged to the finished state.*" And he asks, "*Would the Government have done either wisely or well in demanding from the gunmakers of Birmingham that they should accept the Government arm, and manufacture on a similar principle*" and adds, "*The arms manufacturers of Birmingham are utterly incapable of carrying out any system of this sort upon their present mode of manufacture; and the Government have consequently exercised only a just forbearance towards them in not insisting upon their acceptance of the Enfield-made arm as a model for them to follow.*"

"The London Armoury Company has been established to follow in the course pointed out by the Government, and to this company the Government have granted permission to borrow from the factory every means which can assist them in successfully competing with the Government factory. All the parts of arms, in every stage of manufacture, have been forwarded to the company to help them in their endeavours to turn out similar arms to those made at Enfield. Even Birmingham is taking hints from Enfield, and copies of letters received from Mr. Goodman himself are enclosed, in which he applies for assistance and information. Mr. Goodman has, on the part of the Birmingham contractors, thrown out a challenge to the Government which it is quite possible that they may accept; but I will only caution the authorities, who have still to depend for the supply of every pattern of arm (except the Enfield rifle) upon the arms manufacturers of this country, that not a single arm would be made by the trade — in fact, there would be an immediate suspension of work on the part of the men — if the principle of interchange were insisted upon, or even the same quality of work throughout the entire arm. In proof of this it may be here stated as a fact, that when it was desired lately to introduce the principle of interchange, as far as the sword, bayonets, and ramrods were* concerned, in the new pattern short rifles for rifle corps, the Government officers had to yield the point, even before the work had been put into the men's hands, solely on account of a representation made to the Small Arms Department that the difficulties in the way of executing the work on that principle amounted to an impossibility.* Why do not the Birmingham trade follow the example set by the London Armoury Company, and enrol themselves as a company, purchase machinery, and really, by legitimate means, try to beat the Government out of the field? This is open to them, and would be much more to their credit than engaging in a kind of desultory warfare, and making statements which are easily refuted." With reference to the assertion that the pattern of the Enfield rifle was originally the production of a Birmingham gunmaker, Col. Dixon gives the statement an unqualified denial. "*The arm in question,*" he says, "*was proposed by a committee of officers in 1852-3, and was accepted as the result of that committee. Several gunmakers were invited to send models of arms to the committee for trial, but none were found to possess all the different points which were laid down as essential for a military rifle. All the good points of the various arms submitted for trial were carefully considered by the committee, who finally proposed a pattern which has every right to be considered as emanating solely from the committee then sitting at Enfield, and has in consequence been called the Enfield rifle.*"

Upon this point we can only allow the conflicting statements to stand for the present.

NOTE:

Famous last words. Within a few years John Goodman would completely reverse his position on the superiority of Birmingham "handmade arms." In 1861, Goodman would form Birmingham Small Arms Co and begin work on a huge factory at Small Heath for the purpose of manufacturing military small arms by machinery.

Appendix D
British Arms And Accoutrements
As Issued To Confederate Ordnance Officers And Individual Units

From the CSR of Moses H. Wright, Captain of Ordnance Nashville, Tennessee

Invoice of Stores turned over 25th Day of November 1861 by Captain R.M. Cuyler Ordnance Officer C.S Arsenal, Macon, Georgia to M.H. Wright Ordnance Officer at Nashville TN

    816 Knapsacks and Straps
    816 Mess Tins & Covers
    1390 Pouches, 50 Rounds
    1266 Buff Pouch Belts
    1116 Buff Waist Belts
    1326 Buff Frogs
    896 Buff Cap Pockets
    1915 Buff Gun Slings
    816 Ball Bags & Bottles
    190 Oil Bottles
    350 Canteen Straps
    587 Pouches
    618 Ball Bags
    3039 Bayonet Scabbards

Confederate Navy Subject Files, Ordnance, December 10th 1861
Confederate States Navy Department
Richmond, December 10th 1861

Invoice for Ordnance Stores forwarded by Captain G. Minor per Steamer *Northampton*
To Lt R.H. Henderson, Confederate States Marine Corps

    1510 Cartridges for English Rifles with Caps

From the Complied Service Record of Colonel Leon Marks, 27th Louisiana Infantry
Received this 30th Day of April 1862

    152 Brunswick Rifles
    30 Bayonet Scabbards for Brunswick Rifles

Signed,
L. Marks, Colonel 27th Regiment L.A Volunteers

Organized at Camp Moore in April 1862, the 27th Louisiana regiment surrendered and was paroled at Vicksburg, Warren County, Mississippi on July 4, 1863.

Production of the Brunswick rifle began in March of 1838, and the first mass produced rifles were issued to a few specialized units in 1840. The Brunswick rifle developed a reputation for being difficult to load, but was fairly well received and remained in production for almost 50 years. The rifle was used in England and assorted colonies and outposts throughout the world. Several refinements were made to the design during its production life, and production of the rifle was finally discontinued in 1885.

From the CSR of Captain Lardner Gibbon, 2nd Military District South Carolina Ordnance Department

Invoice of Ordnance Stores turned over by Captain L. Gibbon, Ordnance Officer, Second Military District for transportation to Colonel Goodlett 22nd Regiment of South Carolina Volunteers in obedience to orders for supplies:

        80 Long Enfield Rifles
        80 Bayonets
        80 Gun Slings
        24 Cones (extra)
         8 Screwdrivers
         3 Bullet Molds
        80 Cartridge Boxes
        80 Cartridge Box Belts
        80 Cap Boxes
        80 Waist Belts
        80 Oil Cans
        80 Frogs

> Signed,
> L. Gibbon, Captain, Ordnance Officer
> Charleston S.C.
> May 12th 1862

The first duty for the 22nd SCVI was at Charleston, SC, in the defense of the city. Their first engagement was at Secessionville, on James Island, South Carolina, at Ft. Lamar on June 16, 1862, just over a month after receiving these British arms and accoutrements.

CSR of Captain O.F. West, Co, A, 9th Battalion Mississippi Sharpshooters

Received at Corinth, Mississippi, May 26th 1862

        125 Enfield Rifles and Bayonets with Equipments
        125 Cartridge Boxes
        125 Cartridge Box Belts
        125 Shoulder Straps
        125 Bayonet Scabbards
        125 Cap Boxes
     12,000 Enfield Cartridges
     13,000 Caps
        125 Gun Slings

The 9th Battalion Mississippi Sharpshooters was formed in May 1862 with three companies and was with the Chalmer's/Tucker Brigade the entire war.

From the CSR of E.B.D. Riley, Ordnance Officer of Polk's, Hardee's and Cheatham's Corps, Army of Tennessee
Received June 1862 from Charleston Arsenal the following Ordnance and Ordnance Stores viz:

    264 Bayonet Scabbards
    388 Bullet Pouches (Buff)
      11 Frogs for Enfield Rifle Sabres
    483 Oil Bottles
    800 Rifle Sabre Scabbards
    423 Cap Pouches

Signed,
Lt E.B.D. Riley, Ordnance Officer, Polk's Corps, Army of Tennessee

Received at Atlanta this 2nd Day of July 1862 from Lt Cunningham Ordnance Officer Savannah, G.A the following Ordnance and Ordnance Stores viz:

    68 Cases Enfield Rifles

Signed,
Lt E.B.D. Riley, Ordnance Officer, Polk's Corps, A.O.T

From the CSR of Lt. Brailsford, Captain, 1ˢᵗ Battalion Georgia Cavalry

    June 5ᵗʰ 1862
    73 Ball Bags

From the CSR of O.C. Hopkins, Captain, 1ˢᵗ Battalion Georgia Cavalry
July 10th 1862 (at Camp Penn as part of 1st Battalion, Georgia Cavalry)

    20 English Sabers and Belts

Aug. 26th 1862

17 English Sabers and Belts

The 1ˢᵗ Georgia Cavalry was first organized with five companies during the late fall of 1861, composed of men who had enlisted for 6 months' service. Reorganized after the term of enlistment had expired, the 1ˢᵗ Battalion served along the Georgia coast until January 1863, then merged into the 5ᵗʰ Georgia Cavalry.

From the CSR of Maj. Robert Anderson, Commanding Officer of 1st Battalion, Georgia Sharpshooters
Received at Savannah GA this nineteenth Day of August 1862 from Lt Cunningham Ordnance Officer, Savannah, Georgia, the following Ordnance and Ordnance Stores viz:

    20 Enfield Rifles & Bayonets
    20 Bayonet Scabbards
    339 Knapsacks
    259 Haversacks
    259 Canteens and Straps
    329 Cartridge Boxes
    329 Waist Belts
    329 Ball Bags

329 Shoulder Belts
329 Gun Slings
329 Frogs
329 Mess Tins and Covers
329 Sets Knapsack Boards
1200 Enfield Rifle Cartridges and Caps

Signed,
R. Anderson, Commanding Officer, 1st Battalion Sharpshooters

The battalion was only formed on August 15, 1862 and drew its arms and accoutrements four days later. The battalion was organized by Colonel Robert H. Anderson. It was mustered at Camp Anderson, south of Savannah, Georgia, on the Ogeechee River. The battalion was under departmental command of Gen. John Pemberton. The sharpshooters remained at Camp Anderson with no military activity, except for a review by Gen. P.G.T. Beauregard, who replaced Pemberton on October 27, 1862.

From the CSR of Colonel Charlton H. Way, 54th Georgia Infantry Regiment

Requisition for Ordnance and Ordnance Stores to be furnished to Colonel C.H. Way, commanding 54th GA Volunteers, August 23rd 1862

250 Knapsacks
250 Knapsacks and Boards "Sets"
Received of Lt Cunningham Ordnance Officer, Savannah, GA
The above Ordnance and Ordnance Stores in full of the above requisition

Signed
Charlton H. Way, Colonel Commanding

The 54th Georgia Infantry Regiment was organized at Savannah, Georgia, during the summer of 1862, and contained men recruited in the counties of Lamar, Appling, Harris, Muscogee, Bartow, Chatham, and Barrow. The unit moved to the Charleston area and was involved in numerous conflicts, including the fight at Battery Wagner. Later it was assigned to Mercer's and J.A. Smith's Brigade, Army of Tennessee. The 54th participated in the Atlanta Campaign, Hood's Tennessee operations, and the Battle of Bentonville. The regiment surrendered on April 26, 1865. Colonel Charlton H. Way, Lieutenant Colonel Morgan Rawls, and Major William H. Mann were in command.

From the CSR of Isadore P. Girardey, Military Storekeeper, Ordnance, Government Works, Augusta, Georgia

Received at Augusta Arsenal this Day 10th September 1862 from Lt Cunningham, Ordnance Officer, Savannah GA

1000 Knapsacks and Boards
1000 Bayonet Scabbards
1800 Pouches
1800 Ball Bags
1800 Waist Belts
1800 Frogs
3000 Gun Slings

Signed
I.P Girardey, MSK Augusta Arsenal

From the CSR's of the 10ᵀᴴ Mississippi Regiment, Army of Tennessee

Pvt. J.T. Tipton, Co A, Deserted Sept 24, 1862 Lost Enfield rifle and accoutrements complete & English Knapsack

Pvt. James H. Kerr, Co K, Deserted Oct 5, 1862 Lost Enfield rifle and accoutrements complete & English Knapsack

From the CSR of Captain W.S. Good, Acting Ordnance Officer Trans-Mississippi Department

Invoice of Ordnance and Ordnance Stores by Captain W.S. Good Acting Ordnance Officer to Major William H. Griffin, (21ˢᵗ Texas Infantry Battalion) on the 31ˢᵗ Day of December 1862.

> 200 Enfield Rifles
> 200 Bayonets
> 200 Gun Stoppers
> 10,000 Enfield Cartridges
> 3,000 Enfield percussion caps

William H. Griffin was commissioned a Confederate Lieutenant Colonel, commanding the 21ˢᵗ Texas Infantry Battalion on June 28, 1862.

On the night of Dec. 31, 1862 - the very day that the regiment was issued these British Enfield rifles and ammunition - Griffin and his infantrymen were assigned to attack Galveston Island at daylight the next morning, after crossing over on the new railroad right-of-way to the mainland. They then attacked the 42ⁿᵈ Massachusetts Regiment, then in garrison on Kuhn's Wharf, and 300 of them surrendered intact. At that time Col. Griffin was decorated for his "cool bravery while under fire."

From the CSR of Isadore P. Girardey, Military Storekeeper, Ordnance, Government Works, Augusta, Georgia

Invoice of Ordnance Stores Turned over by I.P. Girardey M.S.K., Ordnance, Government Works, Augusta, GA, for transportation to Richmond VA

> For Major Downer, Richmond VA

> 845 Knapsacks and Boards "English"
> April 22ⁿᵈ 1863

Signed I.P Girardey,
MSK Augusta Arsenal

From the CSR of Lt. E. Mazyck, an Ordnance Officer in the Charleston area

Invoice for Ordnance Stores turned over by Lt E. Mazyck for Transportation to Colonel P.C. Gaillard 27ᵗʰ South Carolina Infantry, January 27ᵗʰ 1864

> 20 Bayonet Scabbards (Enfield)
> 20 Bayonet Frogs
> 20 Cartridge Boxes
> 20 Waist Belts

Signed,
Lt E. Mazyck

In January 1864, the 27ᵗʰ South Carolina were stationed at Fort Sumter, Charleston, SC, before heading to Virginia in May '64 to join Lee's Army.

From the CSR of A.C. Jones, Inspector General of the District of Texas, New Mexico and Arizona.

Headquarters, District of Texas, New Mexico and Arizona
Inspector General's Office, Houston, March 4th 1864

"Arms and Ordnance Stores purchased by the Cotton Bureau from the cargo of the steamer Alice were delivered to Captain H.T. Scott, Ordnance Officer at this post and consist of the following articles:"

860 Enfield Rifles & Bayonets
840 English Muskets & Bayonets 1849

"The Enfield Rifles had all been issued before their arrival had been reported and were not inspected; though the Ordnance Officer informed me that they were in good condition."
The English muskets are of the Tower Pattern of 1849, large bore calibre.75. Buck and ball cartridges are preferred for them and issued with them."

Signed,
A.C. Jones, Inspector General

Ordnance report for issues to Co K, 1st Regiment Engineer Troops
April 8 1864
29 Enfield Rifles
34 Saber Bayonets
31 Bayonet Scabbards
34 Frogs [1]

Of particular importance to the Confederate defensive operations were the efforts of the Confederate Engineering Regiments, which for the first time in modern warfare were true combat engineers. The Confederate government created the 1st Regiment of Engineer Troops in 1863 and the 2nd Regiment of Engineer Troops in 1864.

From the CSR of Lt. J.T. Buck, who was an ordnance officer the whole war, working in Kentucky, Jackson MS, and lastly as the Ordnance officer of Chalmers Cavalry Division in North Mississippi,
May 26th 1864 - To Lt. Featherston Ordnance Officer, 1st Brigade (Slemons) at Columbus MS:

2 Enfield Rifles Cal .58
5000 Enfield Cartridges Cal .58
132 Enfield Cartridge Boxes
132 Enfield Cap Boxes
132 Enfield Waist Belts
132 Enfield Shoulder Straps

In 1864 this Brigade consisted of:
1st Cavalry Brigade - Colonel W. F. Slemons
2nd Arkansas Cavalry Regiment --- Colonel W. F. Slemons
3rd Mississippi Cavalry Regiment--- Colonel John McGuirk
5th Mississippi Cavalry Regiment -- Colonel James Z. George
7th Tennessee Cavalry Regiment --- Colonel William L. Duckworth

Mississippi Battery --- Captain J. M. McLendon
May 26th 1864 - To Lt. J.J. Hay Ordnance Officer, McCulloch's 2nd Brigade at Columbus MS:

>   1000 Enfield Cartridges
>   80 Enfield Rifles
>   87 Enfield Cartridge Boxes
>   68 Enfield Cap Boxes
>   79 Enfield Waist Belts
>   78 Enfield Shoulder Straps

>   In 1864 this Brigade consisted of:
>   Chalmers' Cavalry Division --- Brigadier General James R. Chalmers
>   2nd Cavalry Brigade - Colonel Robert McCulloch
>   1st Mississippi Partisan Ranger Regiment --- Lieutenant Colonel L. B. Hovis
>   18th Mississippi Cavalry Battalion --- Lieutenant Colonel Alexander H. Chalmers
>   19th Mississippi Cavalry Battalion --- Lieutenant Colonel William L. Duff
>   2nd Missouri Cavalry Regiment --- Colonel Robert McCulloch
>   Buckner (Mississippi) Battery --- Lieutenant H. C. Holt

For nearly two years Slemons served with Brigadier Gen. James R. Chalmers' cavalry division in northern Mississippi and Tennessee. In the summer of 1864 – not long after these British arms and accoutrements were issued – Col. Slemons, now in command of the brigade, joined General Sterling Price's invasion of Missouri.

Invoices of QM Stores shipped to the T.M.D. Department by Major J.B. Ferguson and Major J.F. Minter CS Army November/December 1864 (From the Ramsdell Microfilm Collection MF 209B, Center for American History, University of Texas, Austin, Texas)

>   London, November 30th 1864

>   5000 Long Enfield Rifles with Bayonets
>   Snap Caps
>   Muzzle Stoppers
>   Spare Nipples, 35 Shillings each

>   250 Bullet Moulds 8/6 each
>   300 Nipple Wrenches 1/6 each

>   Total £ 8,750.00
>   Commission £235.00

>   (Signed) Sinclair, Hamilton & Co

Invoice of Ordnance Stores purchased by Major Minter CS Army from Alex Ross & Co for shipment to the Trans-Mississippi Department
London, November 1864

>   3000 Bayonet Scabbards 1/4 each
>   Total £200.00

As can be noted from this relatively small sample from invoices and the CSRs of Confederate Officers and Ordnance Officers, British arms and accoutrements were issued in every part of the Confederacy from November 1861 until at least November 1864.

From The Compiled Service Records (CSRs)   U.S. National Archives, Record Group 109 (Fold3) and original invoices

1. Jackson, Harry, L. First Regiment Engineer Troops P.A.C.S, p29

A SPECIAL THANKS TO: Will MacDonald, Lee White, and Marc Averill

APPENDIX E:
Invoice
Major Anderson, 1st Georgia Sharpshooters

Original invoice for British accoutrements from Ordnance Officer, Savannah, GA, issued to Major Robert Anderson, 1st Battalion Georgia Sharpshooters. (Confederate Service Records)

Appendix F
From The Papers of Captain O. W. Edwards,
Military Storekeeper, Ordnance Store House, Richmond Arsenal

Ordnance Stores received from Fayetteville Arsenal and Armory, August 2nd 1862
220 Enfield Rifles and Sword Bayonets
680 Enfield Rifle Muskets and Bayonets

Ordnance Stores received from Fayetteville Arsenal and Armory August 18th 1862
720 Enfield Rifle Muskets
80 Enfield Rifles

Ordnance Stores sent to Knoxville TN for Gen. K. Smith, Sept, 17th 1862
115 Long Enfield Rifles
78 Short Enfield Rifles
60 British Muskets
175 Saber Bayonets and Frogs
75 Saber Bayonet Scabbards

Ordnance Stores sent to the 19th Battalion. Virginia Heavy Artillery, June 2nd 1863
166 English Knapsacks
166 Mess Tins and Covers

Ordnance Stores sent to 4th Virginia Heavy Artillery, June 23rd 1863
32 Short Enfield Rifles
32 Short Saber Bayonets
32 Saber Bayonet Scabbards
32 Frogs

Ordnance Stores sent to Gen. Wise, July 13th 1863
23 Knapsacks with Mess Tins and Covers
3 Saber Bayonets
11 Saber Bayonet Scabbards
13 Frogs

Wise's forces were attached to the division of Maj. Gen. Theophilus H. Holmes during the Seven Days Battles. For the rest of 1862 and 1863, he held various commands in North Carolina and Virginia. In 1864, Wise commanded a brigade in the Department of North Carolina & Southern Virginia. His brigade defended Petersburg and was credited with saving the city at the First Battle of Petersburg, and to an extent at the Second Battle of Petersburg.

Ordnance Stores sent to 1st Corps, ANV, April 20th 1864
1000 Enfield Rifles
50 Screwdrivers
1000 Cones
50 Wipers

Ordnance Stores sent to Richmond Arsenal, April 23rd 1864
Invoice of Ordnance and Ordnance Stores turned over by O.W. Edwards for Transportation to Captain James Dinwiddie, Richmond Arsenal.

3206 Ball Bags in 70 boxes, taken up as scrap leather.

Signed, O.W. Edwards
Military Storekeeper 23rd April 1864

Ordnance Stores sent to Field Train A.N.V., April 26th 1864
For transportation to Captain George Duffey, Ordnance Officer, Field Park, A.N.V., Gordonsville, Virginia

1000 Mess Tins and Covers complete to be sold to Officers only, at $1.50 each.

Ordnance Stores sent to Ordnance Officer, Atlanta GA, April 27th 1864

4000 Mess Tins

Ordnance Stores sent to 1st Corps, A.N.V., April 28th 1864

50 English Box Knapsacks

Ordnance Stores received from Macon Arsenal, June 16th 1864

6 Whitworth Rifles
12 Telescopic Sights
4 Whitworth Moulds
6 Gun Slings

Joseph Whitworth of Manchester, England, was commissioned by the War Department of the British government to design a replacement for the calibre .577-inch Pattern 1853 Enfield, whose shortcomings had been revealed during the Crimean War. The Whitworth rifle had a smaller bore of 0.451 inch (11 mm) which was hexagonal, fired an elongated hexagonal bullet, and had a faster rate of twist rifling [one turn in twenty inches] than the Enfield, and its performance during tests in 1859 was superior to the Enfield's in every way. The test was reported in The Times on 23 April as a great success. However, the new bore design was found to be prone to fouling, and it was four times more expensive to manufacture than the Enfield, so it was rejected by the British government. An unspecified number of Whitworth rifles were imported by the Confederate States which were used together with telescopic sights by sharpshooter units.

Ordnance Stores sent to Third Corps, Army of Northern Virginia, June 28th 1864

23 Enfield Rifles
100 Frogs
100 Bayonet Scabbards

From the *Compiled Service Records of O.W. Edwards,* Fold3
Special thanks to Will MacDonald

Appendix G:
Atlantic Trading Co, Ltd

During the early days of the U.S. Civil War, trade with England was conducted principally by agents of the Confederate States and a few well-known commission merchants. By 1862, a larger portion of supplies was sent by speculators on their own account, with several of them pooling their resources to charter a steamer and make up a cargo with full intent "…to go to America with liberty to run the blockade." Known blockade running companies included Fraser, Trenholm & Co (with subsidiary M. G. Klingender), Charles H. Read and Crenshaw & Co. of Liverpool, Alexander Collie of Manchester, the Anglo-Confederate Trading Company, Albion Trading Co, European Trading Co, Universal Trading Co, and the Mercantile Trading Co, all from London. [1]

One such scheme was the *Atlantic Trading Co Ltd*, a venture put together by S. Isaac, Campbell & Company of London, a firm which had been at that end of the business since the very beginning. The following is correspondence from the U.S. Minister to England, Charles F. Adams, to Secretary of State William Seward. It lends excellent insight into the potential profits available from running the Union blockade.

> Hon. William H. Seward,
> Secretary of State, Washington, D. C.
> London, April 8, 1864
> (Private and confidential)
>
> Sir:
> The business of blockade running appears to be carried on with uninterrupted activity. The present form of agreement is to run the inward cargo on account of the so-called Confederate government, on the condition of receiving cotton in exchange for it, or for bonds for the back trip. It is this plan which has probably contributed to revive the value of the Confederate loan.
>
> I transmit a printed copy of a new project of a joint stock company which has been sent to me anonymously, with the marginal annotations as you will find them. I beg to call your particular attention to the reference to open ports for a full supply of the finest descriptions of cotton. The names attached are those of persons heretofore well known as rebel agents or sympathizers. I have the honor to be, sir,
>
> Your Obedient Servant,
> Charles Francis Adams

> ATLANTIC TRADING COMPANY LIMITED.
> Capital £200,000, in £100 shares, with power of increasing to £500,000 Sterling.
> Prospectus.
> The Atlantic Trading Company Limited has been formed for the purpose of first class paddle-wheel steamers, of light draught, great speed, and an average capacity of 800 bales of cotton, which forms the basis of the business to be transacted, (blockade running). It is intended to employ the steamers in trading with ports in the Confederate States, and participating in the large profits attendant on this business.
>
> The practical experience in the trade enjoined by the promoters(*) affords a guarantee of success, and they are enabled to offer the additional advantage of trading with open ports, where a full supply of the finer descriptions of cotton is obtainable, for which the light draught of the steamers is peculiarly adapted. [2]

Image of paddle wheel steamer. This is the famous blockade runner Robert E. Lee. (Courtesy Library of Congress)

Arrangements are being perfected with C. J. McRae, Esq., agent of the Confederate States, to carry in merchandise, and to bring out on the return voyage full cargoes of cotton, in exchange for supplies, or for bonds of Confederate States cotton loan. The first steamer will be dispatched in April; the second and third in May; the fourth in June; and the fifth in July. The vessels are in the hands of builders of celebrity, the materials of best description, with all the modern improvements in the machinery and boilers which experience suggests, with a guaranteed speed, loaded, of eleven statute miles per hour.

The following sketch of account shows the amount of capital required and probable results.

Five paddle steamers	£125,000
Outfits	£ 10,000
Appropriations for purchase of cotton loan,bonds or [and] merchandise	£ 40,000
Reserved for additional steamers	£ 25,000
TOTAL	£ 200,000

Results of two successful trips.

8,000 bales of cotton, 450 pounds each, sold in Liverpool, to net 2 shillings per pound, free of all charges and commissions	£ 360,000
Freight earned by steamers between neutral port and Confederacy, say = £5,000 per voyage	£ 50,000
SUBTOTAL	£ 410,000
Less working expenses between neutral port and Confederacy	(£ 30,000)
TOTAL	£ 380,000

Allowing as above for only two successful trips of each vessel, the profits realized will amount to £ 180,000. This calculation, however, may be considered the least favorable one that should be taken. The life of vessels of the class to be employed by the confederacy may be computed as worth five trips each, with the following result:

2,000 bales of cotton, net in Liverpool	£ 900,000
Freight earned between neutral port and Confederacy	£ 125,000
GROSS TOTAL	£1,025,000
Less working expenses five steamers, each five trips between neutral port and Confederacy, 25 trips at £3,000	(£ 75,000)
Less Cost of steamers, outfit, merchandise, cotton loan, &c	(£ 200,000)
Total Net Profit	£ 750,000

Source: 38th Congress of the United States, Second Session, "Papers relating to Foreign Relations", Volume I (1864), p. 582

Appendix H
Alexander Ross & Co

The Bermondsey area of London was known for its leather tanneries. Beginning late in the 18th century, they supplied a third of all England's leather. Bermondsey tanners were firm believers in individual enterprise. Alexander Ross & Co was formed in 1760, and from 1829 onwards Alexander Ross' Leatherworks at Grange Mill Tannery grew to become the major supplier to the British War Department for saddles and leather accoutrements. [1] By the time of the outbreak of the American Civil War, the company was building up a reputation for quality and excellence with the British War Department that would eventually lead it to become the biggest supplier of accoutrements to the War Office in the 1880s. The firm would go on to supply millions of individual leather accoutrements, and between 1882 and 1887 supplied well over 1,500,000 separate articles for the British government, with over fifty different contracts, winning three times as much business as its nearest competitor.

All of the goods provided by the firm for the Confederacy were of the British sealed patterns, made (mostly) of the best quality leather and of the highest craftsmanship. (In times of shortage the best leather was reserved for the British War Dept – their main customer). From 1861-1864 A. Ross & Co supplied the Southern Confederacy with large amounts of leather accoutrements, including the waist belt, ball bag, cap pocket, pouch (Cartridge box), and knapsack, as well as British cavalry equipment, including buff carbine belts, saddles, and bulk leather. Confederate buyers Captain Caleb Huse and Major Edward Anderson made an early visit to A. Ross & Company upon their arrival in London in mid-1861. Anderson's first visit to the company was made on August 7, 1861, with Anderson writing: "Called with Huse on Ross & Co in Bermondsey and ordered leather and equipments of various descriptions." [2]

By August 1861, Anderson himself had made contracts with Ross & Co to supply accoutrements, knapsacks, and leather for the State of Georgia, as well as the main Confederate government. On September 24, 1861, Anderson visited Ross & Co to look over the orders placed for the Confederate government and Georgia; he wrote: "I examined the packages he had prepared to send forward for us and finding everything correct and in excellent order, we adjourned to his office where I requested him to make out his account-It amounted to over £10,000 & was reasonable for the articles which I had selected." [3] These £10,000 of goods were purchased for shipment aboard the steamer *Fingal* and invoiced through the commission house of S. Isaac, Campbell & Co. The cargo included many thousands of sets of accoutrements, which included the ball bag, pouch, cap pocket, frogs, waist belt, and bayonet scabbards, as well as other equipment that were needed by the Confederacy to keep her troops equipped for the coming struggle against a vastly armed and equipped Northern foe. Ross & Co would provide equipment and other supplies throughout the conflict. Late war contracts would include goods for the Trans-Mississippi Department, again for all types of war materiel, through their purchasing agent Major Joseph F. Minter.

A pricing document from the company to Minter reads:

Grange Mill, Bermondsey, October 26th 1864

Sir

We shall be happy to supply you with infantry, artillery and cavalry accoutrements as used by the British military.

CAVALRY ACCOUTREMENTS
Black Leather pouches 20 rounds
Buff Leather carbine belts with swivel and strap
Buff Leather cap pouches
Buff Leather waist belt 15/9 per set

Infantry Accoutrements
Black Leather pouches 50 rounds
Black Leather pouch belt
Black Leather ball bag with oil bottle
Black Leather cap pouch
Black Leather bayonet frog
Black Leather waist belt
Black Leather gun sling 16/9 per set

The whole of the above to be of the best quality
Your obedient servant
A. Ross & Co [4]

In one contract in November 1864, Ross & Co supplied the following items for Minter:

3000 Bayonet Scabbards,
   1 Round Pouch,
  30 sets of Horse Harness,
  52 Whips,
  30 Surcingle Butts,
150 Bridle Butts,
  42 Harness Backs,
106 Buff Hides,
  12 Hog Skins,
     Buckles and Blades.

Total £1,944.17s.3d [5]

The following article recounts a visit to the leather works of A. Ross & Co:

During recent years things have in many respects greatly altered with the soldier, and mostly for the better; but all the changes have not lessened his allegiance to leather. If we visit an establishment like that of Messrs. Alexander Ross & Co. army contractors, in Bermondsey, we shall soon convince ourselves of this. By the way a great lull in that industry has now given place to as marked an activity; for a large army contractor's workshop is like the pulse' of the nations, telling how the war-feeling rises or falls, or even the subtler changes of national temper — suspicion, jealousy, and the determination to be prepared. Free trade is observed in this department, and English contractors may be producing outfits for a foreign power. We cannot now do more than follow up some kinds of sheepskin; but it must not on that account be supposed that we are not fully alive to the claims of the heavier leathers in a military point of view. The soldier sits on a leather saddle, he uses a leather bucket, his belts and knapsack are of leather, and so is the scabbard of his sword or the rest of his carbine and of leather are the bags he carries his stable and other tools and often even his rations in. But here at Messrs. Ross & Co's., we must rigidly abide by our sheepskin, else our article would run to inordinate length.

First we see at a table a man engaged in work very similar to what we saw at Worcester. He takes a white skin, stretches it first one way, then the other, and clearly enough proceeds to cut gloves out of it. Having cut the "backs and fronts," he sets together all the little pieces, just as we had already seen, in preparation for the mould at the press; and when we ask him what kind of leather he is cutting, he tells us that it is "mock-buckskin" for soldiers' gloves. But a very little questioning brings out the fact that this "mock-buckskin" is simply sheepskin which has been wrought in a peculiar preparation of egg and cod oil, and afterwards whitened by a process peculiar to itself. These gloves are sent down to Woodstock that quaint, ancient Oxfordshire town where is still to be seen something of old world quiet, undisturbed by railway bustle — and there the gloves, consigned to a master glover, are given out to be sewn by the women of the district, and by-and-by reappear in London, to be seen in bundles at the great army stores in Pimlico, and later on the hands of our heroic defenders. Another piece of sheepskin, which the mounted soldier cannot well do without, is the shabraque. It is prepared in the same way as fur, and forms the covering over the saddle, adding not a little to the fine appearance of the cavalry. The Zouave leather leggings which are to be seen on some of the volunteers who still wear grey, as well as on some of the regiments of the line, are of tanned sheepskin; so are the basils and stable-bags for carrying tools and brushes, with which we can hardly presume our readers to be quite so familiar. [6]

In 1888, Alexander Ross & Co lost all their War Department contracts during a House of Lords inquiry into the "Sweating System" (this is where the modern term "sweatshop" derives). This was basically a system whereby people were forced to work long hours producing goods for low wages. This system and Ross' use of middle men began to lead to poor quality accoutrements being delivered to both the British Army and Navy, which led to the company being struck off the list of contractors. The Parliamentary debates of June 1888 included the following passages on why Ross & Co lost the contracts with both the British Army and the Navy:

He wanted to place the matter on the fairest possible ground, and, therefore, he would take the Government's own pet firm — the best firm on the list — and show how that firm did the work. He would take, too, not only the best firm dealing with the War Office, but the firm which dealt largely with other Departments of the Government — namely, Ross and Company, of Bermondsey. These were the words of the Judge Advocate General — They are now by far the largest contractors for supplying accoutrements to the Government. During the five years ending March, 1887, they have had 56 contracts and supplied 1,687,274 articles. The firm of Messrs Ross get by far the largest share of business from the Government — in fact, three times more than any other firm. This was only in regard to some portion of the contracts sent in, and referred simply to accoutrements. Messrs. Ross sent in an enormous amount of saddlery and other articles, and the contracts obtained by other firms were largely supplied by Messrs. Ross. The next largest contractors were the firm of Messrs Pulman, and it was in evidence that a large portion of the articles sent in by Messrs. Pulman were really supplied by Messrs. Ross. These two firms together supplied the Government at Woolwich with two-thirds of the whole of their requirements, and they did work not only for the War Office, but for the Post Office, the Colonies, and India. In regard to the Admiralty, a representative of Messrs. Ross was asked — Are they more particular at the Admiralty than they are here? No; the inspection is just the same. — They do not reject more there? No; the inspection is just about the same. They had the fact that this large firm sent in to Woolwich a large quantity of goods for the Public Service; and yet, in regard to many of those goods, they were furnished by middlemen, notwithstanding that there was a distinct rule at the War Office that the articles supplied ought to be only bought from the manufacturers, and not from the middlemen. He could not see why that rule had not been observed in this case, and he thought the facts he had mentioned proved that there was no great reason why the Government should go out of their way to select middlemen. But, while they were middlemen in regard to all manufactured articles, they were also sweaters, and sweaters of the very worst kind. There had been startling evidence recently given before a Committee in "another place." Evidence had been given in regard to the accoutrements supplied to the Army by three firms, and every one of the witnesses singled out Ross and Co. as the very worst sweaters in Bermondsey. John Thomas Morris, Army smith, said — The accoutrement business had come under his notice for the last 15 years. As secretary of the Saddlery Trade Society, he had seen the miserable results of the lowering of wages. He referred particularly to Ross and Co., of Grange Road, Bermondsey. The net result was bad work for the Government, hard work for the workers, and riches for the sweaters. John Correy, harness-maker, stated that the practice was for Government contractors to get estimates from sub-contractors, and then give out the work to those who made the lowest tender. Ross and Co. began to employ girls in their place, to whom they paid less than the sweaters received. Arnold Wright pointed out that Bermondsey, the headquarters of Messrs. Ross, the hours were from 6 a.m. to 10 p.m. He also declared that Messrs. Ross were the worst sweaters he was acquainted with. Other sweaters paid men 3s. 3d. for blocking and sewing 12 cartridge pouches for the Navy. It took three and a-half hours to make one. Ross had them made in his workshops for 1s. 9d. a dozen by women. The thread was inferior, because the workpeople had to buy it. The Government, as a rule, ought to be very careful how they gave out these contracts, and should make them only with the men who did the work. The Director of Contracts knew very well what he was doing, and that Government official himself said in his evidence — The specifications describe the very best sort of leather, and I think there is no doubt whatever that such a kind could not be purchased for the prices the Government pay. It came out in the evidence of Mr. Southey that at the time of the Crimean War the best kind of leather was supplied to the Government. Now, the Ordnance Department, in their specifications, describe the very best class of leather, but take it at a price at which no manufacturer could possibly sell it at a profit. Even sweaters would not oblige the Government out of pure patriotism. [7]

Despite losing their military contracts, the firm continued to remain in business, manufacturing saddle stirrups, spurs, and supplying bulk leather well into the 20th century. In 1901, A. Ross & Co became "Hepburn Gale and Ross" and employed a stamp "HGR" on much of its equipment it supplied during the Great War, and in 1920 the company became Barrow, Hepburn & Gale, which continued into the 1970s.

NOTES:

1. Burrow, T.J. *London: Armorial Bearings and Regalia*, Burrow Publishing Co (London) 1964, p. 44.
2. Hoole, S.W, *Confederate Foreign Agent, The European Diary of Major Edward C. Anderson,* Confederate Publishing Co, University of Alabama 1976, p. 43.
3. Ibid, p. 63.
4. The McRae Papers, South Carolina Confederate Relic Room & Museum, Columbia, SC. It is not known whether these accoutrements were delivered, but the fact they were being discussed at this late stage in the war shows that they were still required. Also note that the British infantry "Sgt's" 20 round pouch was being ordered for Confederate cavalry units.
5. Invoices of QM Stores shipped to the T.M.D Department by Major J.B Ferguson and Major J.F Minter CS Army October/November/1864 (From the Ramsdell Microfilm Collection MF 209B, Center for American History, University of Texas, Austin, Texas).
6. MacLeod, Norman (Editor), *Good Words Volume 19,* (London) 1878, p. 260.
7. *Hansard's Parliamentary Debates*, June 1888, Supply – Army Estimates, Volume 327 p 829-920.

Endnotes

INTRODUCTION

1. Johanna Schopenhauer, *Samtliche Schriften*, (All Writings) Frankfurt,, Germany (1830). See "Spinning the Web" City of Manchester, www.spinningtheweb.org.uk.
2. Arthur Walker, *The Rifle: Its Theory and Practice*, Privately Published, (London) 1864, p. 198.
3. John Walter, *The Rifle Story: An Illustrated History From 1776 to the Present Day*, Greenhill Books (London) 2006, p. 34.
4. Accounts and papers, by Great Britain Parliament and House of Commons, Vol XXXII, Published by Eyre & Spottiswoode, (London) July 1863, pp. 69–70.
5. BSA Company factory at Small Heath was operational by 1863, but the Birmingham gun makers kept turning out 2nd grade, handmade weapons for export the old way for another two years.
6. David Williams, *The Birmingham Gun Trade*, Tempus Publishing (London) 2004, pp. 78–79.
7. Birmingham Small Arms Trade Chairman John D Goodman estimated 1,078,205 military arms from Birmingham and London went to America during the US Civil War. See Appendix A "The Numbers Game."

CHAPTER ONE: BRITISH ARMS & ACCOUTREMENTS IN THE CONFEDERATE SERVICE

THE SNAKE "HOOK" WAIST BELT

1. Ian Skennerton, *List of Changes in British War Materials in Relation to Edged Weapons, Firearms and Associated Ammunition and Accoutrements*. Volumes 1-5, with index, self published (1979). Covering the period 1860 – 1920, pp. 118–228.
2. Martin Petrie, *Equipment of Infantry, Part V, Infantry, 1864*.Printed by the Secretary of State for War. Clowes & Sons (London), 1866, pp. 29, 130.
3. Pierre Turner,. *Soldiers Accoutrements of the British Army 1750 -1900*.The Crowwood Press (London, UK) 2008. P 43. Note: This belt appears to be vegetable tanned leather and has been enamelled.
4. *Official Records of the War of the Rebellion* Series IV Volume II, US Government Printing Office (Washington, DC), 1886. pp. 382–84.

THE 1856 - 57 PERCUSSION CAP POUCH

1. John Walter, *Equipment of Infantry* from: *The Arms & Equipment of the British Army 1866*, Greenhill Books (London) 1986. P.14–26, Walter edited this chapter out of his finished book.
2. *Military Percussion Arms*, from the *United Services Magazine*, Part Three (1841), p. 11.
3. *United Services Magazine (1847), Instructions for the preparation for the two grooved rifle*. P. 21.
4. *Military Illustrated Magazine 1987*, kindly supplied by Mr J.D. Spencer. The adoption of this pouch belt mounted cap pouch is undoubtedly from the Crimean War, where Russian units used it. This has to be where the British army got the idea.
5. *United Services Magazine, Military Percussion Arms*, Lucknow March 25th 1858.
6. Martin Petrie, *Strength, Composition and Organisation of the Army of Great Britain 1864-65*, by 14th Regiment Topographical Staff.Her Majesty's Stationary Office 1865 (London), 1866, p. 23-44.
7. The Museum of the Confederacy, Richmond, Virginia. *There were a total of 19 Davis' that served in the 37th N.C.*
8. *The McRae Papers, S. Isaac Campbell & Co Subseries* SCCRR& Museum, Columbia S.C.
9. Martin Petrie, *Equipment of Infantry, Topographical Staff, Part V, Infantry, 1864*, Printed by the Secretary of State for War (London) 1866, p. 46.

THE PATTERN 1861 BALL BAG

1. The Journal of the Royal United Service Institution, Volume IV, No XIV, 1859.
2. Ian Skennerton.. *List of Changes in British War Materials: 1860-1886*, Greenhill Books (London), pp. 43–44.
3. Compiled Service Records of Moses H. Wright, Captain of Ordnance, Nashville U.S National Archives NARA M331, Record Group 109, p. 753.
4. *The McRae Papers, S. Isaac Campbell & Co Subseries* SCCRR& Museum, Columbia S.C.
5. Compiled Service Record of Moses H. Wright, Captain of Ordnance, Nashville U.S National Archives NARA M331, Record Group 109, p. 753.
6. Invoice courtesy of C. Lon Webster.
7. *Compiled Service Records* of Col O. Edwards, Ordnance Store Keeper, Richmond Arsenal, Fold 3.

THE P1860 ZINC OIL BOTTLE

1. Ian *Skennerton,.List of Changes in British War Materials: 1860–1886,* Greenhill Books, (London), p.56.
2. *Circular Memorandum* addressed to the Infantry at Home and Abroad. General No 183 Arms–3 (1859) Horse Guards, SW., 23rd July 1859.
3. Martin Petrie, *Equipment of Infantry, compiled by Captain Martin Petrie, Topographical Staff, Part V, Infantry, 1864,* Printed by the Secretary of State for War, (London), 1866, p. 93.
4. *The McRae Papers, S. Isaac Campbell & Co Subseries* SCCRR& Museum, Columbia S.C.
5. Compiled Service Record of Moses H. Wright, Captain of Ordnance, Nashville U.S National Archives NARA M331, Record Group 109, p 753. (Fold 3)
6. Compiled Service Record of Richard Cuyler, Chief of Ordnance, CS Arsenal, Macon, G.A. U.S National Archives NARA M331, Record Group 109. (Fold 3)

THE PATTERN 1854 'FROG'

1. Martin Petrie, *Equipment of Infantry, Topographical Staff, Part V, Infantry, 1864,* Printed by the Secretary of State for War. (London) 1866, p.15.
2. Pierre Turner,*Soldiers Accoutrements of the British Army 1750 –1900,* The Crowwood Press (London) 2008, p. 24.
3. ibid Turner, p. 26.
4. Ibid Petrie, p. 126.
5. Alvaro de Miranda,,*Creative East London in Historical Perspective,* University of East London, www.uel. ac.uk/risingeast/archive07.

THE P1860 POUCH (CARTRIDGE BOX)

1. Ian Skennerton. *List of Changes in British War Materials: 1860–1886,* Greenhill Books, (London) 1977, p. 34.
2. Francis Wallace, "*Memorial of the Patriotism of Schuylkill County in the American Slaveholder Rebellion*", (Pottsville, PA) 1865, p. 54.
3. Stanley Hoole, *Confederate Foreign Agent: The European Diary of Major E.C. Anderson,* CS Publishing Co (Richmond, VA) 1976, pp. 27–28.
4. *Official Records of the War of Rebellion,* US War Department, Washington, DC, *Series IV Volume II* P 382–84.
5. The Journal of the Royal United Service Institution, volume IV, No XIV, 1859.
6. Martin Petrie, *Strength, Composition and Organisation of the Army of Great Britain 1864–65,* by 14th Regiment Topographical Staff. Her Majesty's Stationary Office (London) 1865, p 124. Note: Tins for the P60 pouches varied slightly. A surviving SIC&Co pouch tin measures: Length 6 ¾ ", Depth 3 1/8 ", Height 3", an original Ross & Co tin measures: Length 6 ¾", Depth 3 1/8", Height 3 1/8", another Ross & Co tin measures: Length 7", Depth 3", Height 3".
7. *Official Records of the War of Rebellion,* US War Department, Washington, DC, *Series IV Volume II,* pp. 382–84.

THE P 1856 KNAPSACK

1. Mike Chappell, *British Infantry Equipments 1808–1908,* Osprey Publishing (London) 1999, p 36.
2. *The McRae Papers, S. Isaac Campbell & Co Subseries* SCCRR& Museum, Columbia S.C.
3. Ibid McRae.
4. *The Compiled Service Records,* Fold3, From the CSR of Moses H. Wright, Captain of Ordnance Nashville, Tennessee.
5. Huse to Gorgas *Official Records of the Union and Confederate Navies, series 2 volume 2, p179.* These must have been knapsacks purchased through A Ross & Co as they contain 'boards'.
6. H799–1060 Letters received by the Confederate Secretary of War, RG 109, U.S National Archives.
7. Personal correspondence with Cody Mobley
8. *Official Records of the War of Rebellion,* US War Department, Washington, DC, *Series IV Volume II* P 382–84.
9. The Compiled Service Records of Captain O. W. Edwards, Military Storekeeper, Ordnance Store House, Richmond Arsenal, Fold 3.
10. Ibid.
11. Jackson, Harry, L. First Regiment Engineer Troops P.A.C.S, p29.

THE PATTERN 1854 MESS TINS AND COVERS

1. Pierre Turner, *Soldiers Accoutrements of the British Army 1750 –1900,* p20, Crowwood Press (London) 2008, pp. 88, 132.
2. Compiled Service Records of Col O. Edwards, Ordnance Store Keeper, Richmond Arsenal, Fold3.
3. Compiled Service Records of Confederate Officers, Fold3.
4. Ibid, Turner. p 22.

CONFEDERATE COPIES OF BRITISH ACCOUTREMENTS
1. *The McRae Papers, S. Isaac Campbell & Co Subseries* SCCRR& Museum, Columbia S.C.
2. *Confederate Citizens File, Business Papers,* Record Group 109, U.S National Archives, November 1862.
3. *Official Records of the War of the Rebellion, Series IV Volume II,* pp. 382–84.
4. *The McRae Papers, S. Isaac Campbell & Co Subseries* SCCRR& Museum, Columbia S.C.
5. Information provided by email correspondence between David Burt and Shannon Pritchard, Old South Antiques.
6. *The McRae Papers, S. Isaac Campbell & Co Subseries* SCCRR& Museum, Columbia S.C.

CHAPTER TWO: Early Confederate Purchases ???
1. Craig L Barry, David C Burt, *Supplier to the Confederacy S. Isaac Campbell & Co, London,* Bright Pen Publishing (London, UK) 2010, p. 27.
2. Stanley Hoole, *Confederate Foreign Agent: The European Diary of Major E.C. Anderson,* CS Publishing Co (Richmond, Va) 1976, p. 4. Other agents that arrived in England to purchase arms and equipment were Colonel John L. Peyton of the State of North Carolina and a Mr Tilton of the State of Louisiana. Tilton arrived with £300,000 from Louisiana Governor Thomas Overton Moore for the purchase of arms and equipment for the State according to Anderson. South Carolina is estimated at have had at least 2,000 P53 Enfields that had been purchased by the State by mid–1862. (SCCRR & Museum)
3. Ibid Hoole p. 43.
4. *The McRae Papers, S. Isaac Campbell & Co Subseries* SCCRR& Museum, Columbia S.C.
5. Ibid, Hoole p. 4.
6. *Official Records of the Union and Confederate Navies in the War of the Rebellion*, Series II, volume II, Mallory to Bulloch p65. To date a total of 19 extant examples of Confederate marked and numbered P–1858 Naval Rifles are known, along with a total of 34 Confederate numbered cutlass bayonets.
7. Ibid, Bulloch to Mallory, p. 86. All of these arms and equipment were to have been shipped on the warship Nashville, but she was unable to sail due to some damage she had received on the inbound journey. Instead most of it was transferred to the SS *Fingal.*
8. Ibid, Mallory to Bulloch, p. 95.
9. Ralph Donnelly, *The Confederate States Marine Corps,* University of Wisconsin Press (Madison, WI), 1989, p. 318.
10. *Official Records of the Union and C.S. Navies in the War of the Rebellion,* Series II, Volume III, p. 291.
11. Letter for sale at, Museum Quality Americana, a division of Cal Packard, LLC. Pickens refers to a man named "Glover" in this letter, and that he had bought "90 Muskets" in England. He must be one of the South Carolina purchasing agents based there.
12. Reports and Resolution of the General Assembly of the State of South Carolina, Columbia S.C. Charles P. Pelham State Printer 1863, pp. 219–222.
13. *Official Records of the Union and Confederate Navies in the War of the Rebellion,* Series I, volume I, Morse to Marchland, p. 227.
14. *Official Records of the War of the Rebellion* Series IV Volume I p. 895.
15. Ibid, Series II volume II p. 179.
16. *The McRae Papers,S. Isaac Campbell & Co Subseries* SCCRR& Museum, Columbia S.C. These items were on three separate invoices, dated February 17th, and March 10th& 20th 1862.
17. H753–1862 Letters received by the Confederate Secretary of War, RG 109, U.S National Archives.
18. Ibid, p. 63.
19. Letters received by the Confederate Secretary of War, Record Group 109, U.S National Archives.
20. *Official Records of the War of the Rebellion* Series IV Volume II pp. 382 –84.
21. *Stanley Hoole, Confederate Foreign Agent: The European Diary of Major E.C.Anderson,* CS Publishing Co (Richmond, VA) 1976, p. 43.
22. *The McRae Papers, S. Isaac Campbell & Co Subseries* SCCRR& Museum, Columbia S.C.
23. *Official Records of the War of Rebellion,* US War Department, Washington, DC, Series IV, Volume One, p. 539
24. Stephen R. Wise, *Lifeline of the Confederacy,* University of South Carolina Press, (Columbia, SC) 1988, p. 50.
25. George Williamson, *Old Greenock from the Earliest Times to the 19th Century,* published by Alexander Gardner (London), 1886, p. 150.
26. *Executive Documents of the House of Representatives, Thirty–eighth Congress, Volume One,* US Government Printing Office (Washington, DC) 1864, "Deposition of Clarence Yonge" p. 224.
27. Ibid, Wise p. 49–50.
28. House of Commons Papers Volume 62 published by the Parliament of Great Britain (London) 1864 p. 31. This contains correspondence between GB and the US about the *CSS Alabama.* The South African firm William Anderson & Saxon, Co of Cape Town was the registered owner of the bark *Saxon.* They were

transplanted English merchants who owned mail ships that ran between Cape Town and London, however during the US Civil War they were obviously a front for Sinclair, Hamilton and the CS Government.

29. John D. Bennett, *The London Confederates*, McFarland Publishing (West Jefferson, NC) 2007, p. 56.

30. *The London Gazette September 14, 1866* provides a lengthy account on the particulars of the voluntary liquidation of LA Co. Val Forgett (owner of Navy Arms and a well-known collector of Kerr revolvers) noted, "*The Confederacy's European bankers did in fact pay all debts, even though it meant financial ruin for them. It appears the liquidation was actually tied to a larger issue with British banks at the time having liquidity issues. Rather than try and sell the company as an ongoing concern, it is believed that the shareholders merely liquidated the assets to shore up these other financial obligations."* See also: Huse, Caleb, *Supplies for the Confederate Army*, Rogers Publishing (Boston) 1904, p. 22.

31. Lloyd's *Register of British and Foreign Shipping*, Volume 2, p. 807. Note: Archibald's son, John James Hamilton is listed as manager for SH&C beginning in 1881.

CHAPTER THREE: The English Gun Trade

1. Official Records of the War of Rebellion. US Government Printing Office, Washington, DC, 1904. Series. 1, vol. 5, pt. 1, pp. 1081 – 82.

2. Great Britain Parliamentary Papers Volume 18 (1854) "Report from the Select Committee on the Cheapest, Most Expeditious and Most Efficient Means of Providing Small Arms for Her Majesty's Service." Also known as "Report of the Committee on the Machinery of the United States."

3. Goodman, John D. "On the Progress of Small Arms Manufacture", Journal of the Royal Statistical Society, Volume 28, 1865, p.498. This paper is later included as part of S. Timmins (ed) Resources, Products Industrial History Birmingham Midland Hardware District: Series Reports, collected Local Industries Committee British Association Birmingham (1866). See also The Enfield Arsenal in Theory and History in the Economic Journal, Vol 78 # 12 (Dec 1968) The War Department was aware that while strikes in the Gun Trade were somewhat uncommon, they did seem to coincide with issuance of large Ordnance contracts.

4. Most of the gun making machinery used by LACo was purchased from Ames Mfg in Massachusetts, and ditto for the Royal Small Arms Manufactory.

5. Dr. C.H. Roads, British Soldiers Firearms 1850–1864: From Smoothbore to Smallbore, Published by Herbert Jenkins Ltd (London) 1964, p84–5. See also: Walter, John, The Rifle Story: An Illustrated History, Greenhill Books (London), 2006, p. 34. It appears that the majority of this information on the initial contracts with Birmingham gun–makers and sub–contractors comes from detailed records reprinted from the hand written notes of G.C. Holden, Assistant Superintendent of Stores, initially written in 1866.

6. Ibid, Roads p. 87. He states fourteen new firms were added to the first four and other sources state sixteen, but do not name any of them. Chairman John Goodman, states there were twenty firms in BSAT by 1865, but also fails to name them. Oddly, although principally known as a London gun–maker Thomas Potts had a Birmingham operation on Shadwell Street which was somehow involved in the early formation of BSAT. Potts made a small fortune on his interest in it and defenestrated to New Zealand in 1854 where he became a famous ornithologist. So who were the twenty firms given by John Goodman in his 1865 report to Parliament? The other two are most likely William Tranter, W & C Scott (a distinct firm not related to W Scott & Sons), primarily pistol makers not involved greatly in the p53 Enfield long rifle contracts.

7. John D. Goodman, John D. In a report to Parliament on the Gun Trade from 1865. See Timmins, Samuel (Ed), Birmingham and the Midlands Hardware District (1866), p. 391.

8. Ibid, Goodman p. 393. Feel free to disagree if you like.

9. Military barrel manufacture was the first part of the gun trade to mechanize. Barrel making machinery was invented in the early 1810s (in Birmingham) and in wide use by the English gun–makers by 1850. The United Service Journal, Volume II, Number 1, December 1850, p. 11 reports "The machinery for rolling barrels was invented by a man now dead, whose patent expired before he could succeed in introducing the plan. Since then, Mr. Clyde has perfected the arrangement, and has been able to make it work well, He is now the largest manufacturer in Birmingham. He says that the government has ordered but little work this year as some change of model is said to be in contemplation;(Pattern of 1851—Ed) last year, however, he had work enough to keep three pair of rollers at work in Birmingham, turning out an average of three hundred barrels a day. Other rollers in the neighborhood were also employed. Stocking machines have been made and put up more than once in Birmingham, but the stackers have always succeeded in preventing their adoption."

10. Virtually all of the Enfield rifles from Birmingham Small Arms Trade (as well as some from the London gun–maker Barnett) sent to America were marked "Tower" despite never passing any inspection with gauges at the Tower. Why? Obviously, the War Department was not paying their inspectors at the Tower to gauge commercial arms being sold overseas to the US and CS, and couldn't care less if the commercial makers future engraved the word "Tower" on the lock plate so that they could charge more to a foreign government. No Civil War-era

Enfield rifles purchased from Birmingham Small Arms Trade are considered class one/parts interchangeable.

11. Thomas H. Hansard, Official Reports of Parliamentary Debates, Vol 4, # 176, Published by Cornelius Buck, London, (1859) pp. 1975–83.

12. Ibid, Goodman p. 404, comparing the Government facility at Enfield to the Birmingham system, he hypothesized that; "By this means great saving has been effected in the outlay for machinery which would otherwise have been required, without prejudice to the quality of the work, as it all passes through the finishing processes in the factory." The Report to Parliament from the Select Committee on Small Arms

13. Ibid, Goodman p. 429.

14. Norman Cheevers, MD, A Treatise of Removable Causes of Death in Europe and India, Bishops College Press, Calcutta (1852), p. 220. Note: These "Minie Rifles" would be the Enfield pattern of 1851, the direct predecessor of the P–53.

15. DeWitt Bailey, English Gunmakers; Birmingham and Provincial Trade in the 18th and 19th Century, Arco Publishing (New York) 1978, p. 45. See also Greener, W. The Science of Gunnery, (London) (1846), p. 188,William Greener is not known to be excessively complimentary and states the firm of Moore & Harris "…can make a gun against any maker in the world, barring none."

16. This was not only the prevailing attitude in Birmingham. At the Liege gun–making complex in Belgium the conventional wisdom was that "…anything made by machine can better be made by hand." In 1858, Royal Small Arms Factory turned out 26,739 and then doubled that amount in 1859.

17. Ibid, Hansard Parliamentary Debates, p. 1937. See also The Civil Engineer and Architects Journal, Volume 31 (1868) p. 23. Additionally, the following quote is from James Burton, former Supt of Royal Small Arms Manufactory dated November 8, 1860:"The cost of the Enfield Rifle as made in the Govt. Manufactory at Enfield, England is about $12.00 [U.S.] each, with the advantage of cheaper materials, and manufacture on a large scale of 2,000 per week."$12.00 [US] at the currency conversion rate in 1860 was about £2 5s. The letter is part of the Col. James Henry Burton Papers (Manuscript Group 117) in the Manuscripts and Archives at Sterling Memorial Library at Yale University.

18. Samuel Buckley was a Banker, Edward Gem was listed as a Merchant in addition to serving as Chairman of the West Birmingham Canal & Railroad, and Sir John Ratcliff was a politician, three times elected Mayor of Birmingham.

19. Official Records of the Union and Confederate Navies in the War of Rebellion, Series I, Vol 6, US Government Printing Office, 1897 (Washington, DC) p. 448. The letter referenced was dated October 26, 1861 and goes on to state that "The Confederates have been very active in this country and (they) have all the armories here (London) at work for them…as well as what they are getting at Birmingham."

20. J.W. Hartley, Marcellus Hartley: A Brief Memoir, privately published (New York) 1903, pp. 30–38.

21. ARMY NAVY JOURNAL, August 26, 1865 (New York) Volume 3 # 1, p. 31.

22. David Williams, The Birmingham Gun Trade, Tempus Publishing (London) 2004, p. 87. The statement is also found quoted on the BBC website on the Birmingham's Historic Gun Trade again by David Williams, their website iswww.bbc.co.uk/birmingham/content/articles. Williams correctly observes that in the gun trade the good times never last for long.

23. Ibid, Goodman. He states "from the Proof–house returns I obtain the following numbers, showing the extent of the supply of arms from this country to America— Birmingham supplied 682,534…making the total number of Enfield rifles sent to America of 1,027,336." In the US House of Representatives, 40th Congressional Edition of the US House of Representatives, Volume 12: Ordnance Department (p. 285) is a letter dated October 20, 1862 from the War Department to Naylor & Co which confirms an order for 200,000 Enfield rifles with deliveries to commence in December 1962. A letter dated November 4, 1862 in response from John Goodman of BSAT accepted the order at the terms specified, except for "strikes, accidents &c." Goodman states that entoto 682,534 Enfield rifles were sent to America from Birmingham, based on data from gun barrel proof. He adds that London gun–makers produced 344,802 which if so, totals over a million Enfield rifles sent to America during the US Civil War. The figure Goodman states does not included any Enfield rifles produced commercially for any other foreign countries. In the 1860s there were wars going on in South America, New Zealand, Italy, Japan, etc. Feel free to disagree with his figures if you like but as Chairman of Birmingham Small Arms Trade, John D. Goodman was considered to be the ultimate authority on the English gun trade.

24. As of 2011, Birmingham gun–maker Westley Richards who began making shot guns by hand in 1812 was still in business, as was Greener who began in 1829.

25. Ibid, Goodman. Note: Many of the same parties in the BSAT were also part owners of BSA Co. The primary shareholders were Joseph Wilson, Samuel Buckley, Isaac Hollis, Charles Playfair, Charles Pryse, Sir John Ratcliffe, Edward Gem, and J.F. Swinburn under the chairmanship of John Dent Goodman. More than a few familiar names appear here but BSA Co is a distinct business venture.

26. Ibid, Goodman p. 398.

27. Ibid Goodman p. 393, .577 caliber or gauge "25" was standard unless the contract specified gauge "24" or .58 caliber for some of the Union contracts.

28. The reason for not revealing the name of the Birmingham firm W. Scott & Sons as the owner of the saw mills in Italy is lost to history. The names of gun-making firms can be confusing at times. There were actually four different William Scotts working in the Birmingham Gun Quarter in the mid–19th century.

29. The following reference confirms BSAT member W. Scott as the principal owner of the Turin saw mills: "Since the closing of the Messrs W Scott & Sons gunstock factory the principle works at Turin are those of a Mr. Ferrato who employs more than 100 skilled workmen and is in a position to supply foreign governments on a large scale." Source: Reports from Her Majesty's Consuls on the Manufactures, Commerce &c of their Consular Districts Volume 20, Part III. Parliament of Great Britain, printed by Harrison & Sons, London (1877) p. 727.

30. Ibid, Goodman p. 393. Estimated 3,000 out of 3,920 employed were stockers, screwers or finishers.

31. The Popular Science Monthly, Volume 2, (London) 1873, pp. 580–582.

32. The Enfield Rifle, Chambers Journal, 16 April 1859, www.researchpress.uk.org

33. Ibid Goodman, p. 388, See also: CH Roads, British Soldiers Firearms 1850–1864.

34. Economic and Social History: A History of the County of Warwick: Volume 7 The City of Birmingham (1964), pp. 253–69.

35. William Greener, The Science of Gunnery, (London) 1846 p. 144. Except of course for barrels made by RSAF and LA Co.

36. H.J.Swinney, Gun Iron and Mild Steel, Muzzleblasts Online, Vol 4, # 3, July 1999. It is interesting to find that the US Armory at Springfield was getting iron for its gun barrels from the Black Country of England. Burton testified to this fact when he was applying for a patent for his barrel making apparatus.

37. The 8th edition of Encyclodpedia Britannica was published from 1853–1860 in 21 volumes, with 17,957 pages and 402 plates and a 239–page Index (published separately in 1861). This is from Volume 11 under "Gun-making." The entire section lends excellent insight into the processes in use in England during the years just before the US Civil War. The name of the author is not provided.

38. Paddy Griffith, , Battle Tactics of the Civil War, Yale University Press (New Haven, Connecticut) 1987, p. 78.

39. Samuel Griffiths,,Griffiths' guide to the iron trade of Great Britain . Published by Newton Abbot (Devon): 1871, p. 72 See also: Hackwood, Frederick William. Olden Wednesbury: its whims and ways: being some odd chapters in the history of the old town. Published by Ryder & Son (London) 1899, p. 37.

40. Ibid, Swinney, Note: Several years ago published a comparative analysis of a known sample of Marshall iron from London, of a sample from a Springfield rifle musket made between 1859 and 1861, and, as a control, one from a Whitney musket presumed to date from the 1830s and presumed to be made of American iron. With full–dress scientific methods, he was able to demonstrate that the London sample and the Springfield barrel were very much alike and of high quality, but the Whitney sample was quite different and of significantly lesser quality. Ibid, Encyclopedia Britannica.

41. Jim Westberg, "Muzzleloaders, Etc" www.muzzleloadersetc.com, see Overview of Locks.

42. J.E. & S.J. Gooding, Arms Collecting.com. Research Report #. 6. AN INDEX OF BRITISH GUN LOCK MAKERS

43. Karl Lippard,The Brazier Gunmaking Tradtion: London & Wolverhampton.www.karllippard.com

44. Clark, C.V. The Wolverhampton Gun Lock Makers. www.wolverhampton–gunlocks.fslife.co.uk.(2009).

45. William Greener, Gunnery in 1858: Being a Treatise on Rifles, Cannon, and Sporting Arms, Smith Elder & Co Publishers, (London),1858, p. 232

46. Wiley Sword, Firepower from Abroad: The Confederate Enfield, Mowbray Publications (Woonsocket, Rhode Island) 1986 p. 12. See also Beck, Tony, The Enfield Rifle Musket: The Southern Contract (2000), www.tcivilwarguns.com.

47. Stephen Wise, Lifeline of the Confederacy, University of South Carolina Press, (Columbia, SC), 1991, p, 51.

48. Ibid, Goodman.

49. Source: The London Review of Politics, Society, Literature, Art, & Science, Volume 9 (1862), p. 114.

50. The "halo effect" refers to the phenomenon of a cognitive bias where positive features in one product extend over to onto the broader brand. In this case, since most "best guns" like the sporting arms from Purdey, Holland, Manton, etc were made in London, the perception is that London gun–makers must categorically make better P53 as well.

51. Comments attributed to various Federal officers about the Enfield such as "…they are rough and tear the men's hands to pieces during the manual of arms" and complaints about "bayonets which did not fit" are taken to suggest that quality may have been an issue with some of the early shipments of P53s to the Union. There are other possibilities to consider as well. Soldiers of all eras are famous for their griping, especially if they had been promised "a fine United States Springfield." In my personal experience, which is limited to inspecting and handling a few hundred Enfield rifles I can fairly report there some variation in fit and finish, but none of them were even to close to rough enough to "tear my hands to pieces." Confederates did gripe occasionally about Enfield cartridges not fitting well in their cartridge boxes, but they were mostly thrilled with the rifle itself. For example, Sam Watkins of the 1st Tennessee H writes quite favorably about his Enfield in his famous memoirs, "Company Aytch: Or a Sideshow of the Big Show"

52. London gun maker JE Barnett would sometimes strike over condemnation marks or try to create what looked like government acceptance marks, such as an arrow under a B to look like the WD crown/arrow.

53. Maj John M. Gould, History of the First–Tenth–Twenty-ninth Maine Regiment, Stephen Berry, (Portland, ME) 1871, page 89. The 1st Maine had originally been issued US Model 1855 rifle-muskets and the reissue of Enfield rifles occurred when the unit was being reorganized into the 10th Maine.

CHAPTER FOUR: History of Some Larger Birmingham Gun Makers

TIPPING & LAWDEN

1. Osborne's guide to the Grand junction, or Birmingham, Liverpool &c, E.C. & W. Osbourne (London)1858 p. 83.

2. Notes and queries, By Oxford Journals, Series V, Volume VII, June 30, 1877, p. 518.

3. The multi–generational passing of gun–making firms from father to eldest son makes it difficult to follow as most elder sons also shared the same first name as their fathers. Others are connected by marriage, which is easier because of the British interest in their family heritage.

4. 1851 Great Exhibition: Official Catalogue: Class VIII.: Tipping and Lawden.

5. Ibid, Ward, p. 170.

6 Harry Horton, Birmington: A Poem in Two Parts with Appendix (1853) General Books (Memphis, TN) 2009 p. 174.

7. Louis Winant, Pepperbox Firearms, Greenburg Publishing (Sykesville, MD) 1952, p. 30. See also 136–140 on the T&L version. See also: J. Kinard, J. Pistols: An Illustrated History of Their Impact, ABC–CLIO Publishing (Santa Barbara, CA) 2003 p. 62.

8. S.C. Robinson made about 1,900 of the Confederate Sharps and the CS Government another 3,000.

9. Nathan Mancaster, The Spirit of Cinco de Mayo, Tafford Publishing, (Bloomington, IN) 2009 p. 209.

10. Royal Blue Book, Fashionable Directory and Parliamentary Guide, Kelly & Co (London) 1897, p. 15.

11. Sylvanus Urban, The Gentlemen's Magazine, Volume 41, JB Nichols & Sons, (London) 1854 p. 330 Hollis & Sheath.

ISAAC HOLLIS & SONS (FORMERLY HOLLIS & SHEATH)

1. www.internetgunclub.com, history of Isaac Hollis.

2. These were the sons of William Hollis.

3. Dr. C. H. Roads, *British Soldiers Firearms 1850-1864*, Herbert Jenkins (London) 1966 p.84. The others were Swinburn & Son, Thomas Turner and Tipping &Lawden.

4. Ibid, Roads.

5. John Walker, *The Rifle Story*, Greenhill Books (London) 2006 p. 35, most of this information is also found in the Chambers Journals (1859) or from C.H. Roads.

6. Williams, David, *The Birmingham Gun Trade*, Tempus Publishing (2004), p. 78.

7. www.oldguns.net, August 2001 see "I. Hollis & Sons." This ad ran in 1868. Sounds like if you wanted it the Hollis firm could make it for you.

8. Great Britain. State Trials Committee, Reports of State Trials, Printed for H. M. S. O., by Eyre and Spottiswoode, (London) 1858, The Queen v Simon Bernard, p. 968.

9. Frederick Llewellyn, *The Volunteer Corps: Their Constitution, Arms, Drill Laws and Uniform*, (1860), reprinted University of Michigan (Ann Arbro, MI) 1997,, p. 29.

10. Ibid, internet gun club.

11. Lazarus Goldman, *The Jews in Victoria in the 19th Century*, Melbourne Publishing,(Melbourne, AU) 1954 p. 376.

CHARLES PHILIPS SWINBURN & SON AND T. TURNER, BIRMINGHAM

1. William West. *History, Topography and Directory of Warwickshire*, published by Wrightson (London) 1830, p.333. There were of course four generations of John Fields associated with the Parker, Field & Son gun-making dynasty, but they were in London not Birmingham.

2. DeWit Bailey, *English Gunmakers and the Provincial Gun Trade*, Aroc Publishing (New York) 1978, p. 34.

3. R. A. Brooman, (ed), *Mechanics Magazine*, Volume LIX, Robertson, Brooman & Co, (London) 1853 p. 198

4. Thomas Turner, patent for improved rifling dated 16 April 1860. (www.researchpress.co.uk.)

5. Official Report of the Parliamentary Debates on the Gun Trade Thomas Hansard & Co, (London) 1854, p. 1412. It reads as follows: *We, the undersigned, on behalf of the gun trade, will undertake (if the Board of Ordnance will enter into contracts for that purpose) to supply and deliver complete 50,000 rifled muskets within the first year, 100,000 in the second year, and a much greater quantity in the third year. We will undertake to find all the materials for the above muskets except the rough stocks, of which the Board of Ordnance have a large quantity in store, and can supply. If the Board of Ordnance will entertain this offer, we will immediately make twenty rifled muskets of the pattern required as samples, which shall be inspected, marked, and scaled by the inspector of small arms, ten of which shall be retained by the Board of Ordnance, and ten retained by the contractors; the whole of which shall be kept for reference in case of dispute.*
We propose that the course of inspection shall be the same as carried out by the Board of Ordnance; that is to say, each part of the musket shall be inspected and marked in each stage of manufacture as being of proper

quality and make. But we will undertake and hold ourselves responsible for the production of a perfect arm, according to the pattern supplied.(Signed) "HOLLIS AND SHEATH. CHAS.P. SWINBURN AND SON. THOMAS TURNER. TIPPING AND LAWDEN."

6. Dr. C. H Roads, *British Soldiers Firearms 1850–1864.* Herbert Jenkins Publications (London) 1964 p. 177.

COOPER & GOODMAN

1. Max Baker (ed), Arms & Explosives Magazine (London) Vol 8, Issue 99 (1900) p. 205 and 246.
2. DeWitt Bailey, *English Gunmakers: Birmingham and the Provincial Gun Trade*, Arco Publishing Company (New York) 1978, p. 61.
3. History and General Directory of Birmingham, Francis White& Co (London) 1849, p. 132.
4. Bill Curtis, www.britishmilitaryforums.uk.org.
5. Journal of the Society of Arts :Volume 4, Published by Royal Society of Arts (London) 1856, p. 80.
6. George Sharswood (ed), *Reports of Cases Argued and Determined in the English Court of Common Law,* Volume 139 (London) 1857 p. 93–106.
7. Ibid, Bailey p. 34.
8. Ibid, Arms& Explosives Magazine, p. 189.
9. Great Britain Board of Trade, Birmingham Labour Gazette, (London), 1915.

W SCOTT & SONS

1. The new combined firm was named "Webley & Scott." Branches of this firm were still doing a firearms business in the 21ˢᵗ century as recently as 2005, even outlasting Holland & Holland.
2. J.A. Crawford, and P. Whatley, *The History of W & C Scott Gunmakers,* Rowland Ward Publishing at Holland & Holland, (London) 1986 pp. 7–12.
3. History and General Directory of Birmingham, Francis White & Co (London) published 1849, p. 247
4. William West. *History, Topography and Directory of Warwickshire*, published by Wrightson, (London),1830, p.435.
5. www.anccstory.uk.org (Scott, William Charles). 18 employees is small for a gun–maker. Charles Reeves, the Birmingham gun, sword and bayonet maker employed 300 hands in 1861 and 400 by 1864.
6. Ibid Crawford & Whatley, pp. 20–33. Earlier in 1863, Eyton Bond purchased the Moore & Harris factory at 36–37 Loveday Street.
7. *Birmingham and District Commercial List*, published by Ethell & Co, London (1876), p. 14.
8. Accounts and Papers of the House of Commons of Great Britain, Commercial Reports Volume 34, London, published 1877, p. 727.
9. Samuel Timmins,(ed) *Birmingham and the Midlands Hardware District,* Published by Robert Hardwicke, London, (1866), See "The Birmingham Gun Trade" by J. Goodman, p. 388.

WILLIAM LUCAS SARGANT

1. William Lucas Sargant, *Essays of a Birmingham Manufacturer* Volume II, published by Williams & Norgate (Edinburough) 1870, pp. 186–192.
2. Henry may have been an absentee partner as he is continuously listed at as a barrister at Lincolns Inn, London, as are his sons and grandsons.
3. Francis White, *History and Directory of Birmingham*, F. White & Co, (London) 1849, p. 41. The lease on the property was for "ninety years, six months less three days."
4. National Archives shows an Indenture "…between Elizabeth Sargant of Edgbaston, widow, and others, being an assignment from the said Elizabeth Sargant to William Lucas Sargant, of Birmingham, sword cutler and gun–maker, of leasehold land and premises in Edmund Street, Charlotte Street and George Street. Endorsed with agreement, dated 18 September, 1839, between the said William Lucas Sargant and Henry Sargant, co–partners, concerning the said premises. MS 3375/408251, *11 September 1839.*"Then later, "…assignment from William Lucas Sargant of Birmingham, gun and sword manufacturer, Henry Sargant of Lincolns Inn, London, esq., and others, to Joseph Gibbins of Birmingham, esq., of leasehold land and premises in Edmund street, Charlotte street and George street. MS 3375/408255, 25 March 1851."
5. Carl P. Russel, *Guns of the Early Frontier,* University of California Press (Berkeley, CA) 1957 p. 107–118,, Barnett was initially the largest supplier of trade guns and considered the "standard" as far as quality for that type musket was concerned. The more established firms disparaged it as "the gas pipe trade."
6. *Congressional Edition, US Government Printing Office, 2ⁿᵈ Session of the Twenty–sixth Congress,* "Report of Select Committee, to inquire into the propriety of establishing a national foundry for the purpose of fabricating ordnance." p. 79.
7. J.E. White, *House of Commons, Second Report from Commissioners on Children's Employment in Factories, Volume 22,* Geo E Eyre, printer (1864), p. 77. The polishing incident was from a visit to Messrs Cooper & Company (Cooper & Goodman) on Woodcock Street. The young man was named Henry Martingale, age 11.

8. William L. Sargant, Essays of a Birmingham Manufacturer, Volume I, Williams & Norgate Publishing. (Edinburgh) 1869, p. 52.

9. George Herbert Sargant, *Farthing Dinners* (pamphlet), p. 10 See also excerpt published by the British Association for the Advancement of Science, (1887).

10. Ibid, W.L. Sargant, Vol I, p. 37.

11. Obituary of William Lucas Sargant, *Birmingham Post and Gazette*, November 2, 1889.

12. New Library World, Volume 18, published by Library Supply Company, Bridge House (London) 1916, p. 52.

BENTLEY & PLAYFAIR

1. Charles Carder, *Side by Sides of the World* Second Edition, Avil Onze Publishing (Delphus, OH) 1997, out of print; p. 20–21. See also DeWitt Bailey, *English Gunmakers: The Birmingham and Provincial Gun Trade* Arco Publishing (New York) 1978, p. 30.

2. *Corporation and General Trades Directory of Birmingham*, published by W. Cornish,(London) 1861, p. 65.

3. Max Baker (ed) Arms & Explosives: A Trade Journal, Number 77, Vol 7, Effingham House (London) 1887, p. 45.

4. Acocks Green Historical Society, www.oldmaps.uk. (re: Sherbourne Road).

5. Barry Ryerson, *The Giants of Small Heath – The History of BSA*, Sparkford (London), 1980, p. 48.

6. DeWitt Bailey, *English Gunmakers: Birmingham and the Provincial Gun Trade*, Arco Publishing (New York), 1978, p. 30. It states Joseph Bentley and Charles Playfair did partner to provide some breech loading small arms to the War Department some years later in a different venture.

7. The Jurist: Alphabetical List of Bankruptcies, Vol 24, part II, Hodges, Smith & Co (London) 1861 p. 10.

JOSEPH BOURNE

1. Max Baker (ed) Arms & Explosives, Vol XVI, December 1908,(London) p. 161.

2. Ian Glendenning, *British Pistols and Guns 1640–1840*, Cassell Publishing (London), 1951 p. 163. See also Robert Dent, *Old and New Birmingham*, Houghton & Hammond Publishing (London) 1880 p. 48.

3. Charles Sawyer *Firearms in America Volume 1*, self published (London), 1910 p. 221. Note: All the Ketlands specialized on the American trade, as did Wilson & Co.

4. Norman Cheevers, MD, *A Treatise of Removable Causes of Death in Europe and India*, Bishops College Press, Calcutta (India) 1852, p. 220. Note: These "Minie Rifles" would be the Enfield pattern of 1851, the direct predecessor of the P–53.

5. William Greener, *Gunnery in 1858*, Published by Smith & Elder Co,(London), 1858, p. 448.

6. Another gun–maker in BSAT, in fact one of the original four, Thomas Turner often marked the bottom of the barrel TT or T Turner, as well as the inside of the lock like Joseph Bourne. However, Turner was a barrel maker and even patented his own form of rifling.

7. Sir Henry Setton, Forms of Decrees in Equity Vol 62, (London) p. 432, *Tranter v Goodman, May 16, 1876, WN (76) 169.* The gun trade was in decline by this time period and significant over–capacity in manufacturing caused BSA Co and others to diversify. Bicycle making was one new area where BSA Co ventured.

WILLIAM GREENER

1. Greener was something of an outsider in the Birmingham gun trade, perhaps because he began in the Newcastle area and moved later to Birmingham.

2. The Minié ball primarily used in the US Civil War was a later design modified by James H. Burton (Harpers Ferry) to do away with the iron plug in the base, instead utilizing a hollow base. Also the Greener design did not use a cylindro–conical shape.

3. W. Greener *The Science of Gunnery as Applied to the Use and Construction of Firearms*, (dated variously from 1841 to 1846). Longman and Company, (London) p. 314.

4. Joseph Rosa and Robin May. *Gun Law: A Study of Violence in the Old West*. Contemporary Books, (Chicago). 1977, p. 61. "Doc" Holliday was reputedly using a custom–made W. Greener shotgun during the famous "Gunfight at the OK Corral" in Arizona.

5. Ibid, Greener, p. 184.

6. Ibid, Greener p. 224.

7. William W. Greener, *The Gun and Its Development*.(1910) Published by Greenhill books, (London) 2003 p. 241.

8. Leon Levi, PhD. *Annals of British Legislation*, Parliamentary Blue Books Vol II, published 1866, p. 833.

9. C.H. Roads, *British Soldiers Firearms 1850–1864*, Herbert Jenkins, (London) 1964 p. 112. Other members of the so–called "original four" Birmingham gun making firms were Tipping &Lawden, Swinburn, and Thomas Turner. Technically, the firm was known as Hollis & Sheath until 1861 and afterwards, Isaac Hollis & Sons.

10. New York Times, *"About Guns"*June 29, 1881.

JOSEPH WILSON

1. Period Advertisement for Joseph Wilson, gun–maker which appeared in the Commercial Directory and Shippers Guide, Birmingham (1862), p. 341.

2. Walter S. Dunn *People of the American Frontier*, Praeger Publishing Co (Westport, CT) 2005, p. 31.Sketchley's Birmingham Directory of 1770 lists one Robert Wilson, Gun & Pistol Manufacturer on Bull Street in Birmingham.

3. The Commercial Directory of Birmingham for 1818 and 1837, Published by J Pigot & Co (London) 1818, 1837 p. 202 and p. 243.
4. The Sessional Papers of the House of Lords, Report of the Commission on Child Labor to Parliament, Volume 8, Eyre &Spottiswoode (London), 1864, p. 107.
5. The Birmingham & Midlands District Commercial List, Estell & Co,(London) 1876 p. 18.
6. Dudley was so shrewd a judge of diamonds that he earned the epithet "Jew Dudley." This was intended as a compliment of sorts as the Jewish community was preeminent in the Jewellry Qtr. See Gary Tenant, "About William Dudley," www.williamdudleytrust.uk.org.
7. E.R. Kelly, (ed) The Birmingham Post Office Directory of 1879, published by Kelly & Co, (London), p. 148.
8. H. White, & R. Trudgeon, "Birmingham Gun Quarter: A Skilled Trade in Decline" Vol. 11, No. 2,,Autumn 1983, Oral History & Labour History, (London) pp. 69–83.
9. UK National Archives, Reference MS 3375 "Deeds and Leases." It also lists premises on Bull Street from the first Wilson & Cogun maker in the mid–1700s. Cottesbrook literally means "cottage by the brook." This should not be confused with Cottesbrooke Hall in Northamptonshire, the estate of a family of London turkey merchants.

R & W ASTON
1. Mr. R. Aston is referring to the "new" BSA Co factory at Small Heath.
2. Interesting observation by Mr R. Aston on the Birmingham "piece work" or outworker system of manufacture from an owner's perspective…that the workers and mechanics would be better served with regular hours.
3. R. Aston seems somewhat unenlightened about the literacy level of his child workers.
4. "Sunday School" in Victorian England was a Protestant attempt to educate the illiterate children of working class parents, which eventually led to compulsory public school education in England beginning in the 1870s. Public opinions in England prior to the time of this report were strongly against state involvement in schools, particularly the aspect of forced attendance. Families needed the wages (however slight) that their children brought in to the household. See Seaman, L.C.B., *Victorian England: Aspects of English and Imperial History, 1837–1901*, Rutledge Publishing (1973), p. 21.
5. Ha'p'orth is an abbreviation of "half penny's worth."

CHARLES REEVES "TOLEDO WORKS"
1. London Gazette Newspaper, May 19, 1852, see "Notices."
2. The Chas Reeves factory had nothing to do with the sword making craft in the city of Toledo (Spain), it was merely chosen for the name recognition, Toledo being synonymous with high quality sword–making. We would call that "marketing" in the modern business world. This is the same reason Chas Reeves had a London address when the factory was in Birmingham.
3. George Measom, , *Official Illustrated Guide of London & NW Railways with Descriptions of the Most Important Manufacturers on the Lines*, (London) 1861, p. 207–10.
4. Apparently between when this was written in 1861 and 1864, the firm of Chas Reeves added 100 hands to the workforce. Interesting that Toledo works in Birmingham was implementing some sort of manufacture by machinery for their bayonets as early as 1861.
5. John Dent Goodman Chairman of Birmingham Small Arms Trade and BSA Co, and partner in the large gun making concern of Cooper & Goodman, was considered the last word on such matters.
6. Gustave Strauss, *England's Workshops*, published by Biblio Bazaar, (Charleston, SC) 2008, p. 18, It must have been producing a greater number of swords and bayonets because their P53 Enfields are less commonly encountered than most of the larger gun–makers from the Birmingham Small Arms Trade.
7. Bankers Magazine Volume 29, Annual for 1869, (London), p. 612.
8. Wilkinson & Son were first gun–makers who evolved out of the Henry Nock firm that began in 1772. Nock was the most influential gun–maker of the 18th century and a famous gunsmith. James Wilkinson (son–in–law), former apprentice was the foreman and took over the firm after Nock passed away in 1804. At that time the firm was the main supplier of flintlock muskets to Ordnance. His son, Henry founded Wilkinson & Son and entered the sword making business in the 1820s. In the 1850s, Henry Wilkinson licensed a sword tang design from Chas Reeves & Co.

CHAPTER FIVE: HISTORY OF SOME LARGER LONDON GUN MAKERS
LONDON ARMOURY COMPANY (LA CO)
1. Peter G. Hall, *London Voices, London Lives. Tales from a Working Capital*, Policy Press (London) 2007 p. 58–60,
2. William B. Edwards, *Civil War Guns*, Castle Books (Secaucus, New Jersey) 1978. The London Armoury Company manufactured Kerr revolvers have engraved on the side of the frame "KERR'S PATENT No.6333" with the "6333"representing the serial number. The "number" on the frame is not the patent number of the revolver.
3. Archibald Hamilton was Superintendent of LA Co, and also a partner in the Commission House of Sinclair, Hamilton & Co. with Alexander Sinclair, in business since the 1840s. He helped Caleb Huse get most of the London gun makers (including Barnett) busy filling orders for the Confederacy immediately, as well as some in Birmingham.

4. Actually, this was true…one of the ironies of the situation was McFarland, who set up the gun making machinery purchased from Ames Mfg by LA Co in the late 1850s beat a path to LA Co's door ahead of Caleb Huse. Also, the exchange rate at the time was $5 (CS) to one £, hence £10,000 = $50,000.

5. Official Records of the War of Rebellion, Series IV, Volume I, US Government Printing Office, (Washington, DC) pp. 343–345. See also Caleb Huse, *The Supplies for the Confederate Army* T.R. Marvin & Co (Boston) 1904, pp. 19–23.

6. Thomas Boaz, *Guns for Cotton: England Arms the Confederacy*, Burd Publishing (Shippensburg, PA) 1996, p. 16, see also: William Albaugh, Edward Simmons, *Confederate Arms*, Bonanza books (Modesto, CA) 1957,p. 60, Chuck Lewis, *A Certain Justice*, Universe Publishing (New York) 2004, p. 313, Library of Congress Desk Reference, p. 489, etc. In addition, D. Radcliffe wrote for armscollectors.com, "*After the opening days of the Civil War there is no evidence whatsoever that any of their (LA Co) products went to supply the North*" and other balderdash. The most accurate statement would be that LA Co was "a major supplier to the Confederacy." The Confederates were believed to have purchased all the Kerr revolvers that LA Co could make after Caleb Huse visited in May 1861. However, they had other customers for their Enfield rifle production, including the Union, sworn enemy of their best customer.

7. Marcellus Hartley, *A Brief Memoir*, privately published (New York) 1903, p. 60. See the Appendix under Civil War correspondence with Secretary of War, Edwin M. Stanton. Hartley was the founder of the New York firm of Schuyler, Hartley & Graham. He was unpleasantly surprised by the duplicity of the English gun–makers who he characterized as "a slippery lot."

8. The Civil Engineers and Architect's Journal, Volume 31, Jan 1866, p. 23.

9. Wiley Sword, *Firepower from Abroad: the Confederate Enfield and LeMat Revolver*, Lincoln, RI: Andrew Mowbray Publishers,(Rhode Island) 1986, pp. 49–53. He counts 7,700 to the US and 35,100 (1,300 x 27 months) to the CS respectively. More recent historians that are better at math put the total figure at 70,000 to 75,000, which is much more likely to be accurate, perhaps even conservative.

10. See *Rifle Practice*, The British Review, Volume 28–29, 1858, (London) p. 283. See also Frank E.Vandiver, *Confederate Blockade Running through Bermuda,* reprinted by Kraus Publishing (1970) page xiii.

11. The figures for the amount of machinery at Royal Small Arms Manufactory and LAC are found in the journal "Proceedings" published by the Institute of Mechanical Engineers of Great Britain (London) 1861, pp. 335–338. Mr Greenwood reports "…at Enfield with two sets of the machines 2,000 gun stocks are produced" and there was "one similar set with London Armoury's works in London." A full set of the Ames Mfg gun making machinery cost £8,000.

12. John Goodman provides a figure of barrels proofed at the Enfield factory of 505,102 for the seven years from 1857 to 1864 which averages out to 72,154 per year or about 6,000 per month. Government–run operations like Royal Small Arms Manufactory are seldom as efficient as private companies, much less 2.5 times more efficient. It is doubtful that LA Co was the sole exception to this rule given the business acumen of the men running it. If I had to hazard a guess on the terms of LA Co's contract with Ordnance, given that it was for 30,000 arms in late 1859 and had 18 months left to go by May 1861, my guess would be that the contract was for 1,000 parts interchangeable rifles per month.

13. Henry Heaton,*Notes on Rifle Shooting*, Spottiswoode & Co publisher, (London) 1864, p. 117, see advertisement for LA Co. Heaton was Capt and Adjutant of the Third Manchester Volunteer Rifle Corps.

14. *http://www.cfspress.com/sharpshooters/arms.htmlsee "Kerr Rifle."*

15. Ibid, Heaton p. 26.

16. Martin Pegler, *Out of Nowhere: A History of the Military Sniper*, Osprey Publishing (London) 2006, p. 68. The cost of the Kerr rifle was on par with Whitworth target rifles, and the Kerr rifles came with two barrels.

17. Val Forgett, *Why Kerrs?http://asoac.org/bulletins/97_forgett_kerr.pdf (1997).*

18. Ibid, IME of Great Britain, p. 335.

19. Patrick Dove, *The Revolver: its Description, Management and Use with tips on the Rifle for Defence of the Country*, Published by W. Clowes & Sons. (London) 1858 p. 2.

20. Craig L Barry, *The Civil War Musket: A Handbook for Historical Accuracy*, Watchdog Publishing (Warren, MI) 2006, p. 32. The rifle is in the collection of William O. Adams of Scotland, Connecticut. The lock is stamped in slanted letters LONDON ARMOURY CO.

21. Extracts from the *Reports and Proceedings of the Ordnance Select Committee*, Volume II, Spottiswoode& Co (London) Jan. 1864, p. 15, 3(d). "The bands should be of the Baddeley pattern." Baddeley tragically passed away from diphtheria later in 1861 at age 32. Brent Wilburn, proprietor of Antique Arms notes "*Some collectors will argue the Baddeley bands were not used on rifles imported during the Civil War... Given how scarce existing LAC guns are now, it's more likely they just have never seen one. A friend of mine who relic hunts has even seen a Baddeley band dug up from the Battlefield at Griswoldville, Georgia from Nov. 1864.*" See Antique Arms website for images of the LAC with Palmer bands and fourth model oval rear swivel dated 1862. (www.antiquearms.com).

22. Ibid, Barry p. 33. A professional researcher and historian known to the author has an original LAC with the Baddeley patent bands in his collection with documented Civil War provenance, dated 1865. It is believed to be one of the last LACs to run the blockade into the Confederacy before the end of the US Civil War. The LA Co type IV rifles were in existence but not widely encountered, most of the LACs exported to America were the type III.

23. The stocks on machine made Enfields all feature the "rounded ear" type washers regardless of whether the rifle is a type II, type III or model four. It is a characteristic of the P53 Enfield long rifle stock making machinery. The Windsor (Robbins & Lawrence) contract from 1855 was made on the same machinery and also has rounded ear lock plate washers.

24. Brian Longman, *A History of the British Economy*, Longmans Publishing (London) 1973 p. 635

25. *Handbook of Birmingham*, British Association for the Advancement of Science, (London) p. 196.

26. George Williamson, *Old Greenock (Articles from the Greenock Herald)* 1886 reprinted by University of Michigan Press (Ann Arbor), 1992, p. 153.

27. Graham Storey, (ed), *Charles Dickens, Letters: 1868–1870*, Oxford University Press (London) 2002, p. 169. It is addressed to *"London Armoury Co, Ltd, James Kerr & Co successors, Gun & Pistol Makers, 36 King William Street EC and 27 Leman St, Goodman Fields."* Apparently Kerr was still producing rifles and revolvers for commercial sale as "London Armoury" at the last known address of the offices of the old LA Co bldg.

J. E Barnett & Sons

1. Bailey II, Dewitt, The Wilsons: Gunmakers in Europe 1730–1832. American Society of Arms Collectors, Bulletin 85. See also:William, Herbert, History of the 12 Great Livery Companies of London, originally published 1837, Volumes I and II. There are presently 107 Livery Companies, and the Worshipful Company of Mercers (Merchants) is # 1 on the order of precedence. During the mid–19th century there were over 150 Livery Companies, but time and technology have reduced their numbers. For example, the Worshipful Company of Bowstring Makers eventually went by the wayside after the English Longbow was no longer a primary military weapon, and so on.

2. Hamilton, T.M. Early American Trade Guns. Great Plains Publishing 1968. American Fur Company order to JJ Henry reads (in part): "…all (Northwest) trade guns must be equal to Barnetts." Though no records exist on Barnett & Sons prior to 1821, several articles on Northwest Trade Company guns make reference to Barnett as a very common gun–maker. Some other familiar names show up on the Board of Ordnance records for the Hudson Bay Co, including a few familiar to Enfield enthusiasts: Moxham, E. Bond, Parker, Field and W. D. Sargant.

3. 1841 London Census.

4. 1851 London Census.

5. Hoole, Stanley: Confederate Foreign Agent: The European Diary of Major Edward C Anderson

6. United States Government: War of the Rebellion OR Series IV, volume I, p. 1003–1005

7. http://southgeorgiarelic.org/enfield.htm. The other Enfields on the Bermuda were from the London firms of LA Co and Field & Son and the Birmingham firms C&W James, E. Bond, W. Scott & Son.

8. Ibid, OR Series I volume 6, p. 455.

9. www.internetgunclub.com Historical Database.

10. Adams, William O. British Gunmakers, Parts Makers, Contractors, Etc. Known To Have Been Active During The Period 1850–1865. Part one: The London Gun Trade. Unpublished.

11. Colin McRae papers, SCCRRMM, Columbia, South Carolina, S. Isaac Campbell & Co. Subseries (1861–63). If these figures are correct, and the Confederate States imported 400,000 Enfields during the course of the US Civil War and not all Barnetts were brokered by SIC&Co, then Barnett marked P53s would be quite commonly encountered.

12. Ibid

13. Goodman, John D. The Birmingham Gun Trade article in (S. Timmons, editor.) The Resources, Products and Industrial History of Birmingham and the Midlands Hardware District, published 1866 (London: Robert Hardwicke) p. 418.

Edward P. Bond

1. Robert Barnett (1761) began doing business at 157 Minories and passed the business to his nephew, which then became Thomas Barnett & Sons (1774–1832). It then became J.E. Barnett & Sons, but was the same firm doing business continuously in London until the firm closed its doors in 1908.

2. Ancestry.uk.com/Bond family. Collectors have noted similarities between EP Bond London guns and those made by Barnett & Sons. At least several EP Bonds were among the first Enfield rifles to reach the Confederacy aboard the *Bermuda*. Rack marked 7240 image is in the SPAR collection.

3. The Jurist, Volume I, Part II, II. Sweet Publishing, (London), 1856 p. 61.

4. The Moore & Harris firm dates from 1840, and while considered a "lesser Birmingham gun maker," W. Greener speaks quite highly of them in his book *The Science of Gunnery* (1846) p. 188. It appears that competition from the Birmingham Small Arms Trade ultimately drove the firm out of business.

5. Birmingham Commercial Directory and Shipper Guide, RE Fulton, Liverpool, (1862) p. 340.

6. Corporation and General Trades Directory for Birmingham and Wolverhampton, W. Cornish, Publisher (1861) p. 194. Charles W. James is the only "James" listed in the section under "Gun Trade." CW James is a fairly well known Birmingham maker who was not affiliated with Birmingham Small Arms Trade. He may have partnered with Bond to better compete vs BSAT.

7. DeWitt Bailey, *English Gunmakers: The Birmingham and Provincial Gun Trade*, Arco Publishing, (1978) p. 43.

PARKER, FIELD & SONS

1. Source: The Police Constabulary Almanac Official Register and Telegraph Code, published by Sowler & Sons, Manchester (1901).

2. HEIC is the Honourable East India Company. Gun makers liked doing business with the HEIC because (compared to Ordnance) "…their standards were laxer and payments quicker."

3. Joachim H. Stocqueler., *The Oriental Interpreter: A Companion to The Handbook of India*, published by James Madden, (London) 1857, p. 345. Big game hunting was a major pastime of Englishmen in India during the Raj.

4. The manufacture of manacles was done at the firm's factory in Birmingham. One account states that 4,000 pairs were manufactured there per year, of which one–half were for foreign and colonial purposes. Large numbers were exported to the Southern states for the slave trade. It also notes that the manacles for English felons are "lightweight, and highly polished."

5. *Punch or the London Charivari*, Volume 20–21, Jan to June 1851, Fleet Street Publishing (London) p. 207. Editor: Now that button popping reference is a mental image that is a bit hard to shake.

6. In *Firepower from Abroad*, Wiley Sword discusses these Georgia contract Enfield rifles from what blockade runners they came on, to where they landed, and even to which regiments they were issued. It is some of the best surviving documentation that exists on which English firms supplied the CS, especially early in the war. The Georgia contract Enfields are often marked on the stock with a large capital letter "G" and rack numbers on the butt stock tang.

7. John D. Bennett, *The London Confederates*, McFarland & Co (West Jefferson, NC) 2008 pp161–163.

8. FH Morse writing to Secretary of State, Wm. H. Seward. Source: Official Records of the Union and Confederate Navies in the War of Rebellion, Series 1, Volume 6, Washington, DC, p. 449.

9. In the Official records of the War of the Rebellion Series IV, Vol III, p. 383 in December 1862, J. Gorgas provides a summary abstract to Secretary of War Seddon of purchases made by Caleb Huse as follows: *"131,129 stands of arms consisting of 70,980 long Enfield rifles, 9,715 short Enfield rifles, 354 carbine Enfield rifles, 27,000 Austrian rifles, 21,040 British muskets, 20 small bore Enfield, 2,020 Brunswick rifles. There were also 23,000 Enfield rifles in London awaiting shipment…"* It appears the ratio of 7:1 is probably about right as the short rifle was about 20% more expensive than the P53 rifle–musket for some reason.

POTTS & HUNT

1. James L. Mitchell, *Colt: A Collection of Letters*, Stackpole Publishing Co (Mechanicksburg, PA) 1959, p. 141. The contract was for 4,000 Enfield long rifles, bright barrels and furniture to the Springfield standard of .58 of which 2680 were ultimately delivered. See also, Barry, Craig L. *The Civil War Musket: A Handbook for Historical Accuracy*, Watchdog Publishing (2006).

2. "Potts & Hunt." www.internetgunclub.com

3. Paul Star, 'Thomas H. Potts and the origins of conservation in New Zealand (1850––1890)' MA thesis, Otago University (NZ), 1991, p. 23.

4. Official Catalog, Crystal Palace Great Exhibition of 1851, London. Category VIII.

5. Paul Star, 'Potts, Thomas Henry 1824 – 1888'. Dictionary of New Zealand Biography, updated 22 June 2007 See also: Star, P. *Thomas H. Potts and the origins of conservation in New Zealand (1850––1890)' MA thesis, Otago University (NZ), 1991.

6. Ibid, Star (thesis) p. 24. Also, the BSA directors after September 1863 were Joseph Wilson, Samuel Buckley, Isaac Hollis, Charles Playfair, Charles Pryse, Sir John Ratcliffe, Edward Gem, and J.F. Swinburn under the chairmanship of John Dent Goodman.

7. See: *Nineteenth Century New Zealand Artists: A Guide & Handbook*. He identified a grey kiwi and a black billed seagull in 1882.

8. *Christchurch Press*, 28 Jul 1888 (Obituary).

9. William Laxton, (ed) *Civil Engineers and Architect's Journal*, (London) Volume XVI, 1853, p. 238. See also The Mechanics Magazine, "Specifications of English patents" p. 196.

10. Thomas Potts found time in 1862 to rummage the "untamed wilderness of Alston's Moor" for buzzards eggs to take back to New Zealand with him, but he apparently did not visit London or the firm of Potts & Hunt.

E. YEOMANS & SON: GUN AND SWORD MAKER

1. The etymology of the word comes from the Anglo–Saxon term for "young man." While *Yeoman(s)* was not a common name in 19th century England, like *Wilson* or *Smith*, it was not unheard of either. It is one of those last names like *Cooper* (barrel maker), *Carpenter* (woodworker) or *Farrior* (blacksmith) that suggests a trade in the family history.

2. *Annual Directory for Merchants & Traders &c of London for 1814*, Volume 15, by Post Office of Great Britain, p. 358.

3. The first James Yeomans died 22 October 1839 (Source: National Archives) and lists his occupation as gun–maker and address asSaint Mary Whitechapel, Middlesex (London) Catalogue reference PROB 11/191. James Yeomans (#2), same occupation and address, passed away 9 October 1851, and in his will left the entire business and all property to his surviving wife Elizabeth.

4. Great Britain. Royal Commission for the Exhibition of 1851, (London), www.gracesguide.com, "....exhibit booth # 231 Yeomans, & Sons, 67 Chamber Street, Goodman's Fields featuring an assortment of muskets."

5. It appears that Horace Yeomans worked in the sword and cutler trade, and ran the retail operation at 35 Upper Street, Smithfield. E. Yeomans & Son, like most gun–makers of the time also made pistols (on the Tranter pattern), various swords, knives and civilian sporting guns.

6. The Proceedings of the Old Bailey, London Central Criminal Court, Reference Number:T18610408–294, dated April 8, 1861.

7. John D. Bennett, *The London Confederates* Published by McFarland (West Jefferson, NC) 2006, p. 98.In other words, the "London Confederate States Commercial League" was founded by James Yeomans to drum up some business for the E. Yeomans firm.

8. *London Gazette*, March 8, 1864, see "Bankruptcies."

9. *London Gazette*, June 29, 1866, see "Leases and Sales of Settled Estates."

10. Collection of National Maritime Museum, London. Images can be viewed atwww.nmm.ac.uk/collections. (Items AAA–2536 thru 2540).

11. *London Gazette,* January 16, 1866, see "Notices."

12. *The Liverpool Commercial List of 1871*, published by Seyd & Co (London) 1872, p.9, See also *Strakers' Annual Mercantile, Ship and Insurance Register*, (London) 1863, p. 13. Oelrichs & Company (shipping agents) originated in Bremen, Saxony but was in England by the 1830s, at least they start showing up in the Court of Common Pleas (see Callender v Oelrichs) by 1838. Liverpool is the "Bremen" of England if that makes sense as far as shipping/commercial agents. The London office at 26 Fenchurch Street of Oelrichs & Co (later Oelrichs, Yeomans & Co) appears to have been in business since the Norddeustcher Lloyd contract of 1857, but dissolved in the mid–1860s, about the same time as the bankruptcy of E. Yeomans & Son. It seems reasonably clear that after Horace Yeomans took over the Sword & Gun–maker business in 1865, it was the family ties between Yeomans and Oelrichs that led the rest of the clan to the move from London to Saxony.

Chapter Six: Enfield Rifle Implements • Appurtenances Issued with the P53 Enfield Rifle Musket

The P53 Enfield Socket Bayonet

1. *Avery Weigh–Tronix web page http://www.averyweigh–tronix.com*

The Salter P53 Enfield Bayonet

1. *A Visit to the Ordnance Factory, Enfield*. The Chamber's Journal 16th April 1859.

2. CH Roads, *British Soldiers Firearms 1850–1864*. R & R books (London) reprinted 1994, p.84–85.

The Pattern 1860 Scabbard

1. *List of Changes in British War Materials: 1860–1886*, by Ian D Skennerton. A large quantity of the obsolete P1842 scabbards, both marked "WD" (War Department) and unmarked, were imported to the Confederacy.

The Sword Bayonet and Scabbard

1. John Walter (ed). *Arms & Equipment of the British Army 1866*, Greenhill Books (London) 1986, p. 27–28.

The Muzzle Stopper

1. *United Service Magazine, Part two 1857 Volume 84* Instructions in Musketry.

2. Reproduced from a hand written set of notes made in 1866, this sample from *War Department Notes* appears courtesy of Adrian Roads.

The P1857 Snapcap

1. *Colburn's United Service Magazine and Naval and Military Journal*, Part One 1857.

2. Reproduced from a hand written set of notes made in 1866, this sample from *War Department Notes* appears courtesy of Adrian Roads.

The Enfield Gun Sling

1. Winfield Scott, *Infantry Tactics or Rules for the Exercise and Maneuvers of the United States Infantry Volume 1*, New York 1835 edition, reprinted by Steve Abholt 1990 Texas ; William J. Hardee, *Rifle and Light Infantry Tactics Vol. 1*. Reprint Green wood Press Publisher Westport CT 1971; William Gilham ,*Manual of Instruction for Volunteers and Militia of Confederate States*, , West and Johnston Publishers, Richmond VA 1861; Silas Casey, *Infantry Tactics for the Instruction, Exercise and Manoeuveres*. Vol. 1. Reprint Morningside Press Clayton 1111 1985

2. *Official Records of the War of the Rebellion, Series IV Volume II*, pp 382–84.

3. Sam Hankins, *Simple Story of a Soldier*. Confederate Veteran Magazine, September, 1912. The word *broncho* means "bronco" or horse.
4. Pierre Turner, *Soldiers Accoutrements of the British Army 1750–1900,*Crowood Publishing, (London) 2007, p. 84.

Conclusion

1. John Walter, *The Rifle Story*, Published by Greenhill Books, (London), 2006, pp. 34–36. The so-called "old four" Birmingham firms (*Tipping & Lawden, Swinburn, Thomas Turner and Hollis& Sheath*) given the first Ordnance contracts for Enfield rifles due in 1854 failed to deliver on their contracts by the agreed upon date, and rejections during the inspection process at the Tower were high. Ordnance decided to adopt a new strategy, namely manufacturing rifles by machine at RSAF.
2. Except for London Armoury, of course. They had purchased one set of the identical machinery that Royal Small Arms Manufactory (or Factory) used to make Enfield rifles, and LAC could produce an early identical copy.
3. Caleb Huse was working through the London commission house of S. Isaac, Campbell & Co and buyers from South Carolina, North Carolina and Georgia were also buying on behalf of their individual states. F.H. Morse, the US Consul in London wrote to Secretary of State William Seward that the Southerners had beaten Union buyers to the punch and "…already secured the production of all the London gun–makers."
4. John D Goodman The Birmingham Gun Trade, *Birmingham and the Midlands Hardware District*, Samuel Timmins,(ed), Cass & Co Publishers, (Abingdon) 1866, p. 386–414. According to Goodman in an address to Parliament, the numbers produced by Birmingham during the US Civil War was 783,404 with all but 50,000 going to America, and London gun–makers produced 344,802 for a total of 1,078,205. This gives Birmingham about a 3 to 1 advantage in output. Goodman's point to Parliament with all this was that the gun trade could meet the needs of the War Department no matter how great the number, but he was about ten years too late with that sales pitch. RSAF was currently meeting their needs at a lower cost. All Goodman got for BSA Co was a small contract for some Snider breech loading conversions of old percussion Enfield rifles.
5. BSA Co was formed in 1861 during a meeting at the Stork Hotel coincidentally owned by John D. Goodman, to build a new factory to produce military arms by machinery. They were somewhat late in deciding on this new course of action and the factory was not operational in time to furnish any Enfield rifles for the US Civil War. The first order for BSA Co was in 1866 from the Turks for 20,000 Enfield rifles.
6. The Union canceled all existing contracts with the English gun trade in mid–July 1863, once they could meet their needs domestically. The Confederacy was the sole remaining American customer. Having the Confederacy as the sole American customer led to some financial trouble for the gun trade when the CS defaulted on the Erlanger bonds.
7. John O'Sullivan, *American Economic History*, Markus–Wiener Publishing (Princeton, NJ) 1989, p. 134. See also the Report of the Royal Commission on Depression of Industry &Trade, Great Britain (1886).

Appendices

Appendix A: The Numbers Game

1. John D. Goodman, *The Birmingham Gun Trade*, from The Resources, Products, And Industrial History Of Birmingham And The Midland Hardware District:a Series Of Reports,Collected By The Local Industries Committee Of The British Association At Birmingham, In 1865. Edited By Samuel Timmins (1866), p. 418.
2. The oddest number from Goodman's production figures is the unsupported figure of 50,000 as the sum total of all Birmingham Enfield rifle exports to all other countries. Where does number this come from? It seems pulled completely out of thin air. There were wars going on in the world throughout the 1860s. And what about the British Volunteer Movement? No commercial Enfield rifles were sold to the Volunteers in the 1860s? My thought is that the hundreds of thousands of Enfield clones produced by other gun–makers such as those in Belgium (Liege) went to facilitate the slaughter in those other corners of the world.
3. *Official Records of the War of Rebellion* Series I, Part I, Vol. 5 US Government Printing Office (Washington, DC) 1866, p. 1081–1082. It states that the Union purchases from England total 428,292 Enfield rifles.
4. C. Lon Webster, *Enterpot*, Edinborough Press (Eden Praire, MN) 2009, p. 242. Webster notes that invoices from Charleston often list small arms generically, such as "small arms," "English arms" or "Tower arms" rather than as "Enfield short rifles or long rifles." See also: Stephen Wise, *Lifeline of the Confederacy,* University of South Carolina Press (Columbia, SC) 1991, p. 227. Note the lengthy appendix and the approximate number of small arms on each of the blockade runners.
5. Official Records of the War of Rebellion, Series IV Vol II, US Government Printing Office (Washington, DC) 1882, p. 383.
6. Ibid, ORs Series IV, Vol II, p. 956. Ouch! The loss of 75,000 stands of arms means the CS had to be importing huge numbers just to keep pace. And Gorgas claims they were gaining ground in small arms? Howard Madaus, John M. Murphy, *Confederate Rifles & Muskets* (privately published 1996), states that it was

sometimes possible to discern what was in a particular shipment as Enfields were packed 20 to a case and Austrian rifles 24 to a case. Madaus estimates 60,000 of the 113,504 from 1863 were possibly Austrian rifles many of which were aboard the Blockade Runner *Miriam.*

7. Ibid, Webster, *Entrepot* (appendix) and private email correspondence with the author. If so, there is your missing 69,944 from Birmingham, plus some.

8. Frank Owsley, *King Cotton Diplomacy: Foreign Relations of the Confederate States of America*, University of Chicago Press, (Chicago) 1931 p. 290. See also: Mary DeCredico, *Patriotism for Profit: Georgia's Urban Entrepreneurs and the War Effort*, UNC Press, (Chapel Hill, NC) 1990, p.166.

9. Or sometimes as "assorted hardware" was in use on manifests to disguise the contents which ran the Union blockade.

10. Civil War letters of Carlos W. Colby, Vault Case MS–10014, Newberry Library, University of Illinois (Champaign–Urbanna, IL), 1863. See also Vicksburg National Battlefield Park. Note: "...after the surrender of Vicksburg, the 101st Illinois, along with about twenty regiments armed with "second class" arms, exchanged its obsolete weapons for captured Confederate Enfield rifle–muskets."

Appendix B: The Enfield Rifle

1. Frederick Llewellyn and William Jewitt, *Rifles And Volunteer Rifle Corps: Their Constitution, Arms, Drill Laws And Uniform* (London) 1860, p. 8.

Appendix G: Atlantic Trading Company

1. In this case the "promoters" of Atlantic Trading Company, Ltd refers to Messrs. Isaac Campbell & Co., 71 Jermyn street, London; along with T. & J. Johnston, Liverpool; Shipbuilder George Wigg, in Liverpool; and Co. Messrs. J. C. Man &. Co.

2. Joseph McKenna, *British Ships in the Confederate Navy*, Published by McFarland & Co (West Jefferson, NC) 2010, p. 210.

Appendix H: A. Ross & Co

1. Burrow, T.J. *London: Armorial Bearings and Regalia*, Burrow Publishing Co (London) 1964, p. 44.

2. Hoole, S.W, *Confederate Foreign Agent, The European Diary of Major Edward C. Anderson,* Confederate Publishing Co, University of Alabama 1976, p. 43.

3. Ibid, p. 63.

4. The McRae Papers, South Carolina Confederate Relic Room & Museum, Columbia S.C. It is not known whether these accoutrements were delivered, but the fact they were being discussed at this late stage in the war shows that they were still required. Also note that the British infantry "Sgt's" 20 round pouch was being ordered for Confederate cavalry units.

5. Invoices of QM Stores shipped to the T.M.D Department by Major J.B Ferguson and Major J.F Minter CS Army October/November/1864 (From the Ramsdell Microfilm Collection MF 209B, Center for American History, University of Texas, Austin, Texas).

6. MacLeod, Norman (Editor), *Good Words Volume 19,* (London) 1878, p. 260.

7. Hansard's Parliamentary Debates June 1888, Supply–Army estimates, Volume 327 pp. 829–920.

About the Authors:

David Charles Burt and Craig Lee Barry are from opposite sides of the Atlantic. They had both become interested in how British companies supplied the Confederacy during the American Civil War. Separately, they started to research the various firms involved, the arms, equipage, and uniforms supplied by these companies. David published his first book, *Major Caleb Huse C.S.A. & S Isaac Campbell & Co* in March 2009, which reached No 1 on the online retailer Amazon charts. After the publication of this book, David and Craig, author of *The Civil War Musket: A Handbook for Historical Accuracy - Lock, Stock and Barrel* and Editor of *Watchdog* magazine (a monthly magazine in the *Civil War News*), got together to write their first joint title, *The Civil War Musket: J.E. Barnett & Sons*. The pair then wrote the first in the Supplier series, *Supplier to the Confederacy; S, Isaac Campbell & Co, London*, a major reworking of David's original book, which also reached No 1 on the Amazon charts. The second "supplier" book, *Supplier to the Confederacy Peter Tait & Co, Limerick*, was published in June 2011.

 Suppliers to the Confederacy: British Imported Arms and Accoutrements is the fourth book the pair have co-written, and the third in the Supplier series. David lives in Congleton, Cheshire, England. Craig lives in Murfreesboro, Tennessee, U.S.A.

David Charles Burt and Craig Lee Barry